The Invisible Empire
Racism in Canada

The Invisible Empire
Racism in Canada

Margaret Cannon

Random House of Canada

To my daughters Jacquelyn and Erin
and my granddaughters
Rebekkah and Alexandra

Copyright © 1995 by Margaret Cannon

All rights reserved under International and
Pan-American Copyright Conventions.
Published in 1995 by Random House of Canada Limited, Toronto.

Canadian Cataloguing in Publication Data
Cannon, Margaret
Invisible empire: racism in Canada

ISBN 0-394-22149-4
1. Racism - Canada. 2. Canada - race relations.
I. Title.
FC104.C36 1995   305.8'00971   C90-095427-2
F1035.A1C36 1995

Cover design: Orbit Design / Gary Stüber

Printed and bound in the United States of America
10 9 8 7 6 5 4 3 2 1

INTRODUCTION:
ENCOUNTERS WITH THE OTHER

Hate is not inborn; it has to be constantly cultivated...Hate demands existence, and he who hates has to show his hate in appropriate actions and behavior...That is why the Americans have substituted discrimination for lynching. Each to his own side of the street.
—Frantz Fanon, *Black Skin, White Masks*

You may say that this is the lot of all, that each of us has a character familiar to those close to us which we ourselves do not see. No doubt: this is the expression of our fundamental relation to the Other.
—Jean-Paul Sartre, *Antisemite and Jew*

THE OTHER STOOD IN THE SHADE of a convenience store on a hot June day in 1994. His name was Clive and he was twenty-two. He stood quietly, watching the milling mass of men and women

waiting solemnly on Steeles Avenue in North York, Ontario. Along
the street, stretching for more than two kilometres, stood an honour
guard of police from across North America. They had come to say
farewell to one of their own—Constable Todd Baylis, aged twenty-
five, killed in the line of duty.

For four hours Clive stood, watching and listening to the mourn-
ful skirl of the bagpipes, the doleful sniffs of the spectators. It was
the largest police funeral in Canadian history. For the Other, it was
a day of fear. He watched the hundreds of people lining the streets
and they watched him. "I wasn't me to them," he said. "I was someone bad, a killer, a drug dealer, a pimp. They didn't know my name
and they wanted me dead, like that policeman. He was one of them
and they wanted me to die in his place."

Clive was not exaggerating. On that day, as the hundreds gathered to pay their respects to the dead and lend support to the living, there was deep suspicion and distrust in the air. As Clive stood,
quietly, hands in his pockets, eyes straight ahead, people looked
over their shoulder at him, turned to their neighbours and nodded
in his direction. No one said a thing. The looks were enough. Clive
was young, Black, male. He was wearing a baseball cap, a comfortable loose shirt over cotton pants and untied Air Jordan running shoes. He looked like ten thousand other young Black men in
Toronto. He looked, in fact, a bit like the newspaper and television
photos of Clinton Junior Gayle, the man accused of the murder of
Constable Baylis.

"I wasn't me to them." Clive had become the Other, the shade of
Clinton Gayle. Gale was twenty-five years old. He came to Canada
from his native Jamaica in 1977 when he was eight years old. His
father, who remained in Jamaica, was a policeman. His mother. who
sponsored him to Canada, had been a domestic. By the time he was
in his teens, Gayle was in trouble with the law. There were arrests
and convictions for assault, for carrying weapons, for theft. After
fourteen convictions, Gayle was ordered deported back to Jamaica
in 1991. Through some oversight or, perhaps, simple ignorance, neither he nor his mother had applied for his Canadian citizenship.
After fifteen years in Toronto, Gayle was about to be summarily

shipped back to a place he didn't know and people who had long ago learned to live without him.

Gayle appealed his deportation order; the appeal was denied. But help was on the way, in the form of the maze of bureaucracy in the Immigration ministry. For one reason or another—and the reasons really aren't important—Gayle wasn't put on a plane and shipped off to Kingston. He was released to his relatives in Toronto on a $2000 bond and, like hundreds or even thousands of others, slipped into the twilight world of the immigrant underground. For a man with petty criminal tendencies, it was fairly easy to deal a little dope, steal a few stereos, survive.

That's essentially what Gayle seems to have been doing the night Constable Baylis and his partner, Constable Michele Leone, ran into him behind a North York highrise. Gayle, who was shot in the arm during the altercation, is pleading not guilty to the charges of murder, attempted murder, possession of a restricted weapon and possession of cocaine for the purposes of trafficking. But according to the published police reports, Baylis and Leone interrupted a deal, gave chase, and were shot.

Baylis, the son of a twenty-four-year veteran of the Metro Toronto Police Force, died. Gayle was arrested and charged within hours. His father, contacted in Jamaica, said that he hadn't kept up with his son over the years but allowed that if Gayle had killed a policeman in Jamaica, he could be hanged. There were plenty of Canadians who thought a good dose of the noose was just what Clinton Gayle and his kind deserved.

"This [killing] is an invitation to racists," said Clive, watching the funeral. "After the Leimonis thing, well, it's going to just be open season on Black men. I mean, already, people are saying that the government should be more strict, not let Black immigrants in, that Black people are responsible for all the crime in Toronto. I mean, Ted Bundy was white and he killed all those girls. That doesn't mean that every white man in America is a serial killer. Why does one bad Black man have to mean all Black men are bad?"

"The Leimonis thing" refers to what a good many people regard as the racial watershed in Toronto's multicultural history: the day the town got mean. Georgina Leimonis, known by her nickname ViVi, was twenty-three years old, blonde, and beautiful and bouncing with life. On April 5, 1994, she was eating a piece of cake in a café called Just Desserts in the Annex, one of Toronto's classier neighbourhoods, when three young Black men entered the café and ordered the patrons, at gunpoint, to the rear. ViVi, along with twenty or so other customers and staff, complied, and the thieves began collecting the patrons' money and wallets. Witnesses, interviewed later, claimed that one man, carrying a sawed-off shotgun, seemed visibly nervous, possibly on some form of drug. For no reason that anyone has been able to discern, the gunman fired, directly into ViVi Leimonis' chest. Four hours later, she was dead.

Within hours of the crime, the police released photos of the suspected criminals. Taken from the café's security videotape, the grainy black and white photos show one young Black man in a baseball cap and jacket, another completely unrecognizable in toque and hooded sweatshirt, and a third merely a shadow in the rear. These photos, repeatedly aired on every television newscast, on the front page of the major newspapers, looked like any young Black man in town. Perception, always the handmaiden of fear, shifted to the idea of the Other, dangerous, sinister.

People who lived in the area were confused and frightened. "If you can't feel safe here, where can you feel safe?" asked one neighbourhood resident. People who hadn't been at the café, but who often dropped in for an evening treat, spoke of the feelings of being violated, of having marauders on their streets. Police Chief William McCormack spoke for a good many residents of Metro when he called the Just Desserts killing a "cowardly, dirty, filthy act of urban terrorism."

The morning after ViVi died, the people of Toronto began turning the café into a shrine. They covered the front of the building with flowers, bedecked it with letters and pictures, festooned it with flags. There was even a little row of votive candles burning brightly in a corner protected from the rain. There were Mass cards for those who wanted to pray for the repose of ViVi's soul. All day long, for several days after the young woman's death, there was a steady procession of people passing the café and pausing. Some of the messages were visible only from the sidewalk but others were large enough to be read by motorists stopped at the lights by the café.

The largest sign was a message printed in black marker on white board. It read: "We grieve for our lost sister, Georgina ViVi Leimonis. Don't let this tradegy [sic] be marred by racist issues. When a white man murders it is not a reflection on the white community. This murder does not reflect the black community." Across the side of the sign, someone had written an answer to this plea for tolerance. "Kill your own. Leave us alone."

Clive is quite right when he says that Toronto might have been a bit more forgiving of the death of Constable Baylis, if it hadn't been for ViVi Leimonis. Her family—hardworking Greek immigrants—described her as "a good girl who never caused anyone one minute of grief." Thirty-five hundred people turned out for her funeral, weeping openly as they passed by her casket. As is the custom for unmarried Greek women, she was buried in her wedding dress, a virgin "Bride of Christ." Tucked into the coffin was her teddy bear. The Other had murdered Snow White.

At the funeral, Bishop Sotirios Athanasoulas, Head of the Greek Orthodox Church in Canada, gave the eulogy for ViVi. In it, he called for greater police powers, more rights for victims and less concern for the rights of criminals, and, in a reference to immigrant communities, "reprimanding ourselves equally," subtly called for the gathering of crime statistics by race. A few days later, Art Lymer, the outspoken president of the Toronto Police Association, appeared at a public rally and demanded the deportation of criminals. He was cheered.

Plenty of people in Toronto, including ViVi Leimonis' friends and family, tried to downplay the unpleasant topic of race. A murder was a murder, they said, and the colour of the killer didn't matter.

But colour did matter, along with class, caste, and custom, because ViVi Leimonis was a white girl murdered by a Black man. Furthermore, she was murdered in a pleasant place located in one of the most desirable neighbourhoods in Toronto. A neighbourhood that houses much of the Canadian intelligentsia, the media elite who

shape opinion, the high-powered consultants and authors and publishers and professors who are called in when there's a matter of
public policy for the government to consider. The people of the
Annex take what happens in their neighbourhood very seriously.
Michael Valpy, senior columnist for the *Globe and Mail*, blasted
Leimonis' murder in his column. When he said, "the barbarians are
inside the gates," he meant it.

Outside the leafy avenues of the Annex, there were plenty of rum-
blings. "All I ask in this world," said LaVonna Bray, a university student, "is that these men don't turn out to be Jamaican."

Other young members of the Toronto Black community had more
immediate concerns. There were very real fears that the vague photographs of the suspects could lead to an open season for attacks on
Black men. There was a rumour, unsubstantiated, that a young
Black man had been attacked by white vigilantes and beaten to the
ground on Yonge Street two days after the murder. Black parents,
watching their sons head for work or school, asked children to call
in upon arrival and to telephone again before they left for home. "I
can't leave the house without calling my mother," said a nineteen-
year-old York student. "I was studying in the library and I had to
call her every two hours so she'd calm down."

Black parents wrote to the newspapers, asking for tolerance,
pointing out that an entire community shouldn't be judged by the
actions of four thugs. Cecil Foster, writing in the *Globe*, broke a
long-term code within the community by calling for Blacks to recognize that too many young Black men were turning to guns and
violence as a way to command respect. He pointed out that violence
was hurting the Black community, keeping people scared, harming
businesses.

It all fell on deaf ears. Toronto wanted action. A lot of people in
Toronto wanted blood. Ten days after ViVi's murder, just three days
after her funeral, Toronto nabbed Lawrence Augustus Brown,
known as "Brownman," aged twenty-five, of no fixed address. He
had surrendered after police, acting on information received from a
Black couple, located his car parked on a quiet West End street.
Information about him was scant but it was known that he had

attended a local high school for two years, had not graduated, had a criminal record, moved around among a group of women friends and had five illegitimate children. The police didn't say whether or not he was Jamaican. He didn't have to be. He was, alas, exactly what the Black community feared and what the disciples of Art Lymer and Preston Manning expected.

A few days later, the police arrested the second suspect in the Just Desserts case. His name was Oneil Rohan Grant. He had been twelve years old when, like Clinton Gayle, he'd come to Toronto to join his mother. No one had secured his citizenship. Like Gayle, he had a history of crime and had been ordered deported. But unlike Gayle, he had been able to convince an Immigration Appeals officer that he was a good citizenship risk. His deportation had been stayed for five years while he supposedly dealt with his drug addiction. They were still processing the case against Grant when Constable Baylis died. That was all it took to ignite the racist powderkeg.

Comments not heard in decades suddenly burgeoned in news articles, were hurled at people on the streets. "I've been called a Nigger for the first time in Toronto," said Clive. Others reported comments that referred to Blacks as apes who should live in a zoo. Killers, murderers, rapists were the kindest charges. Nice people from good homes talked about sending people back to Africa. A majority of Canadians told a polling company that the immigration quotas were too high, that the refugee determination process was too easy, that the immigration appeal process was obviously designed to permit dangerous felons to kill Canadians at will. There was a nasty undertone to the comments, an idea that somehow Canadian good will, Canadian good manners were being abused. Todd Baylis and ViVi Leimonis weren't the only victims. We were victims, too. The Other had killed our innocence, destroyed our faith and we wanted revenge. As one person put it, on the front of Just Desserts: "Toronto the Good or Toronto the 'Hood. It's up to us."

Immigration Minister Sergio Marchi, himself an immigrant, at first pointed out the obvious. Grant and Gayle had been in Canada since childhood. Their Jamaican citizenship was, at best, technical. They were, said Marchi, "a Canadian problem."

That was a noble sentiment, in the face of the howls from ordinary citizens, and Marchi dropped it soon enough. He pulled together a group of experienced RCMP officers and gave them orders to ferret out the estimated six hundred individuals who were in hiding after having their deportation appeals denied. While they were at it, the Mounties could round up a few thousand other people evading deportation orders. To take the sting out of the new roundup, Marchi said that illegal immigrants who were underground, who had been in Canada for three years, had not been on welfare and who had worked for six months could apply for Landed Immigrant status, the first step to citizenship. The Mounties apprehended fourteen people in the first two months of the squad's existence, a record that made them heroes to the right wing Reform members of Parliament. After all, shutting the immigration door and tossing out immigrants convicted of crimes was a plank of the Reform Party, a position that had led Preston Manning's merry band of followers to a hair's-breadth away from becoming the country's official Opposition.

After two decades of relative tolerance, Canadians are once again defining themselves in relation to the Other. There have been Others in the past: the heathen Irish, the dreaded Jews, and the Yellow Peril, but those have all passed, become part of "us." The Just Desserts robbers, Todd Baylis' assailant are something else. Tough, armed, dressed for court in their flashy clothes, grinning at the cameras, proven lechers, with their housefuls of fatherless children, they are not "us"; they are not what "we" are about.

Clinton Gayle and Oneil Grant are no more "representative" of the Black community than I am, a white woman with middle-class roots and a middle-class career. But their act has opened Pandora's Box in Toronto and let out evils long hidden. "I don't want them here," is a mild complaint. Listen to Art Lymer and you'd think that Toronto is rife with crime—all of it imported from somewhere else. How to get rid of crime? Deport it back.

Turn back the clock. Give us back our city. Kill your own. Leave us alone. But there is no going back. The period between 1980 and 1994 has been one of rapid growth for Canadian cities—Vancouver and Toronto particularly—and with the growth has come change. There are many more Black, brown, and Oriental faces. There are more crowds, more traffic, more problems. From our perspective, those of us who have lived here for decades, we have not changed and so the problems must be someone else's fault. It must be the newcomers, the Other.

How we confront the Other in our midst—whoever the other is— is what racism is about. We don't know what forces or powers shaped the events that led to ViVi Leimonis' death. In truth, we don't care. We want the criminals caught, tried, convicted, punished. We want the doors closed to other criminals coming in. If that means considering every young male Jamaican as a potential "urban terrorist," then so be it.

This Canadian racism is, on the whole, more genteel than its American and European counterparts. There is less of the linguistic confrontation one finds in the United States or the sneering superiority of the French or the jackbooted burnouts of the German neo-Nazis. Because it's more refined, people have a tendency to dismiss racism in Canada, to ignore it, or to forgive it. But that opens the door to more dangerous, more violent forms of racism, and those forms are alive in Canada too.

When we begin to talk about racism, particularly if we are decent and civilized people, it's easy to find palliatives: "There is racism between the different African tribes. Look at how the Japanese treated the Koreans. Look at the situation of Native people in South American countries." These are all true and sad, but they have nothing to do with the Canadian experience. Canadian racism, like American and European racism, is unique to the white Christian Eurocentric world. The conviction that the white race is superior to all others is, if you will, our little gift to the world. Whatever tribal hatreds or racial loyalties impelled people before they came to Canada, when they arrived they faced a world in which the white Christian European race and culture was dominant and all others, from the Native people onwards, were inferior.

One of the first questions people asked me was why I, a white woman, was writing a book about racism. The reason is because I know all the forms of racism, from the subtlest nuance to the most virulent epithet. I was born to be a racist. I learned its language in my cradle and its form and face in my earliest childhood. I grew up in the American South in the final decades of segregation, the last brutal gasp of slavery's hold on African America. The world of my childhood was one of Them and Us, of the Other. Segregation meant the fallacy of separate but equal, and so there were separate schools and toilets and hospitals and water fountains and every other detail of daily life for Them and for Us.

In all segregated societies, issues of race are obsessive. What percentage of blood tie separates us and the Other? Are Orientals white or Black? What about South Asians? Racial separation was supported by organized religions, which taught that Black was the mark of Cain for killing Abel. It was supported by science, in the form of Darwin's theories of evolution of species. If man evolved from lesser animals, were there not "lesser" men, ones lower on the evolutionary scale? There were attempts to make it all very intellectual, but, in the end, racism defies reason because it is ultimately irrational—like the Canadians who say all Blacks are criminals. Irrationality is essential to racism.

I was a teenager when segregation began to crumble in the South, and it was a terrible and fearful time. For the first time in my life, I saw Klansmen riding openly, their hoods and sheets blowing in the wind. There were threats of lynchings, of shootings, of nightrider attacks on Black neighbourhoods and homes.

Since that time, I've always known that death is the ultimate racist weapon, whether it's the systematic annihilation of Jews and gypsies by the Aryan supremacists of Nazi Germany or the "Send 'em back to Jamaica" calls from Canadians.

I have known all my life that racism is a lot more than name calling on the playground. It is a way of life, of thinking, a complete worldview that entraps both the believer and his victim, and it has its own moral, social, religious, and scientific imperatives.

This book is about that racism in Canada today—that strange invisible empire of race hate and irrationality, whose loyal, vindictive subjects are to be found in virtually every department of Canadian society. But it is only partly about the dead, cruel heartland of the invisible empire and then only en route to elsewhere. I have no doubt that there are monsters among us: the Jew-baiters, the hatemongers, the swastika painters, the Klansmen. Among these are the not so obvious, the patient bureaucrats who, in another time and place, might have manned the gas chambers and then gone home to a good dinner and a comfortable night's sleep. Such people exist in Canada today. They must be dealt with in any book that addresses the issue of racism in this country.

But the greater part of this book is an excursion through the ambiguous edges, the suburbs, if you will, of Canadian racism's invisible empire—through the familiar places in which most of us work and live and play and raise our children. This emphasis is based on the conviction that, if we are preoccupied with the horrific figures at the centre of the empire, we run the risk of not seeing racism as the corrosive force, eating away at the dignity of both the hated and the hater, as the polluter of all intimacies, as the perverter of decent values, such as kindness and consideration and compassion, into weapons of total control.

This book is about extremists, but it's also about nice people, like the woman in Regina who, in a quiet, aggrieved voice, went on for nearly half an hour about "turbanheads in the RCMP" and the generous, deeply religious Jew who assured me that "there's no such thing as a good Arab. The only good Arab is a dead Arab."

It's about the self-deceptions that aren't that different from all the other self-deceptions that ordinary people use to survive in a complex world except in one crucial respect. The self-deceived smiling very polite people in this book are the agents, witting and unwitting, of an invisible empire that stretches across continents and through time and, I believe, is destined to be a decisive force in Canadian life in the next century.

Change is the handmaiden of racism, and Canada, like the rest of the world, is in a state of rapid change. The immigrants at our doors are part of a huge worldwide migration of people fleeing wars, poverty, fear, starvation. Many of those people are coming to

Canada—many more would come if they could get in—and they are not white, Christian, or of European descent. Today, Vancouver and Toronto are unrecognizable to people who have lived in them for more than ten years. In ten more years, they will be even more unrecognizable. The rapid pace of change has increased crime, pollution, fear, and loathing in Canadian cities. The demands to send back the Jamaicans are a cry from the heart of people who want the process of change slowed.

If, as Sartre and Fanon posit, racism lives in us all, in our need to define ourselves as being distinct from the Other, that we have to have someone to despise and look down upon, then it is imperative that we know that, recognize the sweet stench of racism for what it is, and resist its spell. As one group—like the Jews—passes into the mainstream, they are replaced by another—like Blacks, or South Asians, or Orientals. Whatever the group that is defined as the Other, the method is always the same. The Other is inferior, a bearer of disease, a harbinger of death, a polluter of language, culture, or land. Every racist knows the signs. Everyone raised to be a racist knows how the system operates, whether the fashion of the moment be cross burning or pinstriped suits.

Thirty years after the civil rights marches, after the Canadian Bill of Rights, after endless talk about equity and affirmative action and a thousand skirmishes in the battle to achieve equality for everyone, it still hasn't arrived. Not in America, not in Canada. The Other stands just over the horizon, waiting to come into the promised land.

1

THE OLDEST HATRED

I MAKE MY LIVING AS A JOURNALIST. Most people think that journalism is all about talking and writing, but the real essence of journalism, the difference between being a good and a mediocre practitioner, is listening. You have to hear the words, but you also have to listen carefully to the exclusions and the nuances and then describe those nuances for the reader. What is said is important. What is unsaid, implied, and hinted is often more important. The gaps have to be filled in. When I think of myself, it is as a transcriber of the unrevealed.

I was doing just that, one day two years ago, in an interview with a Bay Street lawyer. He was describing another well-known attorney, one whom he didn't like and who had engaged in a severe breach of legal ethics. He wanted me to understand that he and his firm, his friends and his business partners, were against this kind of dubious legal practice. He described the offensive lawyer as "smart but shallow," a legal trickster who was "all appearance and no substance."

He talked about the man's penchant for bragging endlessly about his rich clients, his large billings, and his "flashy lifestyle items—expensive cars, custom-made shirts and imported suits, forty pounds of gold in the cufflinks and a solid-gold Rolex that impressed him and people like him."

He went on at some length about these things, all the while shrugging his shoulders in his expensive (but not custom-made) suit and discreetly checking the time on his Swiss (but not Rolex) watch. As he went on, he got progressively more irate and less guarded. He was genuinely outraged at the travesty of his profession that this crooked lawyer represented, so he gave me example after example of the man's perfidy and lies.

"You know the kind of person I mean," he told me. "They all stick together."

I nodded. Of course I knew what he meant. *Flashy, bragging, sticking together* are code words in Toronto, just as they are in New York or Little Rock or Dallas, for Jews. I retreated to become a listening ear, to efface my own voice, because I wanted to see just how far he'd go, if he'd actually utter the word *Jewish*, but he didn't. Not because he didn't think it but because he suddenly realized he was talking to a reporter and, today in Toronto, such utterances are bad for business, can even be, under some circumstances, illegal.

To gentile ears, hearing such comments never comes as a surprise. Though our good friend who once referred sneeringly to a cottage down the lake from her Muskoka retreat as "Little Tel Aviv" would never acknowledge herself to be an anti-Semite—after all, some of her favourite colleagues at work were Jews—she is. That's because an anti-Semite, like other bigots, never seems to be able to put it all together: the slur and the poison gas, the slighting remark and the mass shootings, the quip and the pogrom, the private prejudice and the public tolerance.

And, granted, putting it all together is so hard that we usually don't hold the odd anti-Semitic remark against old friends. Perhaps they don't know better, we tell ourselves: It's just the result of poor education, or the family's failure to inculcate liberal values, or the blight of history.

Or perhaps we are just too guiltily aware of how quickly the Jews spring to mind out of that unexamined, unpurged sump at the bottom of ourselves when we need an "explanation" for something that irks us. Christians call this casual anti-Semitism a sin and urge repentance. Liberal pagans call it repulsive and urge better manners. Yet, in all gentile circles, it's far more often ignored and forgiven than not. This casual and continuous anti-Semitism is, as Robert S. Wistrich claims in his book of the same name, "the longest hatred" and it predates all other forms of racism. Look into the annals of any racist organization, from the Nazi party to the Church of the Creator, and you'll find references to Jews and their perfidy and the conviction that they must be driven out or destroyed. The central dogma of the invisible empire's creed is, and always has been, anti-Semitism—the belief that Jews are racially inferior, socially undesirable, and politically dangerous, a belief that has been translated to other so-called inferior races. The Jews "stick together" and form an alien lump in society, controlling men and governments through their control of banking and commerce. This dogma is at least a thousand years old and it's still going strong.

Where did this notion come from? Most believe that it's the fruit of religious bigotry in the Middle Ages, the Jews as Christ killers and moneylenders. But there's plenty of evidence to support the idea that hatred of the Jews is the first recorded evidence of pure racism and the source of all racial prejudice to come.

The Old Testament Book of Esther recounts how Haman ordered the killing of all the Jews when Mordecai would not bow down to him because it was forbidden by his religion. Exodus recounts how the Hebrews were enslaved because they refused to give up their monotheistic God and their dietary and religious beliefs. Dating from the third century B.C., there is a papyrus by the Egyptian priest Manetho, claiming that the Hebrews worshipped an ass's head in their Jerusalem Temple and, once a year, sacrificed a kidnapped Greek to this deity. As far back as then, the Jews were accused of ritual murder in the name of religion. So, even in antiquity, the Jews were seen as separate and exclusivist, a group to move against, "the Other." Even before the word *anti-Semitism* was coined in the nineteenth century, anti-Jewish racism was thriving.

There is no secret about the horror anti-Semitism has led to, and could lead to again. Nobody in my circle doubts that the Holocaust happened, or that millions upon millions of perfectly innocent Jews were put to death on the altar of obscene anti-Semitic ideology. But rare indeed is the gentile who's prepared to give up an old friend, or cut a relative off short, over a little casual joke about "them," to BBBcorrect the nice person who claimed to have "Jewed down" the used-car salesman. These are, after all, just words, holdovers from another time and place, fragments of bad taste that can be corrected with good public education. Can you really equate calling someone a kike with being a member of the Ku Klux Klan?

The chilling thing about anti-Semitism is that it never goes away. It remains at the edge of consciousness, faintly abstract, without an obvious, immediate cause-and-effect relation with anything, like normal sins and peccadilloes (from lying to one's significant other to cheating on an income tax form). During those long stretches when overt anti-Semitism is considered in bad taste, particularly in business, and is even illegal (as it and other forms of racism are in Ontario today), the covert, casual kind continues to exist in non-Jewish circles, undiminished. Whole departments of a newspaper, or a great law firm, or a vast business are discovered not to have a Jew in them. We blink, then go back to business as usual.

We accept without question the idea that nobody purposely designed this outcome. Possibly no Jews or Blacks or, until very recently, women applied for the jobs. It all just seems to have happened by complete accident.

There are also the explanations of why Jews aren't there. Jews aren't good at sports and so won't be able to do business over a squash or tennis game. They prefer to work with their own kind and so will be uncomfortable with gentile clients. Jewish religious and dietary laws make it difficult for them to fit in in the executive suite or to continue business over lunch or dinner. "Some customers," never mentioned by name, "prefer" not to deal with Jewish managers, bankers, brokers. Smart Jewish lawyers and accountants, however, are prized.

Lest one think these stereotypes and beliefs are out of date in today's enlightened world, consider the case of Simon Israel, the British-born, Cambridge-educated vice-president of mergers and acquisitions at the New York office of ScotiaMcLeod, a well-known Canadian-owned brokerage house. In 1991, Mr. Israel was dismissed from his post for "the offensive way he objected to the size of his annual bonus." The image of the moneygrubbing Jew is one of the oldest chapters in the centuries-old story of anti-Semitism and it's one of those quiet subliminal calumnies that are difficult to deny or disprove. Just what did Mr. Israel do that was so offensive to his profit-sharing colleagues? We don't know. We do know, however, that Israel complained in 1989 of anti-Semitism in ScotiaMcLeod, and also claimed he was subjected to eighteen months of harassment and anti-Semitic slurs, allegations denied by ScotiaMcLeod.

Historically, there has always come a day when the prohibitions against open racism, no matter how long or deeply entrenched, seem to weaken, making the ordinary holder of "liberal" values seem embarrassingly timid to himself. One needs to take a stronger stand. The "facts" need to be told. "Reality" must be faced. And hate then feels free to show its less casual side.

It never does so all at once, nor does it ever start in "respectable," traditionally tolerant gentile society. It always seems to start where good gentiles don't go, with people that well-bred middle-class professional gentiles don't mix with. It usually starts at night. It's usually done by unpleasant people and, most often, its cause is unknown, unclaimed, irrational.

B'nai Brith spokesman Paul Marcus is one of those optimistic people who believes that fresh outbreaks of "resistance" have something to do with reality. As he said in 1992: "We've been warning people that there is a new boldness attached to racist activity. A downturn in the economy means an upturn of hate."

During the recession of 1991, says Marcus to support his case, there were 251 "anti-Semitic incidents" in Canada—overt acts of desecration, indictable harassment, violence—which represents a 42 per cent increase over 1990, when times were better. Figures for 1992 show another increase and, in 1993, the worst year since statistics began to be kept, there were 105 incidents of anti-Semitic vandalism, more than double the year before, and 151 incidents of harassment, which included youths who stoned and screamed anti-Semitic insults at children walking home from Netivot HaTorah Jewish Day School in North York.

And what the unpleasant people do is sometimes linked to some incident or current event in the real world. In the summer of 1992, Tom Metzger and his son John, former leaders of the California Klan and current leaders of the White Aryan Resistance (WAR), an organization that advocates the elimination of non-whites and non-Christians from North America, came to Toronto to whip up the troops. The swastikas and anti-Semitic slogans painted on three Toronto synagogues immediately thereafter appear to have been tributes to that visit, the typical memorials that racist thugs leave behind when intoxicated by a fresh breeze from hell.

The Metzgers, who were arrested shortly after appearing at a Heritage Front rally, were jailed briefly before being deported on the prim-sounding charge of unlawful entry into Canada perhaps to commit an indictable offence. Though not as touchy as its American counterpart, the Canadian legal system is edgy when it comes to acts that might be perceived as infringement of free speech. While the right to free speech is enshrined in the First Amendment to the American Constitution, the Canadian Constitution is more ambiguous. It subjects "freedom of thought, belief, opinion and expression, including freedom of the press and other media of communication...to such reasonable limits prescribed by law as can be demonstrably justified in a free and democratic society." Those reasonable limits are open to broad interpretation.

That is the kind of ambiguity that the Heritage Front, and other racist organizations, feeds on, waves its flag about. If you'd rung up the Heritage Front hotline (shut down in 1993 after a lengthy battle before the Canadian Human Rights Commission) in the summer of 1992, you would have heard Front member Gary Schipper, the adopted son of a Toronto Jewish family, crowing that "we totally fooled the enemy about the location of the meeting." Schipper referred to the Metzgers as "our imprisoned heroes" and charged that they were the victims of "an unholy alliance of Trotskyists, Marxists, anarchists and the B'nai Brith." The lunatic message ended by promising that, "beginning June 30, communist Canada will learn the meaning of White Aryan Resistance." So far, the swastikas on the synagogues are the only outcome of this threat.

But if the typical spray-painting antics of the racists can sometimes be pegged on a specific event, they more often cannot be, with any certainty. More often than not, the gesture comes as a surprise, like a certain inexplicable stench on a balmy evening, or an accident of some sort that we never thought would happen to us.

DATELINE: WINNIPEG, OCTOBER 30, 1992. It's Gate Night, a traditional pre-Halloween blowout that usually never ends without a few acts of old-fashioned, non-ideological vandalism, arson, and hell-raising. This year—not a special year, and for no apparent reason—the gang heads for the local synagogue for a small orgy of egg tossing and swastika painting. Not satisfied with the damage, they spray satanist and anti-Semitic symbols on the doors and overpaint them with yet more pro-Hitler and anti-Jewish slogans. It's not the kind of thing that normal, drunken adolescent feloniousness ordinarily leads to. There's a chilling deliberateness that sets these acts apart from hijinks. Oddly enough, nobody in the media or the police seems to notice the difference.

DATELINE: MONTREAL, OCTOBER 27, 1990. Nine teenagers attack a group of Hasidic Jews in the neighbourhood of Outremont, where most of Montreal's 2,500 Orthodox Jews live. When the police round up the perpetrators, they discover seven boys and two girls, all under eighteen, with no previous known links to any radical-right outfit, all from middle-class suburban families. Though the attacks come hot on the heels of the vandalism of a local Jewish school and a synagogue, a spokesman for the town of Outremont tells the press that the attack was an isolated incident. Jewish leaders agree, stating that they "don't believe there are any more attacks against Jews in Quebec than there are in other parts of Canada."

A reflex reaction of disbelief and disconnection often greets such attacks. Such is the nature of good people confronting evil acts of certain kinds—seemingly irrational, symbolic—that they often seem incapable of making connections, even averse to doing so. The more one knows about the pervasiveness of racism, the more closely such disclaimers come to seeming almost normal—until one recognizes in one's own knowing smile a hint of the cynical, blinkered attitude that can allow societies to slide into real, devastating tragedies.

But sometimes—rarely—the point gets across.

DATELINE: TORONTO, MARCH 12, 1990. Zvonimir Lelas, twenty-three, is convicted of mischief in the vandalism of the Shaarei Shomayim Synagogue and the nearby Yesocei HaTorah School. Lelas and a friend had painted red swastikas, and the words *Nazism* and *White Power* on the windows, doors, and sidewalks. Not content with that, they also painted on the sidewalks the words *Smash ZOG* (an acronym for Zionist Occupation Government and a code word in all white supremacist groups). Lelas, a member of the Ku Klux Klan since 1989, when he was barely out of his teens, was sentenced to six months in jail. The judge, remarking on the lenience of the sentence, said he did not want to make Lelas a "martyr in the white supremacy movement."

Jews saw Lelas in rather a more canny light than that in which the spokesman in Outrement saw his racist episode. The attack on the synagogue and school was carefully orchestrated, they believed, and their conviction prompted local police (ever prone to dismiss such actions as "arbitrary" and "isolated") to call it "the worst case of ethnic vandalism in many years."

The care and pointed meaningfulness of Lelas's attack was what set it apart, according to Sherry Kelner, executive director of Shaarei Shomayim. "This is very deliberate. There's vandalism that breaks windows and vandalism that paints swastikas. The swastikas have to be taken a bit more seriously because it's symptomatic of something much larger."

The Crown appealed Lelas's sentence, and three other judges agreed with the Jewish community. They doubled the sentence to a year, adding that the man's potential usefulness as a martyr for white supremacists was of "no consequence." Lelas would never become "a martyr to the vast majority of Canadians who do not subscribe to those views."

At least the judge recognized that Lelas had views, not just a case of nasty high spirits. Here was no crank, no chronic loser, no dimwitted kid with a hate on for the world. Here was a nice young man, very much like so many other young Torontonians nourished in a decent, hard-working family of recent immigrants trying to make good somewhere far from wars and communism. In a way, that pretty much sums up the new Toronto and does much to account for why it is the relatively safe, stable place it is.

But somewhere in a dark corner of the Lelas family's suitcase, along with the dreams they brought with them, a tiny seed of hate from the Old World managed to hide itself and bide its time. The pleasingly simple idea of ZOG—the notion that most everything that goes wrong can be blamed on the Jews running the world for their own profit, pleasure, and power—is old, unassailable in its irrationality, perfectly suited to the racist mind.

ZOG is the defence and the rationale used by people like the Metzgers and organizations like WAR, the German neo-Nazis, the National Front, and the Heritage Front, for their support of anti-Semitic actions. The American government is a tool of ZOG, as are the Canadian and German governments. All governments, in fact, are linked by ZOG. To people like Lelas, action against ZOG is a blow for freedom.

The roots of ZOG and the idea of the Jew as outsider and evil are at least as old as the racist fanaticism that darkens the pages of late medieval Christianity. Anti-Jewish oppression was most virulent and murderous among the scattered pre-Protestant sects that sprang from the chaos of collapsing feudalism, but hatred of the Jews was also part of the common culture of Christian Europe.

The idea that the Jews were irredeemable isn't a religious dogma. The notion that any soul is beyond redemption has never been a part of formal Christian doctrine, nor has it ever been formally taught that intractability to the idea of conversion is grounds for ghettoization, exclusion, or murder. On the contrary, both Catholic and Protestant beliefs support the idea of kindness to one's neighbour.

But religious belief isn't cultural action. Western European

Christians may have known, in some amorphous way, about the idea of the New Jerusalem, where all peoples would live in harmony, but in practice they Christianized with fire and sword, demonized those who did not convert to their beliefs, and created the religious basis for hatred of the Other, the idea that even God turns from the unbeliever.

There were attempts to change the more virulent forms of anti-Jewish action. The Russians might mount pogroms, but the more "civilized" Europeans simply kept the Jews in ghettos, or out of business or universities or professions. Such repellent, ever-popular ideas as anti-Semitism have never proved changeable by "official" organizational doctrine, whether Christian, in the Middle Ages, or good modern liberal, as in our own time. Nor have they ever been failed by the most dependable, strangely durable item in the kit of self-delusion: denial.

We have seen a few instances of denial by people anyone could class as good guys, people on the right side, people who genuinely believe that this can't happen here, that these people are isolated crazies. We shall have occasion to witness more denials by the good, the respectable and law-abiding folk of Canada. We want to believe we are better than this, that we have learned the lessons of history, and they won't be repeated.

Only his widespread circle of Canadian supporters would list Toronto publisher and activist Ernst Zundel, Canada's apostle of denial nonpareil, among the good folk. Like most New Age Aryan supremacists, Zundel hardly looks the part of the unrepentant ultra-rightist. He's dimple-cheeked and balding, with greying hair and twinkly eyes behind spectacles—more like Santa on a Christmas card than Hollywood's snarling, plough-jawed image of a racist hatemonger. Many years of living in Canada—he is a Canadian resident in good standing, and proud of it—have softened but not annulled his German accent.

Zundel is a man with a mission, a mission that can be summed up in one word: Hitler.

In his cluttered little home on Carlton Street, in Toronto's once-trendy Cabbagetown, Zundel has created a cottage industry out of

Holocaust denial and Hitler rehabilitation. "Hitler," Zundel told reporter Victor Malarek in a 1993 interview for the television program *fifth estate*, "wasn't a monster. He was a decent peaceful man." When Malarek reminded him that Hitler, in a speech quoted by Zundel, compared Jews to monkeys in the trees, Zundel replied, "Hey, nobody's perfect."

From his tidy presses come myriad works with names such as "The Leuchter Report," a $37,000 "scientific" study commissioned by Zundel that asserts that the gas chambers of the Third Reich were a hoax. There's his newsletter, *Germania*, which keeps the faithful up to date on neo-Nazi and other white supremacist events worldwide. For those who prefer video, there's his Samisdat Video line, featuring tapes of rallies and mass marches in Europe and North America, along with snippets of history and infomercials from Zundel on getting involved.

Since September 1993, his weekly television program has been beamed via satellite from somewhere in Canada or the United States. Where it comes from is a secret, but it's assumed to be in the U.S. If it was originating in Canada, Zundel could be open to prosecution for transmitting hate literature—but the United States, with its constitutional protection for free speech, allows "alternative" opinions to exist. Once it's on the satellite network, one that Zundel shares, ironically, with radical Black Muslim leader Louis Farrakhan, Zundel is able to broadcast to anyone who'll tune in.

Zundel markets his tracts, books, and videotapes in more than forty countries. His Cabbagetown office is one of the prime suppliers of mail-order anti-Semitic tracts to the ultra-rightist and neo-Nazi organizations in North America. But the big market is in the old country, and he is today the Citizen Kane of printed hate literature in Germany. For while it is illegal in Germany even to say that the Holocaust never happened, it is not illegal to sell documents alleging it, just so long as they've been printed elsewhere.

Thus has Zundel's little Toronto business become a key player in the rise of the new German Nazism. His tracts on the lies of the Allied conquerors and their deliberate, ZOG-inspired falsification of the numbers of Jewish dead are available in most German shops selling neo-Nazi propaganda and regalia. To leaders of Germany's burgeoning neo-fascist movement, Zundel is a distant hero, a lone man dedicated to sending truth back into a Europe dominated by lies.

Along with his publishing business, Zundel runs an informal hostel for transient young Canadians in search of the truth about Hitler. But despite his kindly demeanour and his hospitality, Zundel is a racist felon convicted of spreading lies about the Holocaust, and it's safe to say that he's hardly well liked by most people in his adopted homeland. But that doesn't bother him.

When he was interviewed in 1993 by Malarek, Zundel made no secret of the fact that his 1985 trial and conviction for spreading false news and the attendant publicity were pure gold for him. Before, he was dismissed as just another member of the lunatic fringe. The trial put him on national television and got him coverage in newspapers and magazines that would ordinarily treat him like the plague. Eight years later, he was still making news. He was obviously enjoying his interview with Malarek, smiling, relishing his role as the purveyor of hate to the German masses.

While Zundel was on trial in 1985 Toronto was treated to a little televised circus. Each day of the court proceeding, he and his burly cohorts, a small group of unnamed supporters-cum-bodyguards, muscled their way into court, carrying huge boxes of documents and tracts. They were unmistakable in their bright blue and yellow hardhats, worn ostensibly to prevent a crazed demonstrator, a member of the militant Jewish Defence League (some of whom did attack Zundel and his attorney, Doug Christie), from cracking them on the skull.

For the cameras, Zundel was active, agile, grinning. His adversaries in court, on the other hand, were tottering, elderly European Jews who had survived the German death camps, the very existence of which Zundel refuses to acknowledge.

And that's his mission, and the purpose of all the books and boxes being carted by him and his hearty henchmen into the courtroom: to show up these old Jews as frauds, mere agents of ZOG, continuing the Great Lie against the German people and their great leader, Adolf Hitler.

According to the fantasia in the head of Ernst Zundel and his cobelievers, "orthodox" historians in the West—obviously in the employ of ZOG and its international publicity machine—have created the myth that six million Jews were gassed, shot, starved, and systematically destroyed, all as a way to discredit the German people and promote the interests of the Jewish conspiracy. The "proof" that the ZOG-inspired fabrications are pure lies is in a vast heap of spurious tracts, pseudoscientific "research documents," and other oddments, which all show that only a few thousand Jews—maybe a hundred thousand, maximum—perished in German camps during the Second World War. Not enough Jews, in other words, to count—and certainly not as many as ZOG claims.

And anyway, the death of this insignificant number of Jews wasn't deliberate. The camps were decent, healthy places set up to provide work for the German war machine, but—well, sometimes people get hurt in wars. Surviving Jews shouldn't take the death of a few thousand of their coreligionists personally, and, anyway, maybe even the "authentic" deaths are inventions of ZOG.

When Zundel lost his first trial for promoting this lunacy, he promptly announced that he would appeal all the way up to the Supreme Court of Canada. He did and, in August 1992, his conviction was overturned. Money seemed to be no object, and truth would out. In a less idealistic mood—and with the radical right's typically excellent instinct for the opportunities for self-promotion afforded it by mass media—Zundel let slip that the publicity was worth twice the price of the lawyers, briefs, and appearances.

Where Zundel gets his money is an open question. Rumours tie him to various groups, but the one documented source is his publication empire, and no one disputes that there's big money in pro-Nazi propaganda. Still, amassing personal wealth does not appear to be what's moving him to send those hundreds of informational kits into Germany each week. The hundreds of thousands of German marks and Canadian and American dollars he takes in each year—and the German government confirms that he's raking in plenty—are ploughed immediately back into the cause in Canada, in the United States, and in Germany.

Zundel is a supporter of the Heritage Front. He doesn't always appear at meetings, but that doesn't mean he stays off the road for long at a time. He was on hand for the Toronto gala at an East End banquet hall celebrating the 102nd anniversary of Hitler's birthday, knocking back a few beers with the kids, pressing the flesh with Wolfgang Droege and bikers from the Hell's Angels. Then he was out west, lending his support to the cause of schoolteacher Jim Keegstra, convicted of disseminating hatred. He brought revisionist British historian David Irving, who describes himself as a "hardcore disbeliever" of the existence of gas chambers at Auschwitz, to Canada on a lecture tour to promote his latest book proving the Holocaust was a conspiracy and a figment of the Jewish-controlled media. Zundel describes his support of people like Irving as part of his "intellectual foreign legion."

He was reputed to have been in Vancouver for the birth of the Liberty Net, a western Canadian white supremacist group allied to WAR; and the lads at the Church of the Creator, one of the most militant white supremacy movements, claim he's sympatico, if not a card-carrying member. He defines himself as "the guru of the right."

Zundel also makes regular trips to Europe to meet with his counterparts in Germany and with his soul-brother Robert Faurisson, chief of the illegal French neo-Nazi party. A Swedish documentary on the rising neo-Nazi movement in Germany showed a cheery meeting between Zundel, Faurisson, and Col. Otto Reimer, a friend of Hitler, one of the heroes of the Third Reich (he saved Hitler's life when a bomb went off in 1944), and since the end of the war, chief fundraiser, flag bearer, and general factotum of renascent National Socialism.

First and foremost, in Zundel's view, there's the truth to print and to make men free. But he also recognizes his obligation to serve as an example. He's old enough to remember the good old days when Hitler was around and he wasn't cursed with the postwar, ZOG-inspired German education that made the Third Reich sound like a racist, totalitarian hell. He's living history for the German punks who have few Jews to persecute but plenty of Turks, Cubans, Russians, Vietnamese, and other Ausländer to kick around. A recent neo-Nazi rally in Munich, filmed for the CBC, took one back to old movies of the thirties, an era during which Zundel and his followers believe Germany was on its way to saving Western civilization from communism and America—and, supremely, from the Jews, whom Zundel and company believe dominated both.

To the ultra-rightist mind, the Jews are absolutely crucial. If they did not exist, wrote Jean-Paul Sartre in his essay "Antisemite and Jew," they would have to be invented. They constitute the menace the racist personality needs to exist, bearers of a virus so lethal that even the slightest brush with it is enough to pollute the blood, ruin the soul, destroy the mind. Like AIDS, it's everywhere, and permanently a menace—of immense danger to the casual or ignorant, of no danger to those who read and believe the prophylactic literature produced by Zundel and company and thus learn ways to keep themselves pure. One of the horrible things they see about ZOG is that it behaves just like AIDS or cancer: at the beginning, it's silent, invisible, lethally slipping up on the unwary host.

Although old in inspiration, modern anti-Semitism is as new as the era in which it took root. Like so many other things about modernist culture, the new anti-Semitism sprang to life in the era of emancipation from traditional religion that swept Europe after the failed revolutions of 1848. It was a wonderful time for Jews, who were granted unprecedented freedoms in the Austro-Hungarian empire and Germany and who grasped those freedoms with enormous energy. The *stetl* and ghetto and other overt vestiges of traditional Jewish repression were abandoned, and many of the Jews of central Europe quickly joined the upwardly mobile, secularized professional and managerial classes with enormous enthusiasm and a complete freedom like nothing they had ever known before.

For the Jew-haters, it was a headache. When Jews suddenly began to be good bourgeois citizens, shedding all the trappings of religious stereotype, what was to be done to keep hate alive? How could they be the Other when they were sitting across from you at dinner eating the same food as you, sponsoring the opera, making witty conversation at the local coffeehouse?

But then, in the 1870s, the scientific-sounding term *anti-Semitism* was born, apparently the invention of German journalist Wilhelm Marr, who'd been searching for a way to describe "the non-confessional hatred of Jews and Judaism which he and others like him advocated." The term, and the movement, which emphasized the racial as opposed to the religious inferiority of Jews, was helped along by its putative modernity, but that didn't keep it from striking fire in some of the least modern backwaters of Austria, Hungary, France, and Russia. It was respectable, inasmuch as it made a nice distinction between its adherents and the less enlightened Jew-baiters of earlier times.

Anti-Semitism, writes Robert Wistrich in *Anti-Semitism: The Longest Hatred*, was "a self-conscious reaction to the emancipation of the Jews and their entry into non-Jewish society." In that sense it appeared to be a novel phenomenon; the new anti-Semites were at pains to stress that they were not opposed to Jews on religious grounds but were motivated by "social, economic, political, or 'racial' consideration."

This "scientific" rationale, which replaced the older anti-Semitism (holding that Jews were inferior because they killed Christ, and clinging to the medieval image of them as moneylenders and usurers), was eventually applied to all non-European races. It was fostered by Darwinism, which encouraged the concept of superior and inferior stages in the development of all species; by religion, which taught the concept of one true God; and by capitalism, which equated worldly success with both Darwin and religion. Progress was the catchphrase of the day, survival of the fittest the philosophy, and heaven the true reward.

But not for everyone.

In his book *The Occult Establishment*, James Webb charts the reaction against the twin gods of reason and materialism. He records that, even as the forces of reason were consolidating their successes after Napoleon's defeat, the forces of irrationalism were growing strong. The radical societal changes of the eighteenth century led to fear and anxiety in the nineteenth, which in turn led to what Webb calls "the flight from reason," a rejection of reason and a movement towards faith and "the spontaneous generation of causes of an exalted or mystical nature, whose concept might be no less religious for being clothed in the vocabulary of politics." Among those concepts can be found such disparate groups as the Theosophists, Christian Science, Utopian socialism, and Marxism. All believed man (and society) was perfectable and all believed that conventional wisdom denied the "truth" of their message.

Scientific anti-Semitism became part of the grand worldview needed by European irrationalists as they rejected everything else materialistic, crude, merely operational, whether it be capitalism, individualism, the quest for profits, or "standard" medicine, physics, and philosophy. "This Underground of rejected knowledge," Webb writes, "comprising heretical religious positions, defeated social schemes, abandoned sciences, and neglected modes of speculation, has as its core the various collections of doctrines that can be combined in a bewildering variety of ways." The foundation stone of this body of rejected knowledge was "modern" race theory, the matrix that, magically, made all the paranoid, disparate delusions seem to work. It is what also gives the broader culture of anti-Semitism its durability and endless flexibility, simply by arming it and its adherents against reality. The centre of the invisible empire, as we shall see, is a strange place of ghosts that many of us thought were laid to rest long ago.

The empire's documents and "proofs" are updated versions of nineteenth-century tracts that purport to reveal secret information and alliances between Jews and other groups. The most famous—and infamous—of these documents is a pamphlet called "The Protocols of the Elders of Zion," a forged report allegedly written by the Czarist secret police that shows the "Jewish master plan" for world domination. The "Protocols" were widely challenged as forgeries, even in the nineteenth century when they were first printed, but that didn't stop them from being believed and disseminated. Translated into German and then into English, the "Protocols" are still trotted out as "proof" of a Jewish and, now, Israeli Zionist world conspiracy.

Another favourite "scientific" rationale for anti-Semitism was *The Secret of the Jews*, a jumble of occult and historical information that attempts to link Judaism and Freemasonry. This work doesn't pretend to be for a general audience but claims to be a report by a person possessed of "secret information" who is passing this research on to higher authorities. The text combines the evolution of monotheism—a mishmash of East Indian and Chaldean religious practice—as well as the revealed wisdom of the Egyptian hiero-phants (the Emerald Tablets of Hermes Trismegistus), and Essene Jewish practice. It holds the lost wisdom of the ancients and the sup-pressed truths as proof of a worldwide conspiracy against Christian Europe and uses key episodes in European history—the Crusades, the coronation of Charlemagne, the American War of Independence, the 1864 International—as examples of the conspiracy's powers to influence history.

Bizarre as these ideas may seem, both the "Protocols" and *The Secret of the Jews*, along with dozens of similar tracts, still make reg-ular appearances in more recent writings by scholars of the invisible empire. As well, the research plans—the careful and systematic gath-ering of obscure facts from ancient and occult sources, the insistence that truth has been suppressed for centuries—are appealing to those who like to possess "secret" wisdom, information not shared by the general public or taught in schools. These students of "lost" history jump upon such books as *Other Losses*, James Bacque's study of Eisenhower's treatment of German POWs immediately after the Second World War. Although Bacque never denies the Holocaust, his work does point to other evils. In the twisted world of racism, the fact that German POWs were starved and frozen somehow "bal-ances" the Jews, gypsies, Slavs, and POWs who died in the German extermination camps.

What is remarkable about the supposedly suppressed works is their endurance and their flexibility. The same books, the same occult references, the same types of rigorous recounting of "fact," sometimes even the same language, are used today to support today's racist research. The Atlantean myth, for instance, appears over and over again. In this tale of the sinking of the continent of Atlantis and the diaspora of the Rays—the founders of the various groups around the world who evolved into today's races—all Rays were not equal and so all races are not equal. Whites are destined to rule, all others to bow.

The myth of Atlantis gives credence to the most egregious racial cant. Blacks, for example, are lower on the evolutionary scale and gave the world AIDS. Jews and Orientals have a worldwide conspiracy that seeks to undermine Western civilization. Secret Muslim cabals plot against Christians worldwide. It may have all begun with the Jews but it has become the universal language of racism.

All of this arcane knowledge comes to vivid modern life in the figure of Carney Nerland, the once and future "Führer of Saskatchewan." It's difficult for decent people to understand Nerland. This product of the beautiful Saskatchewan prairie is just twenty-nine, born in the 1960s, the decade that was going to change the world. He is the very picture of red-blooded, white-skinned Canadian manhood. With his Beaver Cleaver grin, his chubby chipmunk checks, short hair, and neatly trimmed moustache, he's the kid next door, the boy on the bike, the boy your daughter brought home from the school dance. In his neatly pressed khaki uniform, he looks the part of the perfect boy scout, except for the slick black reflector shades covering his eyes.

Prince Albert, Saskatchewan, is a pretty little town of 35,000 curving along the banks of the North Saskatchewan River. This is western Canada as the settlers dreamed it. The grass is green, the air is pure, and the high blue sky goes on forever. People like to think of this as God's Country, a place to stand in, and where a man can fantasize about having to defend his family with firearms—though he never has to—and hunt down his evening meal. Hunting is what firearms are really about in Prince Albert, and are taken seriously as such. Unless you believe there's something intrinsically evil about hunting, then handsome, well-kept, clean firearms come with the territory.

Carney Nerland grew up here in a family that nowadays would probably be condescendingly described by an easterner as "dysfunctional" and which seems to have been considered weird in Prince Albert even then. Carney's mother was a Jehovah's Witness, believers in blood salvation and one of the many new religions born in the nineteenth-century religious renaissance. Then and now, she plies her religion on the street corners of Prince Albert, handing out copies of *Awake* and *The Watchtower* to possible recruits.

Carney's father, Big Bob, roared around town on his Harley-Davidson sporting a German army helmet complete with an Iron Cross. He wrote "Big Bob on Bikes," a chatty motorcycle column for the local newspaper. He was a character. Every little town has one. And this was, after all, the sixties. Bikers were respectable after a fashion—dealing a little dope, guarding rock concerts, being pictured as fashionable antiheroes in films like *Easy Rider*, and playing out the fantasies of the wild and free that straighter townsfolk pretend to dislike but secretly smile about.

At public school Carney, then known by his middle name, Milton, seemed almost ostentatiously average for a Biker Brat. Like the rest of the Prince Albert pack, he chased girls, drank beer, and grew up knowing how to handle a hunting rifle. By junior high school, he was immersing himself in Second World War history and, according to neighbours interviewed in *Saturday Night* magazine, "spray-painting swastikas anywhere he could find a flat surface."

By high school, where he spent two years before dropping out, he was into the brushcut and jackboots. His teachers remember him as a smart kid with an encyclopedic knowledge of German war lore. They recall a boy who, even then, knew exactly what he was doing and had a plan for his life.

By 1984, Nerland was living out his plan. He was a member in good standing of the KKK and the violently racist Church of Jesus Christ Christian—Aryan Nations. In that year, he showed up at a congress of the Aryan Nations at its headquarters in Hayden Lake, Idaho, publicly proclaiming himself a Nazi. Thus, Nerland allied himself with the two most popular (and best-financed) ultra-rightist organizations in western Canada. It also meant he was in touch with the best-organized and best-financed, as well as the most militant, organizations in the U.S.

The Aryan Nations is not to be dismissed as a bunch of beer-bellied rednecks with rifles. It is part of an international movement with connections and cash across Europe and North and South America. It holds regular meetings and rallies and it sallies forth from its Idaho redoubt to spread the gospel of racial hatred and race war. Carney, full of Nazi lore and belief in white Christian superiority, was an eager recruit and he took his message home to Prince Albert.

Nerland headed home because it was the place he knew best but he also went back to Prince Albert because he knew he could find more recruits to the cause there. That's because there's another side to Prince Albert, not nearly as folksy and down-home. Prince Albert is known, with reason, as the City of Jails. Six federal and provincial correctional facilities call the town home. Though nobody intended it, that makes race an issue in Prince Albert, simply because more than six hundred local residents, almost all white, make their livings guarding a prison population that is largely aboriginal. Forty per cent of the convicts in the maximum-security Saskatchewan Penitentiary, bristling with barbed wire and surrounded by high stone walls, are Native peoples. In the provincial jails, aboriginals make up more than 80 per cent of the population.

While most of the residents of Prince Albert are white, ranchers or farmers, one-third of the town's citizens are Natives. There is a large Métis population in the area, as well as the Whitefish Indian reserve nearby. Police, Mounties, and prison guards are taken seriously in Prince Albert; they are upstanding citizens. Aboriginal people, on the other hand, are widely portrayed to outsiders as ne'er-do-wells, drunks, and common criminals. These are, of course, just images—one-sided pictures of a perceived reality that people carry around in their heads. Most of the time they stay hidden in the nastier recesses of the human brain but sometimes they bubble to the surface, get an exposure to the light and then someone acts upon them. That's what happened on January 28, 1991.

It was minus 27 when Leo LaChance hit town. The tall, greying man was known to take a few drinks, but he was hardly the lazy, no-good Indian of local white fantasy. He made his living the hard way, as a trapper living alone most of the time in the wilderness above the Whitefish reserve, coming into town regularly to sell his furs. The few people who knew this reclusive, middle-aged bachelor described him as a friendly, quiet man with frugal habits built up over a lifetime of poverty, tough work in the bush, and bad luck.

On the last day of his life, his luck didn't change. He headed into town with a small load of furs for wholesaler Arnold Katz, of Katz Fur and Metal. He had, according to his family, less than a dollar in his pocket. While he was there, he told Katz he had an old .303 rifle back on the reserve that he wanted to sell. Katz suggested he go next door to the Northern Gun and Pawn Shop and see if there was any interest. Katz told him that Carney Nerland, owner of Northern Gun and Pawn, was a local firearms expert and collector.

It was just about 6:15 p.m., cold and dark, when the trapper entered the store. Nerland was behind the counter, chatting and nipping on a bottle of whisky with two visitors, Wallace Brownbridge, a social services worker, and Russ Yungwirth, a provincial jail guard: typical of Nerland's customers, many of whom were guards or police.

A lot of people wonder why Leo went to Northern Gun and Pawn. Everyone in town, particularly the Natives, knew that Carney didn't care for Natives, was insulting, had fired shots at them.

Later, there were disputed claims of who was where and who knew whom and said what, but no one disputes what happened next. Leo LaChance didn't speak to Nerland, but he did offer his .303 to Brownbridge or Yungwirth for $100. There were no takers, and so LaChance turned to leave. Nerland fired two shots into the floor from a European-made M-56 7.62-mm assault rifle. Brownbridge later said that LaChance "got a disgusted, annoyed look on his face" and stepped outside. As he closed the door, Nerland fired a third shot. The bullet went through the doorframe, through LaChance's arm, spleen, pancreas, gallbladder, and liver. It also sliced through his portal vein, a main vessel to the heart. LaChance kept moving, but the wound was mortal.

LaChance staggered approximately 35 metres down the street before he collapsed. Brownbridge took a peek outside, to make sure his car wasn't hit by the bullet. He claimed he didn't see LaChance, lying face up on the sidewalk. Nerland evinced some concern that the Indian had been hit, saying that it might hurt his business. A few moments later, a passerby found LaChance on the sidewalk. He came into the gun shop and asked Nerland if he could use the telephone to call an ambulance. Nerland refused. Then he and his friends left the store.

Six hours later, Leo LaChance died in a Saskatoon hospital. Shortly after, Nerland turned himself in to the local police. "If I'm convicted of killing that Indian, I should get a medal and you should pin it on me," he told a police officer shortly before he pleaded guilty to manslaughter.

There were some questions raised among some Prince Albert residents about how shooting an unarmed man in the back constituted manslaughter, but none were asked or answered by the local police, the local merchants, or the Royal Canadian Mounted Police investigating the case. At Nerland's bail hearing, the Provincial Court judge, Tom Ferris, inquired about how a firearms expert and collector could "accidentally" fire three shots. Nerland said he didn't know there was a round in the chamber when he pointed the weapon at LaChance. Judge Ferris expressed scepticism and wondered aloud whether the charge might be raised to murder. The response came from Crown Attorney John Field, who said, "I think he [Nerland] showed a distinct lack of remorse. But the police held the view that this was manslaughter and that was their honestly held view."

Then local aboriginal organizations, as well as the Canadian Jewish Congress, raised the matter of Nerland's political and racial beliefs. He was, after all, an active member of three major white supremacist groups. Nevertheless, he maintained that he didn't hate aboriginal people and that his political and racist beliefs played no part in the killing. He pointed out that his first business partner was a Native man and he rented his store from Katz, a Jew. At Nerland's sentencing in 1992, Mr. Justice Frank Gerein of the Saskatchewan Court of Queen's Bench concurred. He sentenced Nerland to four years in prison on the manslaughter charge. Just a nice boy playing around with firearms. A tragic mistake. Accidents happen.

At first, it is almost impossible to understand how Nerland's political and racial beliefs were so completely disregarded at the time of his sentencing. But here again we encounter the strange blindness of ordinary justice when it comes to making connections between violent acts and the tenets of the invisible empire, perhaps because those tenets, and their iconography, belong to a world of thought so foreign to the one most of us live in. Carney had a picture of Hitler prominently displayed on the wall in his gun shop. His personal association with white supremacist groups was as well known in Prince Albert as the Hitler photo.

In 1985, barely out of his teens, he was refused entry to Canada after arriving from the States with a carload of Nazi propaganda. He was posing as a U.S. citizen and gave the name of Kurt Meyer, a Nazi SS officer notorious for the murder of Canadian POWs after the Allied invasion of Normandy. (Meyer is one of those hallowed heroes of the neo-Nazi underground who most Canadians have never heard of.)

Through the years, Nerland had attended neo-Nazi survival camps in South America organized by the Aryan Nations and other Nazi groups. His Chilean wife, Jackie, filed for divorce in 1992, claiming that he physically abused her and threatened to kill her and all her Spanish-speaking friends. Later, Jackie Nerland recanted her allegation and, according to one source, she and her daughter live in fear of Nerland and his pals.

Throughout this time, Nerland was in contact with other white supremacist groups in Canada. By the time he was a young man, he was an open member of the Ku Klux Klan and the self-proclaimed leader of the Saskatchewan "congregation" of the Church of Jesus Christ Christian—Aryan Nations. He was an insider, and he wanted people to know it.

Just a year before his manslaughter conviction, in 1990, Carney had appeared voluntarily before the Alberta Human Rights Commission, then investigating a cross burning at Provost, Utah. Nerland told the commission that "because of the media coverage of this event and Jewish coverage of this event, a blatant accident has been turned into a racial incident." He couldn't explain how a cross got on a lawn, or how it happened to catch on fire. And, far more important, who cared? Nerland seems to know the legal ins and outs of western American and Canadian bigotry.

He was also, through his association with Aryan Nations, linked to a network of white supremacist organizations across North America and Europe. His contempt for non-whites was well documented. At a lunch break during his bail hearing, he wanted to know who prepared the Chinese food that was brought to his cell: "I will not eat that...gook food. I won't eat that Chink food. I'll starve first. I won't eat anything unless it's prepared by a white man."

I have before me a photo of Nerland taken at the 1990 Alberta Aryan Fest. Carney is natty in paramilitary uniform, black shades, and assault rifle, manning the KKK booth. He waves his rifle and seems to be either giving the press the finger or beckoning to someone. His sign reads "White Power."

With this image in mind, it's hard to believe that respectable and well-respected white men leapt to Carney's defence, or conspicuously kept their counsel. But they did. Sgt. David Demkiw of the Prince Albert Police said there was insufficient evidence to prove that the shooting of LaChance was anything but accidental. Roy McKnight, a former jail guard and brother of Tom McKnight, a high-ranking official of the guards' union, offered to post bail for Nerland. Brownbridge and Yungwirth, the two witnesses, kept silent about the shooting until the next day.

Nerland himself called the police six hours after the shooting (presumably just after he learned that LaChance was dead) and said that two men "he didn't know" were in the store around 6 p.m. and fired some shots, giving him the jitters. He returned to his store just after 3 a.m., ostensibly to collect the gun shop's books. The police barred him from entering. Two days later, Roy McKnight, a known sympathizer of neo-Nazi ideals and a man who claims to have been Nerland's newly appointed business partner, came in and removed the books. They haven't been seen since. Gerald Morin, a Prince Albert lawyer and chairman of the Indian-Métis Friendship Centre, questions whether the ledgers were an ordinary record of sales. "Was it a list of the Aryan Nations membership? Were any of them jail guards or police officers?" The questions were never answered.

Nerland's expertise with guns and the fact that he had police permits for dozens of restricted weapons give rise to another, even more sinister possibility. What if those ledgers showed not only a record of who belonged to the Aryan Nations and KKK but what arms they had bought from Nerland? Sam Katz, Nerland's neighbour and former business partner, told *Saturday Night* magazine that there was a police car outside Nerland's store "every time I looked out my window." When he asked Nerland about the police, Nerland told him they were customers. When asked about the LaChance shooting—and anything else—Katz said to ask the cops and told the interviewer, "You think I want my store burned down?" He also pointed out that the local synagogue had been vandalized in 1985 and there had "always" been racism in Prince Albert.

These were some of the questions no one asked before or during Nerland's guilty plea and sentencing, despite the pleas of Native people and members of the militant Jewish Defence League. Rumours of collusion between Nerland and the police, and police membership in white supremacist groups, abounded in the days leading up to Nerland's sentencing. And when he was sentenced to only four years, with the judge explictly ruling that racism and politics played no part in the killing, those rumours intensified.

Rumour then led to fact. Senior Crown officials in Saskatchewan revealed that in the fall of 1991 Nerland and two Calgary men were under investigation. They had been distributing anti-Semitic and anti-Native literature in Prince Albert. Once again, there were rumours of police implication and coverup. Three months later, the Saskatchewan government convened a commission of inquiry into the LaChance killing. They were to decide if race had, indeed, been the motive for the shooting.

The three-person tribunal, headed by Mr. Justice Ted Hughes, a former Saskatchewan judge and B.C. conflict of interest commissioner, and consisting as well of Toronto lawyer Delia Opekokew and law professor Peter MacKinnon, convened on May 27, 1992. On its very first day, Staff Sgt. Arnold Sommer, a police ballistics expert, said that the bullet taken from LaChance's body could not possibly have been fired as Nerland and his witnesses claimed. It wasn't damaged enough to have gone through a door and then into LaChance. Sommer's testimony opened up the possibility that LaChance was deliberately shot in the back as he left the shop.

But before the tribunal could digest the idea that Nerland's "accident" was a cold-blooded murder, the RCMP stepped in. Their lawyers wanted an injunction to prevent the tribunal from delving too deeply into RCMP intelligence data on white supremacist groups in Canada. The reason the Mounties wanted the injunction was to protect a "key" RCMP informant. The informant was unnamed, but the RCMP did reveal the name to the LaChance family on the proviso that they not tell. After months of fruitless legal wrangling, the leaders of the twelve Indian bands that make up the Prince Albert Tribal Council decided to lift the lid. At a crammed press conference, Chief Allan Feliz stated that the tribal council leaders had been told that the informant was none other than Carney Nerland himself.

In November 1993, three weeks before Nerland's scheduled release from prison, Saskatchewan Justice Minister Robert Mitchell released a seventy-five-page report detailing the findings of the Hughes inquiry. The commission claimed it had uncovered the truth of the death of LaChance, "to the extent it can be known." The police and the justice system were acting in "good faith" when they charged Nerland with manslaughter. There were shortcomings in the investigation—like the failure to take into account Nerland's avowed hatred for Natives and his history of involvement in the KKK and the Aryan Nations.

While these shortcomings were "unfortunate and serious," the inquiry found that racism was not an issue in the investigation. The role of the RCMP or police in giving Nerland possible special treatment in the form of a reduced charge wasn't mentioned. The Aryan Nations movement in Saskatchewan was dismissed, having "dwindled into oblivion." It also stated that the facts of the case would not have supported a murder charge because Yungwirth and Brownbridge claimed that Nerland looked suprised when the gun went off.

On the first or the third shot?

At the end of the day, the $400,000 inquiry made only two recommendations: that the Prince Albert police force have a Cree-speaking officer on duty at all times and that police officers and prosecutors engage in more cross-cultural training.

The Carney Nerland story raises a lot of questions in my mind. Was this the best the Mounties could do? Protect a grinning neo-Nazi with murderous tendencies and a cache of guns? A man who once brandished his rifle in front of a group of journalists and dubbed it "Native birth control"? Did they really think he was a good guy? Are we supposed to believe he was play-acting at white supremacy, all in the name of justice?

Tell that to Leo LaChance.

Carney Nerland was just what he said he was and what he's been for more than ten years. His commitment to the cause of the Aryan Nations, the cleansing of the Canadian prairies of everyone except the great white Christian race, was firm. If he was working for the RCMP, it was because he believed that working with them would, in some way, further his ideological and personal goals.

That people close to him and even people who disagreed with him refuse to talk about him and his beliefs and that he and his unnamed friends and supporters are able to keep the lid on his actions, get him off with a light sentence, and maintain a steady silence about the whole affair, despite the publicity and the work of the Native councils, is indicative of the kind of power and influence he wields, even from a prison cell. And there are still those who believe that Nerland's views are merely eccentric, not dangerous. He is, after all, only one man.

But statistics have a way of coming back to haunt the imaginations of good people prepared to isolate Nerland and his strange beliefs. A survey done by a human rights group in the United States found that the Ku Klux Klan and the Aryan Brotherhood were the organizations of choice for prison guards. The Klan claims thousands of adherents in the small towns of northern Alberta and Saskatchewan, and, although these numbers are probably inflated, there's no doubt in my mind that their membership is in the hundreds. The organization may have dwindled but it's not dead, and

Nerland, since December 1993, is out of prison and ready to reorganize his troops. According to Warren Kinsella, in his book *Web of Hate*, Nerland is in the RCMP's witness protection program, an irony not lost on the aboriginal groups who fought to get him to justice.

Still, it's easy to write off Nerland and his buddies. After all, this is Canada. We have our crazies, but we also have laws against hate literature and human rights councils to deal with race hatred. We have laws and a Bill of Rights and a formal policy of multiculturalism. We believe that we can deal with the Carney Nerlands if we just have the will.

But under the present circumstances, that's a very big if.

DATELINE: TORONTO, JANUARY 25, 1993. It's 8:45 a.m. and the highrise canyons at the corner of Bay and Queen are uniformly grey, grim, and imposing. Nathan Phillips Square, in front of City Hall, is a vast open space surrounded by hills of grimy snow, and the wind whips in and saws through the warmest coat. Office workers scurry from subway to doorway without a glance at the little crowd huddled and waiting. In front of City Hall, a man smokes, swearing about Toronto's new bylaw forbidding smoking in the building. "Last one until lunch," he snarls at no one in particular.

He is joined in the doorway, safe from the wind, by a couple of kids, part of the demonstrators converging on the square. They haul out their smokes and hold the matches in freezing fingers. They are here to save Canada from ravaging hordes of Native peoples and Jews. The Heritage Front hotline is rallying the troops for an all-out battle "for Euro-Canadian free speech." Today the Front has called for every right-thinking Canadian to demonstrate. At issue is the right of the hotline to continue to relay its recorded messages. The battlecry today is "Rights for Whites."

The Canadian Jewish Congress and the Native Canadian Centre have launched an attempt to shut down the hotline. Today, the Canadian Human Rights Commission is hearing the case. If the CJC and NCC are successful in proving that the hotline disseminates hate, the Front will be forced to abandon Gary Schipper's raspy-voiced taped messages available to anyone who calls. Today is the big day, and the Front wants its supporters out in force.

By eight-thirty there are about two dozen bedraggled kids in cheap leather jackets, tight jeans, and unseasonably light shirts. Despite the freezing weather, there is not a mitt, toque, or scarf in sight, even on the ever-so-slightly snarling skinhead with his little Nazi thunderbolts tattooed on his temple. Everyone shivers as Wolfgang Droege, leader of the Front, delivers a pep talk about how they are defending free speech and saving the Charter of Rights for everyone. This fight isn't about race, the Heritage Front claims, it's about equal rights.

The Heritage Front doesn't like to be compared to the Nazi Party. It's members, uniformly white and less-than-upper-class, think of themselves as the representatives of "real" Canada, the founding races who "made this country what it is today." It's considered in bad taste to mention that Droege, with his little beard and sibilant German accent, isn't descended from the Family Compact. In fact, Droege is an immigrant, one of the millions who came to Canada after the war to find a new life in the New World. And, like a few other émigrés, he found it difficult to leave the philosophical trappings of the Old World behind.

In Droege's case, the trappings meant jackboots, uniforms, Jew-baiting, and rabidly racist ideas about people of colour. A lot of little ideas picked up from his Nazi grandpa, who was, according to Wolfie, a buddy of Julius Streicher, the notorious Nazi butcher. Wolfie is always quick to point out that he's not a Nazi. "The Nazi Party died in 1946," he says.

There is a tendency on the part of many people to dismiss Droege, to see him as a cartoon fascist with a tiny following and no base of support. This morning, that tendency is irresistible. It's cold. He's boring. Let's go. The Heritage Front supporters start a straggling march towards the University Avenue court building, where the human rights commission is to meet. There are police everywhere, a comforting sign to those who are white and who believe they are right. They hoist their signs demanding equality. The boy next to me blows on his cold hands and tells me there are some Jews demonstrating at the courthouse.

He is somewhat understating the facts. Just around the corner, the Front meets a counterdemonstration. Where Droege's group has managed to get thirty or forty members, more than four hundred antiracism demonstrators, including Jews, students from colleges and universities, and a large contingent of Native people, are out. The leader is Rodney Bobiwash, the Native leader of Klanbusters, a group that, like the Canadian Jewish Congress, opposes, monitors, and makes public racist incidents. Bobiwash and Klanbusters have been targets of racist slurs and attacks, and their headquarters in the NCC have been vandalized by white supremacist groups.

It takes less than a second for the demonstration to turn ugly.

The Heritage Front, outnumbered and outyelled, is quickly surrounded by people carrying placards that read "Save Our Land, Smash the Klan," "Hate Is Not Hip," and "Evil Is Evil." The antiracism demonstrators link arms in front of the doors, attempting to keep the Heritage Front leader and his supporters from entering. At this point, the police intervene. The Canadian rights code is clear: even the Heritage Front has a right to entry for its hearing. The police, in protective riot gear or on horseback, wade into the mêlée to escort Droege and his supporters into the courthouse. Droege is smiling and triumphant. Behind him he can hear the whirr of the Pentaxes and minicams. Tonight, he'll be the lead story on every television newscast. Tomorrow, he'll be in every Toronto paper. This is what he wants. Before he even enters the courthouse, Droege has won.

Droege wears the new face of North American white supremacism, one based upon the ideas and practices of Louisiana politician David Duke, whom Droege refers to as "my hero." This new face is what is almost certainly going to make their tactics and their doctrines more difficult to deal with in the future.

Noticeably absent, or downplayed, from the tactics are the wacky revisionist histories, the showoffish denials of the Holocaust, the cross burnings. Droege, Duke, and their kind represent a move—common in the second generation of right-wing populist movements—in a new direction, designed to bring them from the fringe into the mainstream of politics, from the purist dogmatic shadowland of lunatic race theory and myth into something approaching respectability. "Sieg Heils" and robes and chains are discouraged. Front supporters might appear at their meetings in black boots, black jeans, and black T-shirts with the Front logo, a variation of the swastika, but not today. Today, everyone is in civvies for the camera. The leader himself is dapper and sleek, shoes shined to a gloss, in a navy blazer and maroon tie. After a morning in court, he could blend right in at the faculty club at any university. He understands how the media works, and how to work it. It's a message that's already catching on in Germany, where skinheads are letting their shaved locks grow and replacing their leathers with London tailored tweeds.

And unlike the old-style fanatics of the Nerland sort, Droege, Duke, and company are prepared to give and take with ZOG, compromise like real politicians, and let themselves be co-opted by a mainstream party. One like the Reform Party, for example, for whose meetings Front members provided security and of which several of them were members until Reform leader Preston Manning ousted them under pressure from the would-be respectables in his populist movement. It was an ouster that wounded Droege. Was it not his right to join the political party of his choice, exercise his rights as a citizen?

Droege's attempt to join the Reform Party indicates that the petit-bourgeois, genteel look pioneered by David Duke is moving into Canada. What's surprising to me is that hardly anyone takes it seriously. Aside from the vociferous demonstrators outside the courthouse and a few passionate people attached to watchdog groups like the Canadian Jewish Congress or Klanbusters, not many Canadians see the Front as a threat. Seasoned colleagues in the Canadian media, among them most of the reporters dispatched to cover the demonstrations, are largely convinced that the Heritage Front and groups like it are simply hateful little anachronisms, with no future in this country. I was even told by journalists whose opinions I greatly respect that I was crazy to waste my time on a few ancient Nazi-minded fanatics, most of them presumably old, eastern European, of Second World War vintage, that by giving these people's ideas print space, I was encouraging them in their racist ways.

When I replied that many of the Front members were young adults or teenagers born and reared in Canada, I was ignored. Evidence of hundreds of Front members across Canada, as well as thousands of telephone calls for information on the hotline, was dismissed. The standard answer for everything is that this is, after all, Canada, a multicultural mix, home of the vertical mosaic, a veritable model for democratic letting-be. We do not want to see our cherished ideals of the peaceable kingdom threatened and so we turn away from people like Droege and all he represents.

But the good liberal wisdom of decent Canadians strikes me as more and more hollow. Preston Manning's attacks on immigration policy, his insistence on reducing numbers, is supported by many Canadians. He is stating publicly ideas and possible solutions that, ten years ago, would have been considered heresy. For all their blinkered view of politics and reality, Droege and the New Rightists are correct in assuming that Reform will be the opposition in the next election and they are correct in assuming that immigration will be the major issue.

The facts of immigration and public policy seem to reinforce the picture of Canada the good and Canada the open. We take in more refugees than any other country except Sweden. Immigration policies instituted by the Liberals and reinforced by the Conservatives favour family reunification. Reunification and the new categories of business immigration have opened Canada's doors to hundreds of thousands of members of visible minorities. A country that once barred Jews, declaring "none is too many," now routinely accepts Chinese, Arabs, East Indians, Africans, and Caribbean peoples. That's the public image.

At the same time, even among liberals, a private language of "them" and "us" has arisen, with growing anger attached to it. There is the feeling that, given the right spark, a bonfire could ignite. In private conversations, immigration is blamed for worsening unemployment, high welfare costs, increasing crime, and problems in the schools. There are too many of "them" coming in, over-whelming the resources of Canada. The Other is among us. "They" are accused of being too demanding, of wanting to hang on to their old country ways. They are fractious tiles in the Canadian mosaic, refusing to fit in. They want to wear turbans in the RCMP, to have Black history classes in the schools.

In Vancouver (now openly referred to as Hongkouver), the new Hong Kong Chinese immigrants are seen as too rich and flashy, destroyers of neighbourhoods, insular, and unwilling to play their part in the community. In Toronto and Vancouver, Blacks and Asians are accused of bringing in gangs, of creating a new criminal class that invades homes to steal and terrorize and settles scores by gunning each other down in Chinatown restaurants or on quiet downtown streets. East Indians are stereotyped as petit bureaucrats who insist on being Indian rather than Canadian and who are responsible for making it legal to carry weapons in suburban schools—a reference to the religious daggers carried by devout Sikhs. Arabs are seen as sneaky and sly, oppressors of women, responsible for bringing the hideous practice of genital mutilation to the Far Shore. Our Native Canadian brothers and sisters, once dis-missed as drunkards unworthy of note, have emerged after the con-frontation at Oka, Quebec, as a gaggle of land-grabbing thieves, ready to commit murder for their right to hold bingos for cash and sell black-market cigarettes. (We tell ourselves that the kinds of racial confrontations we see in the U.S. can't happen here. Yet what was Oka but a Canadian version of the L.A. riots?)

You may not agree with any of those stereotypes, but you've heard at least one of them. I've heard them all...and worse. They are the newest flowers on the old anti-Semitic root, and some of them, sad to say, are uttered by Jews themselves.

With all those images before us, Canadians still think of their society as multicultural, one where there is equality of opportunity and equal justice for all. But what justice?

One final note. Julius Melnitzer, a respectable and well-known Ontario lawyer, was sentenced to nine years for fraudulently obtaining millions of dollars in loans from banks. Carney Nerland got four years for shooting an unarmed man in the back. Melnitzer, who defrauded people of money, is still in prison. Nerland, who killed a man, is back at home. Our justice system is flawed.

And in this unsettled and unforgiving time, anti-Semitism, which we once thought was wiped out or at least driven underground— in North America anyway—has reappeared. Not in the virulent form of "none is too many," but in the more veiled form of my lawyer confidant. There is the slighting reference. A real-estate agent of my acquaintance refers to a particularly gaudy form of interior decoration as "nouveau Jew." Comments about cheapness or pushiness once again are heard. "They've gotten so showy," says a local investment manager of his Jewish clients. "Lots of flashy cars and jewellery on the wives. That's how Jews like to stand up and be seen."

Just words: but they're the first step into the world of Carney Nerland.

2

Equal Rights for Whites

ON A DAMP, CHILLY SEPTEMBER NIGHT in 1991, I went to meet the Canadian Nazis. My invitation to this gathering was a flyer placed on a friend's car in an upscale Toronto neighbourhood. I had a telephone number, which introduced me to the Heritage Front. A recorded message bemoaned the attempts of destroyers of democracy to crush free speech by preventing the Front from holding its meeting. I was advised to keep calling in order to find out the location, which was being kept secret to minimize the chances of demonstrators.

Finally, after several calls, a scratchy male voice that sounded like he was yelling into a tin can informed me that the cause of free speech could be served tonight at the Latvian Hall on Broadview Avenue in East Toronto. There would be a $10 donation to the cause at the door. I was warned again that there might be demonstrators.

Broadview Avenue is the heart of old Anglo-Saxon working-class Toronto. From Victorian times through the 1930s, it was home to families who lived frugally and comfortably in the district's pleasant turn-of-the-century row houses and semidetached dwellings. The area is still known as the "tough East End," even though the tough kids who gave it this reputation long ago moved up the social ladder to bourgeois respectability, or moved farther east, into genuinely tough neighbourhoods.

And as those original inhabitants moved along in the wake of the Second World War, they were replaced by new and then newer immigrants, making the area yet another microcosm of Toronto's incredibly rapid, chaotic, hugely dynamic postwar growth. Along the north boundary of the district is Danforth Avenue, where you can get great Greek calamari at one of the innumerable restaurants run by Hellenic newcomers, or you can buy organic salad greens at the Big Carrot in Carrot Common. The Common, Toronto's first ethically correct shopping centre, is one of many signs of the invasion of the new middle class, politically conscientious exercisers and recyclers who've displaced the white toughs.

South of the Danforth are the renovated row houses that shelter much of postindustrial Toronto's burgeoning upward-bound—until the recession of the early 1990s, anyway—class of "information workers." Television and radio producers, advertising designers, consultants, architects—a constituency that is largely white (though ethnically diverse), in punishingly high tax brackets, blessed with left-wing compassion for the environment and such, and cursed with left of left-wing guilt about making so much money. Here and there, in the old taverns, you can still see remnants of the East End's former population and catch whiffs of beer and Export A smoke on the summer breeze. But for most of the current residents of the upper East End, recycling is the state religion, natural fibres and French immersion for the kids are de rigueur, and green thinking is right thinking.

Farther south are the shops of Chinatown III, a shabby area into which the less well heeled Chinese greengrocers, proprietors of tiny hairdressing shops, and other small business-folk moved when Toronto's first two Chinatowns, in the heart of the city, became too expensive. And with the move of those little businesses came the local Chinese, most of them fluently anglophone, Toronto-born, and quickly rising to affluence but who still like to be within walking distance of an old-fashioned, crowded store where the bok choy is wonderfully fresh and the platter of dim sum deliciously untouristy.

Beyond Chinatown III are the skimpy remains of the industries that once made Toronto rich and provided jobs for the thousands of workers and immigrants who packed themselves into the area's cottages and creaky hotels. They were mostly battery plants, meat processing facilities, tool and die shops, distilleries, and the like. Most of them are gone now, the buildings converted into inexpensive theatres, churches for the un-WASP religions of Toronto's most recent newcomers, from Asia, South America, and the Caribbean, or spiffy offices for the information proletariat.

In this context, the Latvian Hall stands as a reminder of a time that seems long ago but was no further back than a generation. Then, in the brief postwar period when East European immigrants dominated the area, a strong man could get off the streetcar and walk from factory to factory until he found a job. He didn't have to speak English or French or have a college diploma or Canadian experience. He just had to be strong and willing, and the work was there.

He might have been Latvian, or Lithuanian, or Estonian, Croat, Serb, Hungarian, Italian. Whatever passport he carried, and whatever the nationality of his wife and kids, he was a European in search of something better than life in the ruins of a war-ravaged homeland. Such were the people who came in the hundreds of thousands to the big city by the lake and built the skyscrapers and suburbs and the shiny new factories and who, for the most part, made good.

And while they were at it, they changed Toronto from a small Anglo-Canadian bastion into a city of immigrants and children of immigrants largely from the south, east, and Iberian peninsula of Europe. When they were finished remaking Toronto, in the 1970s, they had created a city that would be unrecognizable to the old British bourgeois and elite who'd laid out Toronto in the first place.

Yet in the twenty years since then, another revolution has taken place. The multilingual white Christian European ascendancy that succeeded the British one has now been displaced by one that is black, brown, yellow, and probably not Christian at all. On your way down Broadview Avenue to the Latvian Hall, in a space of only about 3 kilometres, you pass a Sikh temple, a shop that specializes in traditional Asian remedies, a laundry that serves as a front for illicit traffic in peculiar tropical fish, and the home of a nice lady who sells voodoo amulets by appointment only.

I used to know Broadview Avenue well. I thought I still did. In the early 1970s, when I worked as a community organizer in a nearby public housing project, I knew Broadview as the place needy people went to scrounge food or buy merchandise that had fallen off trucks rumbling over the rough brickwork, and where some went to get the drugs that took them, however briefly, away from unpleasant reality.

But as I parked my Volvo in a lot at Broadview and Queen—a dead giveaway of how much I'd lost touch, since the lot was crammed with older-model American cars—I knew I was in alien territory. I looked across the lot and saw the signs and heard the chants. There was indeed a demonstration. Reporters and a camera crew milled about.

I had not declared my journalist's credentials to the Heritage Front. Instead, I had simply arrived. I was prepared to pay my money and meet the gang. I was, in a word, scared. I had taken pains to look right. Yet what does one wear to a Nazi rally? I was fresh out of swastika scarves and leather and chains. I settled for conservative denim and running shoes, just in case.

I arrived at the hall at precisely eight so I wouldn't be early. I knew there would be press at the meeting, and I didn't want to risk running into someone I knew.

As soon as I left the lot, I was surrounded by vociferous demonstrators. A group of Native people held up a banner. Some young college types in jeans and Reeboks glared at me and reminded me of my duty as a woman and a human being to oppose these groups and all their works. Three older women pointed to the numbers tattooed on their forearms and made sure I saw them. It was a bad moment for me. These people were my natural allies, could even be my friends. I believed in what they stood for, for the most part, and in the past I've often supported their causes. I pushed past them towards a group that, under ordinary circumstances, I wouldn't allow to pick up my garbage. Behind me, I heard them calling "Nazi! Bigot!" They made no attempt to stop me. They simply emphasized the sidewalk that divided us.

At the door of the hall, two serious young men in dark suits welcomed me and took my money. In contrast to the yelling, self-dramatizing demonstrators, the Heritage Front ticket-takers were quiet and polite. And young. That wasn't what I expected to see, and not what I wanted to see.

This experience was much more disconcerting than being called things I knew I wasn't. Stereotypes are powerfully attached to our psyches, and they hurt when jostled too sharply. To my surprise, I found myself wanting the Heritage Front people to look like the rednecks and morons that liberal, middle-class doctrine says they are, that they must be. The image of a neo-fascist, I abruptly realized, was a confection spun, uncritically, from TV specials and magazine articles about the Nazi menace in our midst, and concocted over a lifetime spent distancing myself (psychically, geographically) from the jocks and jerks I'd grown up with in Hot Springs, Arkansas. Though I'd thought I'd come through this distancing operation an intelligently sceptical observer of the social and political scene—such is the witchery of all stereotyping—I quickly found myself disoriented, even dismayed, by the absence of slobs in biker regalia, or greaseball girls with Confederate flags stitched on their jean jackets and hotrodding out of some teen rocker movie, or goons sucking at beer cans while giving the old "Sieg Heil" salute.

Instead, I was greeted warmly by a nice-looking young man with an Arrow-shirt-ad haircut, a good blue suit, and a walkie-talkie, who (without the phone) could almost have been an usher at my Anglican church.

Once I'd passed the threshold, a cheerful, healthy, and apple-cheeked teenager in jeans and a sweatshirt took over. Naturally enough, under the circumstances, he misread my obvious apprehension as the understandable fears of a decent white woman for her precious skin. "Don't worry, lady," he said consolingly. "We'll look out for you. There's nobody out there, just a bunch of Jews and commies."

Presto. I was back in the place I had been allotted at birth—the place reserved for white, middle-aged, middle-class women who deserved protection and a kind of reverence. In my real life, I'd been fighting to keep from falling into that place for forty years. Now apparently too old for sex, too young for death, but just right to become an embodiment of matriarchal propriety, I had finally become—at least for one protective teenager—Every Mom, the eternal feminine ideal that haunts white supremacist ideology. Above all things, the cause is in favour of family values so long as they are white, Christian, and heterosexual. I didn't need to wear camouflage; I *was* camouflage.

At the inside doors stood two unsmiling giants that fit my white supremacist fantasy: big guys in black jeans, boots, and black T-shirts with Heritage Front logos on their chests. Like the tidy boys who'd been manning the front doors, each of these tough lads had a walkie-talkie. They also carried huge flashlights that, it occurred to me, could be used in a pinch as truncheons.

"Security," said my newfound friend, the apple-cheeked teenager, who introduced himself as Dave.

It didn't take long for me to realize that there was danger in and around the Latvian Hall—real danger, contained at the moment, but with the potential to break out into full nastiness at any moment. I flashed back to the civil rights demonstrations I'd taken part in during the 1960s, times when I'd marched and sung and tried not to see the screaming crowds or the silent, faceless National Guardsmen.

What was surreal to me in this place was that I wasn't able to put on my moral armour. At any other time, in any other place, I would have been with the protestors. They were obviously outraged, and, should their own non-violent resolve break down, should they give these guys any reason, then those flashlights would crack some heads.

As matters stood, I was a lot more likely to get a whack on the head from one of the rowdy anti-fascists outside than from any of the Heritage Front folk, with their tidy literature tables, all carefully arranged beneath the portraits of Latvian anticommunist "freedom fighters," long-dead and, by most other people beyond the walls of this building, long forgotten.

In those powerless images were the only reinforcements of liberal stereotypes to be found in this place. One wood carving seemed to embody it all, amateurishly but carefully done. A worker in an old-fashioned billed cap—the iconography of anarchist, communist, fascist alike—stared out of one panel; next to him, a similarly unsmiling older man, a peasant farmer perhaps, stood stolidly. Then, ominous in helmet and with his steel-eyed glare, was a man in the uniform of a Second World War German trooper. Below all three hung a carefully carved sword. I don't know exactly what this curiously old-fashioned heraldry meant, but it was not necessary to know the precise wheres and wherefores. Here was a sudden, telling glimpse of a world of thought that lay behind the walkie-talkies and nice haircuts—memories to which I was not privy, but whose power I could imagine, reaching across time and oceans and great cultural changes, and keeping old, dark angers alive behind the glittering multiracial facade of Toronto the Good.

My generation, coming of age in the sixties, had wanted to make things new, to cut loose the ties with the past, and we did, casting aside history and tradition and embracing every current craze from dope to madness-as-liberation. The noble worker and peasant, the soldier with spine and soul of steel—all that belonged to a history we wanted to be rid of. But here in the Latvian Hall, it was precisely that history of wars and hatreds and ancient norms that spun the electricity, galvanized the apple-cheeked young man, put the thrill in the air that everybody wanted and that perhaps nobody except me found both vaguely fearful and vaguely familiar.

A couple of large guys in white T-shirts strutted by, showing off some muscle. There were a few tattoos and another slogan, "The Canadian Alliance for the next generation." But that's just what they weren't. Above the futuristic slogan, rippling with the chest, was a picture of a blond Viking in full horns and hair, a nineteenth-century vision reborn in the New World.

Everyone but me chain-smoked. Here was a generation with no vision more compelling than a return to generations and ideologies past, to an age of cartoon heroes, of Chicago movie gangsters, to the "basic values" of the body-building studio, the pool hall where the guys could come in the evenings, speak the language of their cradles, ignore Toronto's prim official smoking regulations, find a little corner of community in the megalopolis, through identification with dead fighters, destroyed empires, disgraced ideologies. In the midst of all the strangeness, the craziness, the endless adaptation to change that is life in any big city, these kids had found a home, a community, a family.

There were very few women, and that made me uneasy because it made me obvious. A couple of girls in tight jeans and black T-shirts sat slouched and puffing away, faces averted and shadowed by frizzed hair. I recognized the universal female posture of rebellion, whether of the right or of the left. I recalled the days when I cast off my petticoats and slipped into Levi's, pulled out my Camels, and marched for civil rights and the greater glory of Martin Luther King Jr. These kids were ready to hit the road for White Power and David Duke. I remember how committed and how foolhardy my friends and I were in 1965. These kids had the same look of proletarian dedication, of vigorous commitment, of outrage at the status quo. What past infamy or resistance was embodied in those pictures of long-dead soldier, peasant, worker that had the power to do for these women what a living activist had done for me?

The collision of my past and their present was disorienting. Then two women my age drifted in, dressed in nice suburban tweed and twinsets, looking as though they were on their way to a bridge lesson. They didn't seem to know anyone, but they also seemed at home. A couple of giggling young women in micro-minis came in accompanied by a young man in an Armani suit with sleek moussed hair. They reeked of money and style, and I could only wonder at their attendance here. The women chattered and giggled, until a well-dressed youth spoke quietly to them. Obviously, any lack of seriousness was not to be tolerated.

Then there was a lot of whispering and exchanges of hard looks among the security guards. I wondered if the demonstrators were going to charge the hall, or if the police were coming. I had a horrible thought: if there's a confrontation, I will have to trust my safety to these vigilant hunks. I looked around at the television news cameras, thought of the other cameras outside, and had a vision of myself on the eleven-o'clock news heading out of the hall as my guardians strongarmed a couple of aged concentration camp survivors.

One of the security men gave me a warm and encouraging smile, rich in the soothing balm of "Don't worry, lady. Everything's going to be all right." That smile hung in the space between us, pulled me into his world. Why not? I'm one of "them," white, over forty, and speaking with the remains of a Southern accent I can't lose. These guys know me and I know them. I lived with them for the first half of my life. "I'm here," says the grin, "looking out for you. You're fine." There wasn't a doubt in my mind that this vitamin-enriched young man would happily crack a skull to get me safely to my car. I had a feeling he really wanted to do just that—to turn me into a cause, to save me, so he could brag about it. Like all his kind, he was looking for an excuse to let it all go, to flex his arm and smash his way out.

The meeting was delayed and that made everyone edgy. The kids in suits looked nervous. The familiar volatile, toxic smell of testosterone ready to ignite emanated from the security troops. I've sniffed it before. It's the odour of anger and violence, of frustration and hatred, and it's also the scent of sex. Not the warm and comforting sex of love and intimacy but the quick and harsh sex of rage and power. You could read it in the security men's spread-legged stance, see it in the faces closed off and hidden behind black glasses. That was all boxed in in this room, waiting for the slightest encouragement to let it all out, to smack a head or kick a shin. Or much, much worse.

Just as I decided that I'd had it—to hell with the Front, the image, the book—the Heritage Front managed to surprise me again. A quietly handsome young man went up to the grand piano in the corner and began to play, beautifully, a Beethoven sonata.

There had never been any secret about what the Heritage Front stands for or the tactics of racist smearing they're prepared to stoop to. They had made no bones about being behind a hate hotline, spewing venom and bile over the phone lines about Native Canadians, Jews, or some other alleged deadly enemy of white civilization. But listening to the Beethoven sonata, surrounded by other appreciative white people who smiled and clapped, I felt, for one terrible instant, and despite decades spent fighting it, a part of the camaraderie, the atmosphere of reassurance, the soothing whiteness.

After all, these were people who looked like me, who enjoyed the music I love. Like it or not, I am part of the white firmament. I may not always feel proud of this whiteness, and I'm well aware of the crimes against humanity and common decency routinely committed in its name. But for that instant in the Latvian Hall, I let myself slip into the insidious, irrational comfort that, along with the permission it gives to equally irrational violence, is at the heart of the hard-right racist ethos and of its ever-broadening appeal in our society. For the length of a sonata, I was at home.

While I sat there, Beethoven soothing at least one savage breast, I considered the idea that these people were not supposed to exist. From the day I began this project, I was told that racism in Canada was minor, that the white supremacists were an isolated bunch of ignorant crazies, that there were no Klansmen in Toronto. More than one friend assured me that I was wasting my time, was bewitched by media hype, was in search of incidents to assuage my own guilt.

I'd have felt a little less riven if I'd known then, as I do now, that Grant Bristow, one of the Front's founders, was an agent in the pay of CSIS—the Canadian Security Intelligence Service—and was using funds received from them to finance the Front's activities, including the hotline. When the news of his infiltration was broken in August 1994, he went into hiding, but his fellow Front members were quick to claim they'd known for months about his CSIS connection and that he'd still been a most valuable addition to the clan. "I wish we'd had ten more like him, said one grinning Heritage Front spokesman.

But I didn't know all that then. All I knew was that I was in

Toronto, surrounded by a hundred or so people, listening to the distilled racist cant of the past 150 years pour out of the mouths of kids whose parents hadn't been born when Hitler was alive.

As I sat listening to the speakers of the Heritage Front calling for a ban on non-white immigration that September night three years ago, I could hear the same old science, old morality, old ideological arguments against "mixing" that I'd grown up with. No one openly raised the ancient spectre of rape and sexual domination of women, those staples of Southern racist fear, but it was there in the background, on the literature tables, in the air. Once you've left that atmosphere behind, you never lose your ability to sniff it out.

The longer I sat and listened to these people, the more I recognized them from my own history. I could imagine their homes, meals, lives. I recognized the code words, the plausible, almost invisible twisting of history, the strange way science has of coming up, again and again, in the cause of making racism plausible, even inevitable.

Dave, my self-appointed guardian angel, gave me a running commentary on the speakers and speeches. He told me that he was from the Ottawa Valley and that he'd been in Toronto for two years. What he saw in the city shocked him. "There's no place for white people here." He heard about the Front from a friend, called up the hotline, came to a meeting, and joined the cause. He told me he was twenty years old. He looked closer to sixteen.

When he noticed that I was taking notes, his sweet smile and diligent concern turned sharp. "You sure do write fast," he said. "What are you writing down?"

I assured him that I was just jotting down the speakers' ideas for my own future reference. I made a weak comment about having to write things down to remember. But I deliberately slowed down my note-taking. It was a reminder to me that Dave's nice manners were window-dressing, part of the David Duke theory of reality. Wearing a suit was okay. Writing wasn't. The danger to me wasn't outside this room. It was in it.

I wanted to know more about the lives and times of the young people in the Heritage Front but I found communication difficult.

Simple questions like "Where are you from?" were often greeted with hard stares. I couldn't take notes without admitting I was a journalist and I didn't want these people to know who I was because I was afraid of them. I was left with Front members' dull and desultory comments on the speakers ("Real good, very interesting") and on Front leader Wolfgang Droege ("Smart guy. He tells it like it is").

Droege was in his glory that night, laughing with the kids, greeting everyone like an old friend. He'd managed his media coup—getting the meeting to be held—and even the demonstration played into his hands, guaranteeing him a space on the late-night news, insuring an interview or two, reaching more potential recruits. Dapper in suit and tie, smiling at the ladies and chaffing the guys on the arm, Droege was the perfect politician manqué. All he needed was a baby to kiss.

It was a stellar performance, worthy of a man who advises his youthful followers not to haul out the Nazi regalia, calling it bad public relations. According to Droege, the Heritage Front is simply a peace-loving organization dedicated to "a whiter, brighter Canada." But there's more to it than that. Despite his soft-spoken demeanour and his Brooks Brothers appearance, Droege is a convicted felon, a member of four other ultra-right groups, and a man who believes that Hitler was right.

Droege learned about Aryan supremacy at home, at his father and grandfather's knees. He was born in Forchheim, Bavaria, in 1949. His father, Walter, was a veteran of the Luftwaffe. His grandfather was an unrepentant Nazi, a friend of Julius Streicher, hanged in 1945 for war crimes. Little Wolfie grew up on a diet of stories of German glory and Third Reich might, a "pride in being German." He was eight or so when his grandpa told him about the Jews, zog, and perfidy.

He learned his lessons well. To this day, he is convinced that the Holocaust never occurred, that the white European race is superior mentally and morally to all other races, that there is a Jewish-led cabal out to discredit him and those who think like him, and that the "true" history of Germany and National Socialism has been hidden, replaced with false stories of genocide and mass murder.

When his parents' marriage collapsed in 1964, Wolfgang immigrated to Canada with his mother. He returned to Germany in 1967 and attempted to join the German army. Rejected because he was only seventeen, he hung around briefly with members of the neo-Nazi National Party. When he returned to Canada and his job as a printer, he joined the white supremacist Western Guard. His first arrest came in 1975 for spray-painting white power slogans along the route of an African Liberation Day march. Since that day, he's never looked back.

Droege's mother lives in Toronto and, according to Droege, fears for his life. His brother and sister live in Germany. One is a paramedic, the other a doctor, and they aren't interested in having him around. He modestly admits that they might have been upset when his photo appeared in *Stern* magazine as "part of the international racialist, nationalist movement" and as an associate of David Duke.

The white rights movement is Droege's life and his livelihood. No one knows where his income derives; he is a printer, had a bailiff's licence (revoked by the Ontario government in 1993), and does occasional work repossessing goods from defaulted creditors. It seems impossible that the Heritage Front donations would be sufficient to support him and his work unless, as has been rumoured, he receives money from ultra-right organizations in Canada and Germany.

Droege doesn't drink or smoke, isn't married, and draws his female companions from the young women who hang around the Heritage Front. His friends are members of the Front or other white supremacist groups. When asked by a Toronto *Star* reporter if he could be a friend to a Jew or a Black, Droege replied that he could not "because they work for the interest of their race and I work for the interest of my race. These are opposites which cannot be overcome."

Two years after that meeting at the Latvian Hall, Droege's little empire is in some disarray. A group of irate antifascists trashed Gary Schipper's home after it was revealed in the papers that he was the "voice" on the Heritage Front hotline. The Front claims plenty of new recruits, all under twenty-five, but one of Droege's teenaged female followers has been accused of disseminating hate for handing out Heritage Front pamphlets. His newsletter is published infrequently, and the hotline was shut down by the courts after he lost his case before the Canadian Human Rights Commission. When he attempted to set up a new hotline, called Equal Rights for Whites, a judge found him in contempt of court and ordered him, Gary Schipper, and Front lieutenant Ken Barker to appear in court.

On November 24, 1993, the day Droege et al. appeared, along with Front heroine Elisse Hategan, a dimpled, redheaded teenager accused of promoting hatred (a charge later dropped), a crowd led by students from Anti-Racist Action marched on Ernst Zundel's house, carrying signs and chanting slogans. Both Zundel and the police were well prepared for the crowd, which numbered about 150. While Zundel—hardhat in place, the front of his house protected by a plastic curtain—snapped photographs out of his second-story window, more than sixty police kept the kids in line. Four demonstrators were arrested and charged with assaulting police officers. Aside from a lot of litter—paint cans, eggs, pieces of tile— Zundel and his house were unscathed. The case against Droege was postponed until March 1994 when Droege, in a surprise move, pleaded guilty. The hotline messages were subsequently toned down.

By the summer of 1992, I'd managed a few non-informative conversations with the followers of the Front. The kids were mostly like Dave, young, a bit confused, deeply distrustful of anyone not committed body and soul to the cause of white power. I was curious about what brought them, particularly the girls, to the Front.

Elisse Hategan, eighteen, and Droege's own little Evita Peron, is the most understandable. Hategan is no longer a Front member and is now speaking out publicly against her former colleagues. She arrived in Toronto in 1991 fresh from the horrors of Romania. She hates communists with a passion that few of us well-fed, well-housed North Americans can understand. After a childhood spent in the cold, damp, hungry deprivation engineered by leader-for-life Ceausescu, she is unwilling to believe that any form of socialism is beneficial.

Along with her good looks and her zeal, Elisse carries a whole bagful of old country prejudices against Jews and non-whites. She is an admirer of the Iron Guard, the fiercely anti-Semitic and nationalistic movement that emerged in Romania just before the Second World War and allied itself with the Nazis after Romania's defeat by Hitler. It was, she reminds me, "an anticommunist movement, dedicated to the freedom of the Romanian people."

After Elisse, there are other girls, whose commitment is no less strong but whose motives are fuzzier. The Front pays lip service to women's equality, but most of the women are moms, bods, or workhorses. Status is based upon your proximity to Droege or one of the other leaders. It goes without saying that independent action or thought is discouraged, but I found little inclination in any of the youths to utter more than slogans. What they liked was belonging, having a cosy little world, complete with rules, banners, and religion that they could sink into. Why they chose this path, rather than the Hare Krishnas or the Moonies, was vague. The usual answer, always brought out, was their desire to save their country from "them."

Nature or nurture? Did it all begin in the family? Droege's sorry tale of childhood indoctrination and old country immigration baggage would seem to explain his attachment to the hardcore tenets of white supremacy, but I wanted to talk to a homegrown supremacist. Carney Nerland was in jail. So I went in search of someone else, someone who could tell me how a nice Canadian kid with a good multicultural Canadian education could turn to the invisible empire. It didn't take me long to find Lorne.

I located him through one of my students, and we agreed to meet at a corner by the Royal Ontario Museum. There was a demonstration that day by the Coalition for the Truth About Africa, protesting a display at the museum. There weren't many demonstrators, but a few folks had shown up to jeer at the ones who were there. In the summer heat, both sides seemed a bit dispirited. At the time we met, Lorne was waffling about whether to join the Ontario Branch of the Knights of the Ku Klux Klan. He couldn't make up his mind to commit himself, but he had attended some meetings and liked some of what he heard. He was also "sort of" interested in the Church of the

Creator and the Reform Party, which he told me was "the last hope for real Canadian politics."

"I mean, those guys in Ottawa are all alike. All out for themselves. Just get elected and collect the pension." He attended a couple of meetings of the Heritage Front but didn't like it. "I don't like that guy Droege. He's a foreigner and that's what's wrong with this country. Too many foreigners telling us what to do." I point out that Droege is a member of the Klan as well as a friend of David Duke. Lorne is surprised. "They don't say too much about that."

In fact, the Heritage Front talks about it all the time. Duke is the coverboy for a Heritage Front newsletter. His exploits, his books, his words are parroted endlessly. Is it possible that Lorne just managed to miss all those references? "I don't read much of that stuff. I go to the meetings and I talk to the guys. I'm more interested in who's there."

So we have my vision of the life of the true believer in the hard right—no books, no ideas, just a few beers with the guys and a few nostrums about white rights. Lorne doesn't deny it; he seems to find it all comfortable. He defines his life not by what he likes but by what he dislikes, and what he dislikes are non-white immigrants. "All those dope pushers and pimps from the Caribbean. That's why this country is going broke, keeping those deadbeats and criminals on welfare."

Lorne also didn't like what he was seeing at the museum. The protest was against an exhibition that was felt to be a misrepresentation of Black history.

"Just what do these people mean, 'truth about Africa'?" he asks with contempt. I explain that they believe the true, brutal story of Africa's colonization by the European powers was being misrepresented by the museum. "Look at these guys," he says, waving an arm at the demonstrators both Black and white. "They ought to be out working. Bet they've never had a job. Just came here and got on the old welfare tit."

Lorne doesn't want his real name used, because he doesn't need "the aggravation" of people demonstrating at his house or business. "That's what these people do. Look at that professor. They went to her house." (Jeanne Cannizzo, the curator of the "Into the Heart of Africa" display at the museum, was the target of demonstrations.)

But Lorne isn't ashamed of what he believes. "I don't mind standing up." He's no biker stud or skinhead punk. He's a slim man with short brown hair who looks a decade younger than thirty-two. Dressed in jeans, running shoes, T-shirt, Blue Jays cap, and sunglasses, he could be any sports fan on his way to a game. In fact, that's where he's headed later in the day. "It's my day off," he says politely. "I don't mind my boss seeing me, out cheering the Jays. I heard about this demonstration and thought I'd just take a look."

I offer to buy him lunch in exchange for an interview. He chooses a pizza restaurant across the street. "I guess I should hit you for a steak and champagne, but I like pizza."

I want to dislike Lorne. He is a self-confessed racist, a blatant homophobe—"If the general population gets AIDS, it's because of the queers"—and probably sexist to an extreme. But he's also not fearsome, in the way that some of the Heritage Front males are. He has the kind of charming edge that makes Michael J. Fox's right-wing characters so appealing. He says all the wrong things but it's forgivable because he doesn't really seem responsible for it. It's just his nature.

There's also my own bias. I'm always charmed by liars and con artists, and Lorne has a lot of that kind of spirit. He's adamant about one thing. He developed his own cosmology and isn't living out some blighted family fantasy. "I never heard about these groups before," he says. "I suppose my parents voted, but I can't say I ever heard them discuss politics or immigrants even once. It just never came up."

Lorne was born in a small town on the Ontario-Quebec border. "We moved around a bit," he recalls. "My dad followed the jobs. Cornwall, Kingston, Brantford, the Ottawa Valley. By the time I was in high school, I guess we'd lived in all of them."

Lorne wasn't unhappy with the frequent moves, although he wishes he'd stayed in one place "long enough to get some real roots. It's important to kids." His schoolwork suffered. "I was never gonna be a brain." He compensated by being an "average" athlete and "great" with girls. By the time he was eighteen, he was out of school, working and on his own. At nineteen, he was married. "You know how it is. She got pregnant and we got married. We were too young." The marriage ended two years later and Lorne drifted to Toronto, looking for excitement. "It was the place to be," he says.

At least that's what he thought. Then, as far as he is concerned, his Toronto disappeared. Swallowed up by "them." Work was hard to find. "It was like, everywhere I went, there were Pakis or Dreads and they were only interested in hiring each other. You know how it is, one gets in and then he gets all his buddies on the payroll. I've heard they pay the guy who sets them all up a little percentage."

Lorne eventually located a job in Brampton, a suburb city near Toronto. "It was far enough away from the bad things and close enough to enjoy the good," he says. He was earning good money, and after a few years on the singles circuit, he decided to settle down. It was at this point, about three years ago, that he decided Ontario wasn't his place any longer. "I mean, you look around and you see who's getting ahead. Who's buying houses. Who's driving the new cars, shopping in the plaza. It wasn't me or mine."

Toronto's red-hot real-estate market was too high for Lorne's salary, even though his fiancée was also working full time. "I couldn't even afford the down payment on a condo. And rents are going up all the time." As Lorne sees it, wherever he looked, "they" were already there, taking over. "Look at the big expensive housing projects—all for Chinese. They should be building housing I can afford, but instead they're just building million-dollar mansions for them. There's a whole plaza that's all Chinese, they don't even speak English. Even the bank is Chinese. I mean, this is Canada and here are these people refusing to speak English. And we're stupid enough to tell them it's okay."

His country—white, English-speaking, and recognizable—has been stolen from him. "Fucked away" is how he puts it. He is vague about just who did the fucking, but he knows that some of them were Black. "Those people are apes," he says. "They should be in zoos. I mean, look at the crime. Look at the break-and-enters. Look at how, wherever they go, there's dope and prostitution and AIDS.

This was a decent town before we let all them in and nobody's going to stop them now, because they'll scream racism and get on TV and take you to court. That's what we've done to ourselves in Canada. We can't even keep them out because they'll say we're racist.

"As if they're not. They don't want to mix. They don't want to be multicultural. Look at them in Africa, those tribes are killing each other all the time. I see those kids in Ethiopia on the news. Who's starving those kids? Who's keeping the food from getting to them? Then they come here and they want to get the jobs and keep them for themselves and their friends. Just like back in Africa. 'Truth About Africa.'" He sniffs. "That's the 'truth' about Africa and everybody knows it, but nobody says anything because they're scared of being called racist. You know what I say to that? Sticks and stones can break my bones, but names don't hurt me. Call me a racist. I don't care, and my friends don't care, either."

Lorne points to other signs of the lowered estate of white Canadians. "Look at the streets. Who are on the streets, sleeping on the streets? White people. You don't see any Pakis, no Blacks or Chinese. Just white people. We've lost this country. I mean, look at Quebec. All they have to do is squawk and the government jumps. Anything they want they can have so long as they don't go separate. I say let 'em go. Same with the Indians, let 'em have their separate state. No more tax money. Let 'em get out and work for a change."

If there is a typical recruit for the white supremacist movement, Lorne certainly strikes me as it. He's convinced that he's been done out of the job, the home, the future that was his by birth. In his comments about Blacks and Orientals there's an echo of fear, the fear and cowardice that Frantz Fanon says is the core of racism. Somewhere in Lorne's mind, he's afraid of life in the open without a scapegoat to fix his perceived failures on. If he is typical, then he doesn't understand much of what he's buying. He doesn't read much of anything, preferring the wisdom of hearsay and television.

He has never heard, for instance, of the "Protocols of the Elders of Zion," the revealed "truth" of anti-Semites. In fact, until I told him, he didn't know what an anti-Semite was. "I don't know about that. I mean, I've heard about the Jews and all that but I don't know any." As for Hitler, "I don't know about any of that stuff. I mean, I've seen movies and I know he was crazy, but that's all a long time ago. I'm interested in the here and now."

For information on the here and now, Lorne likes the tabloid press, television, and what he hears from people like Pat Buchanan in the U.S. "That's what we need up here. Someone who really says it like it is." And, of course, he likes David Duke. He is also a tepid fan of Paul Fromm and his group, Citizens for Foreign Aid Reform. Fromm, he says, "is really smart, and he's got the right ideas. But he's kinda dull." The same goes for Preston Manning of Reform. "We need somebody up here with some—I don't know—some..." I suggest the word *pizzazz*. Lorne's never heard it, but it fits. "Yeah," he says. "Pizzazz. I like that."

I suspect that Lorne is moved by demagogues, although he doesn't know it yet. He's not being *lured* by the radical right so much as he's being pushed towards it by fierce, half-understood grudges in his own belly. Grudges of Lorne's sort are things the white liberal experts on racism don't ever seem to understand. These grudges affix themselves to the difficulty of finding work or housing or a long-lasting career, but do not spring from them. They are deeper, more angry than mere disappointments.

And they are hungry. Lorne's grudges don't get enough blood from the pale speeches of Preston Manning, or even from the patient discourses of Paul Fromm. And they want blood—the whole irrational thing. Lorne speaks warmly of the need to have someone who'll "speak up" for whites and "tell the truth" about multiculturalism. He wants a fighter. "Here and now" means jobs and advancement and opportunities for Lorne and "ordinary Canadians." He wants the fight to begin now. He tells me that other countries don't allow immigrants or refugees to take jobs from citizens. I ask him what countries, and he says the U.S. and Germany. His grudges cry out for Duke, or the handsome, serious-looking young hatemongers who lead the "respectable," non-punk far right in Germany.

Like most people smitten with grudges, Lorne hasn't paid much attention to the history and social story of the Klan since he found out that it was more or less what he was looking for—righteous, heroic, bloody. "I know it's American and was started to protect women and kids from slaves when they killed people," he told me. He supports the Klan's position on Catholics, which is strongly anti: "I've been in Quebec and I know how much power the Pope has. They want to run everybody's life. I'll tell you something, you can believe it or not, there are a lot of Klan members in Quebec." The fact that the Klan's virulent anti-Catholicism is no more than a reflection of its small-town Southern American Protestant roots is lost on him. Anti-Catholic rhetoric is a message he wants to hear.

Lorne's Klan doctrine comes from the lips of new-era believers like David Duke, whose wisdom he does not question because Duke is successful. Duke's middle-class yuppie image is attractive to Lorne, and to other people similarly afflicted by a sense of powerlessness, because Duke is how he'd like to see himself. "Ordinary" but "getting on with things." Getting the house, the nice car, the good job, elected to office—getting the power, that is, from the cowardly conspirators, the elected officials, the fat-cats, who are keeping it out of the hands of ordinary people. (Perhaps Lorne hasn't heard about ZOG yet. He will.)

Duke has a following in Canada. His message carried on television, his life story parroted in the Heritage Front and Klan newsletters, his exploits are well known among Canadian white supremacists, as they are in Europe. Even though Duke has publicly abandoned his Klan leader past, his white-power views make him a hero to Lorne and people like him. In Lorne's eyes, Droege's friendship with Duke is his one asset.

If there is to be a revolt of the right, it will be a revolt of people who've worked hard for what they've got and see it being taken away from them—people like Lorne, that is, not punks. "I mean, you don't want just skinheads and that. Some are okay, but not everybody."

He also likes the message of rights for whites and taking control of his country. "We just sort of handed it over. Now we have to pay for all these people on welfare, all these immigrants coming in and living on welfare and getting drug cards and dental benefits. I mean,

I can't afford to get my teeth fixed and these guys just come in here and get it for free. I heard about a man claimed he was a refugee. He brought in his whole family. They got all kinds of stuff. The kid had open-heart surgery. All of it on the taxpayer. Then they went back to Tobago or someplace, I forget where. Just came in to take advantage of us. Could I go down there and get away with that? I mean, just hop down in November and say, 'I'm a refugee. I want to live here free'? Get a house, get money, medical, live there for six months and then say 'Adios' and go back to Canada?" He laughs. "Hey, not a bad idea. I'll just be a refugee every winter."

Listening to Lorne's hodgepodge of history and urban folktales is a bit like listening to horrid fairy tales created for the young, with saintly knights and wicked witches and damsels in distress. These are stories well worn—the Pakis with the roaches in the matchboxes, rising crime rates, the jobs lost to the new migrant, the refugee-welfare scams—and all have been refuted by reputable sources and even disreputable ones time and time again. But they linger on, developing lives and legs, travelling across the country. The same stories are told at meetings of the Association to Preserve English in Canada in Vancouver, at church supper Reform fundraisers in Alberta, at dinner tables in Toronto, and over beers in Saint John. They pass from one grudge-laden person to another, and, as the taxman bites deeper into middle-class Canadian incomes and middle-class Canadian aspirations, those stories of immigrants scamming and stealing become more respectable, less the province of the fringe and more the beliefs of the beleaguered ordinary Canadian worker.

There's one other thing that's noticeable about Lorne. For all his apparent openness, there's a guarded quality, a feeling that in a pack of his fellows Lorne would be a lot more aggressive, a lot less polite. In concert with like-minded men, Lorne would find a vent for his simmering hatred and grudges.

I thought about that when I read, sometime later, that the Klan is openly recruiting in Georgetown, an attractive commuter village near Toronto. I wonder if he's there, or recruiting somewhere else. Or whether he has withdrawn into his hatreds, to await the emergence of the leader with the drive, the ambition, the rage he is waiting for.

I was disappointed in my conversations with the members of the Heritage Front and the Klan. I wanted to know what made them tick, what combination of forces led them to join a discredited cause. Of course they were there because they wanted to be, because they found something to keep them there. That goes for most of us. But I wanted to know more. I wanted to believe that they were aberrations, freaks, people out of time; what I saw were people who were, aside from their supremacist beliefs, fairly ordinary. They came, just as people come to any religion or cause, for many reasons—family training, deeply held beliefs, rebellion, a need to have a community. But this was no ordinary community. It was a community that defined itself as outsider, deliberately placed itself at the fringe.

Ultimately, I realized that what really troubled me about Lorne and Elisse and even Droege was that they had made a decision to go with a movement that I consider evil. If I, who had been educated and trained to be a racist, could see the fallacies, the hollowness of the racial-purity line, why couldn't they?

That caused me to rethink my own history. It was outside circumstances—the civil rights movement, changing times—that led me to the first steps in my own journey. Maybe these people were just doing the same. The difference was that the change for them was to see their cities becoming multiracial, to hear that able-bodied white males need not apply for jobs, that spaces were to be reserved for "designated groups"—women, aboriginals, francophones, visible minorities, the disabled. I had fought to gain power for the dispossessed. They were fighting to hang on to power for themselves and their children.

While I mulled over just what appeal Droege and his ideas have for students, I heard my own university students telling me they were afraid that they wouldn't have jobs because of what they called "reverse discrimination." I listened to Ontario premier Bob Rae outline the NDP's righteous crusade for employment equity and then heard the parents of my students—most of them immigrants, all of them dedicated to the Canadian Dream—erupt in rage because *their* sons were about to be denied precisely what they had come to Canada to obtain.

I listened to a radio show in which a bitter young university student called himself "an endangered species" and insisted that all he wanted was to be judged on his merits. He was sternly reminded by Marion Boyd, Ontario's Attorney-General, that the merit principle seemed to be applied only when the applicant was a white male. Certain merits—height and weight requirements for police, for example—discriminated against certain groups and so these merits had to be rethought. "All we are trying to do is level the playing field," said Boyd.

That's a phrase I've used many times. I'm in favour, of course, of pay equity, but I have to admit that the levelling doesn't negatively affect me or mine. My daughters and granddaughters stand to gain from equity. I already have. I'm not like Lorne or Elisse or Dave or any of the other young white people who see their hopes for the future closing before their eyes, see themselves as left out of their own country.

This is exactly the way that Boyd's designated groups—minorities, aboriginals, the disabled—have always felt here in their own country. In our quest to rectify the sins of the past, we've dropped Lorne and all those like him into the ashcan of history. He is now, in his own eyes, the victim and, to him, the enemy is the Other.

The first time I heard of CSIS, the Canadian Security Intelligence Service, was at a rally for injured workers who had been denied Worker's Compensation. I was there with a stalwart little group of leftists who believed that there was an international conspiracy of the Right hard at work undermining good Progressive organizations. The centre of the conspiracy was Langley, Virginia, home of the American Central Intelligence Agency. In Canada, protesters assured me, the CIA lackeys were in CSIS. It was formed in 1984 after a scandal where the RCMP Security Service was found to be engaged in an assortment of questionable activities leveled against the Quebec Independence movement. I didn't take all the talk too seriously.

For me, the news was a strange little bit of déjà vu. Back in 1970, I had briefly been part of the Young Socialists Alliance in

Albuquerque, New Mexico. We met sporadically to talk and theo-rize over meals of cheap red wine and fire-hot chili con carne. There were, as I recall, less than a dozen of us across all of New Mexico. We occasionally joined up with fellow socialists to do volunteer labour at the local Catholic ADD Worker truck farm. It was there that we learned that J. Edgar Hoover, genius of the FBI, had declared the YSA the most dangerous left-wing group in America. We knew, from experience, that Hoover's announcements were generally accompanied by infiltration. Would our skinny ranks soon be strengthened by FBI stalwarts? It had done wonders for the Communist Party of America, now composed almost exclusively of agents. But no new people came to join our band and, eventually, we drifted away to communes, or new movements or the Democrats. Our danger to America was forgotten.

I thought about the YSA when I saw the headlines about Grant Bristow, the alleged CSIS mole in the Heritage Front. I only saw Bristow in the flesh once. He was with a group of other Front males and he made so little impression on me—compared to the more colourful Front lads—that I didn't even bother to follow up on him. I knew that he was one of the original handful of people who found-ed the Front. I knew that he was very close to Front leader Wolfgang Droege. He made the usual inflammatory statements about Blacks and Jews but he lacked the abrasive vocal style of Gary Schipper or the polished pectorals and youthful élan of Droege's protege, George Burdi. He appears in my notes as a minor player. Front lore claimed he was responsible for the hotline, for the harassment tactics against Front "enemies" like the leadership of the Anti-Racist Action group. But the voice and persona of the hotline was Gary Schipper's and there was nothing to show any particular Front member was more opposed to anti-racism than any other. Bristow seemed to be simply another garden-variety white racist. Nothing significant about him at all.

In August 1994, I learned, along with the rest of Canada, that Bristow was supposedly a paid informer for CSIS, had been one since the Front's foundation in 1989. More than that, the money paid to Bristow—reputed to be around $60,000 a year—had gone directly

to the Heritage Front coffers. The repulsive hotline, with its changing messages of hatred and bigotry had been financed, inadvertently, by taxpayers. Bristow also appeared to have been eager to build
the organization. His cash had helped to print *Up Front*, the
Heritage Front newsletter with its glowing messages about David
Duke and White Rights, the public meetings to recruit members, the
cheery little pub night to celebrate Hitler's birthday. He'd been there,
leading the movement, from the beginning. Front spokesperson
Gary Schipper appeared on the Toronto evening news to give an
upbeat report of Bristow's participation. Schipper claimed that Front
members had suspected Bristow of being a mole but that it hadn't
bothered them because he did so much good for the organization.
"We could use ten more like him," Schipper told reporters.

csis has never confirmed that Bristow was on the payroll—theirs
or anyone else's. They didn't deny it, either. In true Cold War style,
they refused to give out any information and then declared the
whole incident to be protected by the Official Secrets Act. The
Toronto *Sun* and the Toronto *Star* newspapers, who first broke the
story of csis involvement in the Heritage Front, were asked to reveal
the sources of their information and to hand over documents used
to substantiate the allegations. The *Star* refused. It then appeared
that there would be a confrontation between spies and journalists
when, in a fashion more attuned to a television drama than real life,
Brian McInnis, former press secretary to Doug Lewis, the solicitor-
general under Prime Minister Kim Campbell, revealed that he was
the source of the information. McInnis said that he had made the
information public, despite consequences to himself, because he was
"disgusted" by the idea that csis could use Bristow as a paid
informer.

McInnis said what he had to say on television and then disappeared from public view. In October 1994, in a detailed interview
with Kirk Makin of the *Globe and Mail*, he outlined what life was
like before and after he blew the whistle on Bristow and csis. Shortly
before the August broadcast, he was arrested by the RCMP. His home
was searched. Cabinet documents from the previous Tory government were found. These documents, which are alleged to prove the

link between CSIS and Bristow, should not have been in McInnis' possession. Because they were, he could be charged with a violation of the Official Secrets Act and—theoretically—sent to jail for as long as fourteen years. That's a fairly severe price to pay for what some journalists believe is a bit of grandstanding. McInnis ignored that cavil, pointing out that Canadians are too complacent about their government's actions. "There are two stories in the country right now," he told Makin. "This [CSIS] is one of them. The other is the tainted-blood scandal. There is no concern about that one either. There was a quote in the *Globe* last week about the hottest place in hell being reserved for those who remain neutral in times of moral crisis. I think this is a moral crisis."

No one believes that McInnis will go to prison. Most Ottawa pundits think that, once the media hue and cry is over, he'll become a minor footnote in the story. As of November, McInnis was in Toronto, working in a refugee hostel, his future up for RCMP grabs. But the story he broke has developed, as we say in journalism, legs. It travelled and the road led to allegations of Tory dirty tricks against the Reform Party, to claims of spying on Jewish groups, the CBC, to clandestine work in Germany. CSIS isn't talking and so, aside from the usual denials, none of the allegations has been proven. Grant Bristow has disappeared, after telling his buddies that he had a job in New Brunswick. The Security Intelligence Review Committee (SIRC), the parliamentary watchdog for CSIS, is delving into the matter and is expected to release a report that will say as little as possible. Meanwhile, questions arise. The first of which is What on earth was CSIS doing infiltrating and, inadvertently or knowingly, funding the Heritage Front?

At least one Ottawa insider of my acquaintance—"not for attribution, off the record, etc."—believes that it was a simple matter of survival. The spymasters of CSIS, suddenly finding themselves without a Cold War to wage, were desperate to find a reason to justify their existence. Anti-communism became, overnight, anti-terrorism and the first terrorists to feel the sting were the ones closest to hand. Like J. Edgar Hoover, in his quest to find the motherhood of leftist hordes in the U.S., they targeted a group and turned it into an enemy. If there were neo-Nazi terrorists to fight, espionage could carry on.

That's an easy analysis and it does beg the question of just how dangerous the Heritage Front was—and is. Droege and his pals, including Grant Bristow, have never made any secret of the fact that they believe that White Rights should be preserved by force, if necessary. Droege's armed infiltration of the island of Dominica and his links with the White Aryan Resistance and the Church of the Creator clearly show his willingness to move from public relations to violence. Furthermore, in 1992, a police raid on the Toronto home of a Front leader netted a cache of arms, including automatic weapons. There was, and is, some justification for a continued surveillance of a group that has, at its core, a belief that certain races are subhuman.

Front leaders have also shown themselves to be highly cunning when it comes to maintaining their organization. The Anti-Racist Action group—a somewhat disparate group of students and members of various community groups, chose direct confrontation with the Heritage Front as their method of striking back at Zundel, Droege, and the others. While the ARA trashed houses—Gary Schipper's—the Front was able to hack into telephone lines in order to ferret out ARA members targeted for verbal harassment. The Front denies doing it but ARA members claimed they were threatened and Grant Bristow is the one who people believe thought up the idea and who had the connections to get names and addresses of arrested ARA members from the police. If this is true, then Bristow was using his connections to frighten and harass Canadians deemed "enemies" by the Front.

The Canadian Jewish Congress, the B'nai Brith, Black and Native Canadian groups took these allegations very seriously. Droege has always given the impression that he has connections in the police and the military. At least one Toronto policeman was proven to have attended Front meetings and there are Front groups close to Canadian military bases, including CFB Petawawa, outside of Ottawa. The Hate Crimes squad of the Metropolitan Toronto Police Department monitors Front activity so it seems logical, to me, that the national police would want information as well. What is at issue is whether Grant Bristow was a mole or a racist masquerading as a mole and whether his connection with CSIS was merely a front to obtain money to advance the cause of white supremacy in Canada.

One of the best defenses of CSIS came from former CSIS officer Peter Marwitz in the October 10th *Globe and Mail*. Marwitz, a retired intelligence officer, with twenty-nine years of experience, spent time in both CSIS and the Department of External Affairs. In his article, he said flatly that SIRC should make public information about the Front and Bristow public, if such information exists. According to Marwitz, the incentive for CSIS to infiltrate Canadian right-wing extremist groups came directly from SIRC in 1986-87. The domestic counter-terrorism branch of CSIS, formed in 1988, was a response. Marwitz maintains that SIRC has been aware of CSIS involvement in the Heritage Front all along and has had "full knowledge of all CSIS operational files related to the Heritage Front since 1990, having reviewed them annually and found nothing adverse." The justification for these actions was keeping tabs on a potentially violent group.

Plenty of people, including those groups targeted by the Front for suppression or extinction, disagree with that idea. Brian McInnis did and that's why he turned to the media. "Infiltration and creation are two different things," he told Kirk Makin. "The Heritage Front is now the most sophisticated and noxious group in the country and your tax dollars may have gone to help set it up."

Was Bristow told to set up an organization? Only the most devoted spy-haters can believe that. What is more likely is that he found it necessary to justify his existence. A group, meeting regularly with leaders and followers, would keep him in information and cash for years. Graham Greene gave the complete blueprint for it in his novel *Our Man in Havana*. But there's also some evidence that Bristow took his role too far. Ultra-rightists who attended a 1984 conference in Libya sponsored by Muammar Khadaffi, recall him as the loudest of the crowd, with views that startled even that ideologically driven group. Was it window dressing? A little screaming to impress the flock? Or was it the real Bristow? A white-rights believer who saw

CSIS as a source of cash for his views? Those questions, along with others about Bristow—who he is and where he came from—remain unanswered. He is in hiding, reputed to be protected by the RCMP or CSIS. Front members now refer to him with contempt as a burnout case with a drinking problem and little influence on Front activities.

One person who sheds a little light on the Bristow affair is Elisse Hategan, now an ex-member of the Front. Hategan, whose criminal charges have been dropped by the police, has become a vocal critic of her former friends. She claims to have provided the police with information about Bristow's harassment of anti-racists over a year ago. No action was taken. Hategan, now in hiding, appeared on several Toronto area news and television shows speaking out about her life as a Front member. She spoke about her involvement as a kind of addiction, where despite harassment and sexual demands, she saw Droege and the Front members as her family. It was only after her arrest for distributing hate literature that she lost the support of the Front. It was that, she claims, that opened her eyes to the reality of the people she had been working with and caused her to turn them, including Bristow, over to the police.

It's difficult for me to take Hategan's conversion seriously but I try to believe. She is, after all, only nineteen. She was just fifteen when she joined the Front. But she was one of their most aggressive and public supporters and it's hard to forget the violent tenor of her words.

That brings me back to Bristow. Could he really have been acting? If so, it's an Academy Award performance, one which he kept up for years both in public and in private. As for the image of him as a hard-drinking dud, history doesn't bear out that view. Three years ago, along with Droege and a handful of other Front members, Bristow joined the Reform Party. He even acted, for a while, as Preston Manning's security person and it was on his advice that the Reform Party hired an agency manned by Heritage Front members to provide security for one of Reform's largest Toronto rallies. Those actions, when they were made public during the 1993 federal election, were damaging to the Reform Party image in Ontario. Preston Manning believes that the Heritage Front-Reform connection may have cost the party four seats in Ontario and, therefore, kept Reform from becoming the Opposition. The question for Manning and Reform is Did Bristow join Reform on his own initiative or was he acting on instructions from CSIS?

Peter Marwitz disputes this theory out of hand. "CSIS," he writes, "is made up of a broad spectrum of the Canadian mosaic, a mix of well-educated officers of both genders, of a wide variety of ethnic backgrounds representing all races. CSIS officers vote, like other Canadians, including some for the Bloc Québécois and Reform Party." In Marwitz's view, this merry multicultural mix prevents CSIS officers from forming a cabal against any group. Furthermore, there are the safeguards built into the system—the SIRC reviews, reports to the Inspector-General, the Solicitor-General.

But, the nasty fact remains that only the Tories stood to gain from a discrediting of the Reform as the spokesmen of the far-right and, during the campaign, the Tories were still in charge of all the apparatus of power. Doug Lewis, the Solicitor-General, wasn't disinterested. He was running for the election of his, and his party's, life. Preston Manning has made plenty of political hay out of that fact, even though there isn't, thus far, a shred of evidence to prove that Bristow was acting for CSIS—or anyone else—when he joined Reform. Manning has kept up the media heat, asking if Bristow was acting for CSIS when he joined Reform and brought five other Heritage Front members with him. Tory dirty tricks to discredit or was there more to Reform and the Front than even Manning knew?

The connection between Reform and the Heritage Front surfaced during the 1993 election, the result of the usual media leaks. Even before Preston Manning expelled six Front members, including Wolfgang Droege, from the party, there were tales of Grant Bristow's close watch on Manning, of Front members being hired to provide security for Reform rallies in Toronto, of Front members or sympathizers running as candidates.

Tales of Front sympathizers as candidates were never proven. One Toronto candidate, John Beck, was accused of making racist remarks at York University. Beck denied the charge but the party was embarrassed and he resigned as a candidate. Manning moved quickly to deal with charges but, in some circles and particularly in sensitive areas like Metro Toronto, the possibility of a connection between the Reform Party and ultra-right organizations was a real fear. While Reform's stand on immigration was music to the ears of those who saw Toronto growing too ethnic too fast and while it's impossible to estimate whether Reform candidates lost two or twenty thousand votes, it's safe to say that the Heritage Front connection did damage the party's message.

As the parliamentary subcommittee began its investigation into the CSIS-Heritage Front affair, Grant Bristow was still missing—the committee were forced to admit publicly that they had no idea where he was—and CSIS was still hiding behind its legislative wall of the Official Secrets Act. Doug Lewis laid all the blame at the feet of his predecessor Pierre Cadieux. Meanwhile, more allegations against Bristow surfaced. There were published reports that he handed lists of members of the Canadian Jewish Congress over to White-supremacist groups in the U.S. The CBC claimed he reported on their investigation of the Canadian far-right. Everyone had questions. No one had answers.

In the midst of all this, SIRC announced that they could contact Bristow. They were, they said, intending to interview him in private.

On October 29, 1994, the Ontario Provincial Police raided two homes of Heritage Front members in the Ottawa area—one in Gloucester and another in Petawawa. They were looking for detonators, explosives, and firearms. They found nothing in Gloucester but in Petawawa, they seized firearms including a submachine gun and a sawed-off shotgun. Seven Heritage Front members were arrested and four were charged with firearms violations. A Heritage Front spokesperson who refused to identify himself said that the raids were politically motivated and "there is no evidence whatsoever that any weapons were going to be used for some kind of violence." He did not say what other use a submachine gun could have.

3

MOULD THE CHILD
AND YOU HAVE HIM FOR LIFE

IN THE SPRING OF 1993, the Ontario government, stung by con-
sistent reports of systemic racism in the province's justice and
education systems, decided on an all-out offensive in the public
schools. By September 1995, every school board in the province
must establish pro-active policies on racial and ethnocultural
biases and barriers in the system. Curriculums must be changed to
incorporate the histories and cultures of non-founding races. In a
season of austerity, when hard-pressed boards are reducing
English as a second language classes, upping class size, laying off
teachers to meet budget reductions, Education Minister Dave
Cooke allocated $1.5 million for the assault, calling it "a new way
of doing business."

In that same spring, Prof. Robert O'Driscoll, a well-connected
and well-established professor of English at the prestigious St.
Michael's College of the University of Toronto, published his twentieth learned tome, a fuzzy peek at New Age religion, entitled *The*

New World Order and the Throne of the Anti-Christ. Within days, the Canadian Jewish Congress had lodged a formal complaint with St. Michael's against O'Driscoll, and critics were comparing the book with the "Protocols of the Elders of Zion." Bernie Farber of the congress called it "a really filthy piece of hate literature," and St. Michael's spokeswoman Joan Foley stated that it wasn't a scholarly work at all and that "the university and St. Michael's were not involved in encouraging or sponsoring this publication and reject Professor O'Driscoll's claim that their scholarly reputations are associated with this work."

A good thing too. Within days, the Heritage Front is promoting O'Driscoll's work as another piece of "proof" in the cabal against truth. O'Driscoll states that he merely edited the book from work by Des Griffin and provided the introduction, but in that introduction he quotes Hitler, and the collection of essays is the usual mishmash of "lost" information that manages to blame the Jews, along with Mormons, Catholics, and Masons, for just about every problem on earth.

O'Driscoll, tenured at the university for more than twenty-five years, is unassailable, so the university suggests that he take a medical leave. Colleagues, appalled at the book's content, delicately hint that the learned prof has had a nervous breakdown.

While O'Driscoll is shouting his innocence and his commitment to academic freedom and free speech, it is revealed that his coauthor, pseudonymously named His Excellency J. J. Wills, is in fact John Ross Taylor, former head of the Western Guard and a member of the Aryan Nations. Taylor has been linked with white supremacist groups worldwide.

O'Driscoll, in defence of his and Taylor's work, claims that he consulted Taylor only because of his extensive knowledge of the pyramids and numerology. (It's worth noting that numerology was a favourite among the many occult practices of members of the Third Reich.) O'Driscoll says he is mystified by the controversy around his book.

"It bewilders me. I am not pro-Nazi, I am not anti-Jew, but I am a person who will speak up. I won't be silenced.

"Anyway, why am I being interrogated about my associations? I can associate with who I want."

Just another attempt to silence the voice of "truth."

The Ontario education minister's brave new world belief in education and Dr. O'Driscoll's fervent defence of the student's "right to know" information that most people don't like and won't agree with are two skirmishes in the battle to shape the hearts and minds of students, to change the shape of the future. It's no accident that Quebec, much further along the road of education for social change than English Canada, has held the line against English culture in the schools. Students in Quebec learn Quebec history, Quebec culture, Quebec sports, games, jokes. The old Catholic maxim of my childhood was "mould the child and you have him for life." In these days of fragmented family life, of confusion over "family values,"and the absence of organized religion, people increasingly turn to the state to influence minds and eradicate problems.

Please, state, we pray, make our kids smart and kind and caring and tolerant. While you're at it, teach them that sex before marriage is wrong, that drugs can kill, not to drink and drive, to prevent the spread of AIDS by using condoms, not to talk to strangers, to save money and pay bills, and all the other things that used to be taught in extended families where parents and aunts and grandparents, friends, teachers and churches and neighbours all shared the kid-rearing load. If we're too exhausted from jobs and stress to teach family values, then let the schools do it. If we can't cope with the violence in the world, educate the next generation about peace. Keep tinkering, we ask, until we find a way to educate children into good adults.

Of course, this isn't a problem for white supremacist parents. They know what their families value and what they hate and despise. All that concerns them is that the schools will use their liberal educational ideals to counter good racist thinking.

The problem is for ordinary parents of goodwill who want their children to be good citizens, to grow up with solid values but who find, in an increasingly complex world, that families have less influence on children than friends, television, and what is euphemistically referred to as the learning environment. In some Canadian schools, that environment includes weapons, drugs, gangs, and violence. "Should I teach my son not to fight?" asks one father of a Scarborough, Ontario, teenager, at a public rally for zero-tolerance proposals on violence in schools. "I teach him to be non-violent and then someone kills him at school because their parents didn't teach them that violence was wrong. Just what am I supposed to do?"

Faced with that dilemma and others equally contrary, many parents are understandably confused about what should be taught in school and what kids ought to know, besides reading, writing, and arithmetic.

Which takes us back to the ministry and Professor O'Driscoll. On the one hand, we have the ministry's conviction that all forms of bigotry and prejudice can be overcome by revamping the school curriculum, making the formerly invisible visible and affirming—to use a favourite buzzword—alternative views, histories, religions, and ideas. Negative images, like those of Blacks in *Huckleberry Finn* or the stereotypical Jew in *The Merchant of Venice*, will be taught only within carefully explained contexts. Truth, in this educational model, is real. It can be determined, described, taught.

On the other hand, we have Professor O'Driscoll and a good many people like him who sincerely believe that the only possible route to knowledge is the one paved with all kinds of conflicting information. Academic freedom may not demand that students believe the ideas that Hitler, or any other writer, espouses, but they should be exposed to *Mein Kampf*, to know what it is and reject it on their own. Truth here is less concrete. Students can and do become confused, can make choices that many adults won't approve.

What is essential in both these educational models, though, are teachers. They aren't the ideal role models they might have been forty years ago, but they are still the conduit by which ideas flow to eager students. They aren't the only conduit, however, and these days they share the learning stage with plenty of others.

It shouldn't surprise anyone that the radical right has targeted Canadian secondary schools as their front line for recruits. The young are, as Wolfgang Droege accurately says, "impressionable."

Just how impressionable, and tractable, they are is borne out at any Heritage Front rally or meeting. Droege is forty-three, which is old in this crowd. Most of his lieutenants are younger, and the audience is composed mainly of white-skinned Canadians on the young side of thirty.

When Elisse Hategan decided to hand out her pamphlets, one of several in a series called "Animal Life," the gist of which was that Blacks are apes and should be treated as less than human, she chose to do it at her high school in East End Toronto. According to at least one student who knew her "very, very casually," Elisse also took every opportunity to state that AIDS originated in Africa and that starvation and war in Somalia and Ethiopia were the result of African stupidity and ineptitude. In short, Elisse, a devoted member of the Heritage Front, was telling her classmates the "truth" that was being kept from them by the left-wing pinkos who control Toronto public education. When she was arrested for promoting hatred and her literature banned from school property, she defiantly claimed her rights of free speech. It was an educational institution, wasn't it? She was simply presenting an "alternative" view of history and sociology.

Droege needs the kids because, for the racists, the struggle has been uphill. When the Heritage Front began its concerted effort to win the hearts and minds of suburban Toronto youth in 1990, teachers and administrators quickly forbade Droege and his group from coming to speak to assembly or on Civics Day. It was a response Droege still resents, wondering how, "in a democracy," this could happen. There should be, he argues, equal time for alternative views.

Totalitarians, of course, have always loved to exploit the ideas, and the particular civilized latitudes, of "democracy," tolerance, and fairness. When the American Nazi Party chose to march in the predominantly Jewish community of Skokie, Illinois, they were protected by a constitution that enshrines freedom of assembly and, above all, the very first Amendment to the American Constitution, the right to free speech.

That's one of the knottier problems of living in a free society, one where the lines between pornography and art are thin to extinction, one where the borderlines between hate and freedom are closer than any of us likes to admit. Just where do we draw the lines, shut off the words, ban the images?

It's at this edge that we find strange confrontations between those who believe in controlling the dissemination of hateful thought and those who believe that to censor one idea is to open Pandora's box to all forms of censorship. That borderline is where Droege and his followers live and flourish. As far as they are concerned, they are simply an alternative viewpoint in the historical debate. We believe that the Holocaust happened. He believes it didn't. We believe Hitler was a monster. He sees him as a good German leader. Just a difference of opinion in a climate that encourages and fosters differences of opinion.

There are altogether too many people who agree with Wolfgang Droege, but most won't air those views publicly. What he does is articulate the position for them, and his public remarks give us a glimpse into the strange circuitry of the racist mind. In a democracy, reasons Droege—if what's going on in his mind can be called reasoning—nothing should prevent a man who happens to have a list of felony convictions as long as your arm, and is also wholly unrepentant, from going into a high school to give presumably inspirational talks.

Perhaps his long FBI file should not be held against him. More than one upstanding Canadian citizen who came to this country from the United States to avoid the military draft some twenty-five years ago has the same thing. But Droege has been deported from the the United States three times for being convicted of illegal acts, including possession of drugs and firearms and an attempted takeover of a sovereign state. (He and a group of white supremacists planned to use Dominica as an economic base to fund white supremacist groups worldwide.) That should be enough to give any school principal pause before letting this man have at the hearts and minds of teenagers, as one might expect Droege to know. But somehow that image of himself as a felon, a bad example, doesn't click in his mind.

And—who knows?—that may account for his success and the remarkable popularity of his ideas among young people. Anyone with a teenaged child knows that the culture of irrationality and out-sidedness—whether expressed in a non-stop blast of rap music, dab-bling in hallucinogenic drugs, dressing tough, or whatever—holds an extraordinary fascination for the mind poised between childhood and adult consciousness.

If this phase of fascination is often arduous for parents, it's prob-ably normal, and in any case is inevitable. Almost everybody out-grows it. The problem is that a considerable number of people do not, remaining forever trapped in a fantasy of being "outside." Crankdom, the addiction to the ecstasy of being outside, always starts as a phase, or an experiment that's usually quickly over. The neo-Nazis, like the drug pushers, have figured out how to make it last.

Not that the Heritage Front and its clones are having much suc-cess, so far, in the upper-income, and often largely Jewish, schools of Forest Hill or North Toronto. Inoculation against this kind of thrilling high starts early. But in the urban schools populated by the children of the ever-sinking middle class—in the ethnically mixed, potentially explosive neighbourhood of Riverdale, and in far-flung suburban Pickering and Scarborough and Mississauga, where Black gangs are confronting white gangs for the first time—the message of the far right is falling on fertile ground. That's where you find cute girls, the classic cheerleader types, handing out racist leaflets on the playground and telling everybody about the hotline. Just call and get the truth about white rights, the kids are told. And they do.

DATELINE: TORONTO, FEBRUARY 22, 1993. The Heritage Front hotline case is due back in the courts tomorrow. On the CBC news, Droege's kids are telling the story as they see it. They are five attrac-tive, articulate white boys from Pickering, a sprawling township just east of Metro Toronto, telling what life is like for them in a large suburban high school nowadays. These sharp kids, decked out in the latest jeans and newly popular grunge-look shirts, are the good-looking boys next door. Their hair is clipped and styled in the casual look favoured by Tom Cruise. Slouched on the floor, relaxed and enjoying their moment of stardom, they're as typical a quartet of high-school heroes as you'll find anywhere.

"The Blacks," says one of them, "stick together. So white people have to stick together. They beat up one of us. We get even. That's how it always is."

These boys are regular callers of the Front hotline number. They haven't joined anything yet, but they certainly like what they hear. What they get from the voice on the other end of the line is tough, bracing, don't-take-it talk. What they hear from the liberal voices around them is encouragement to keep quiet, be polite, take it. In other words, be powerless, which is not exactly good advice for anybody, especially teenagers just learning the powers and limits of being independent.

"There's no point in telling a teacher, the principal," says one young man. "They can't do anything. You say anything about a Black and you're a racist. No one is going to help us. We have to help ourselves." Almost inevitably, the kids end with an ominous discussion about weapons and escalation. And, as in any such discussion that keeps circling around a certain unspoken hopelessness, it's not easy to decide whether the talk about weapons is flavoured more by the grim inevitability or the exciting desirability of violence. The line from one boy is: "Someone could get killed." It would be an easy thing—requiring only a little more anger, frustration, and sense of futility—for that verb to change from *could* to *will*.

From the other side of the racial divide—a divide that traditional Canadian liberalism has always insisted does not exist—CBC has summoned three Black youths, as attractive and articulate as the white group, and students in the same school. Like the white kids, these young Blacks wear their uniforms: razored haircuts and colourful athletic jackets and baseball caps. They confirm everything the white kids say, but emphasize that they stick together because they feel unwelcome. One young man provides the context: "There never used to be any Black people in the suburbs. These guys all grew up here, lived here all their lives, they feel like they own this place. Then a couple hundred Black people move in, and they are upset. They think we're taking it away from them."

All of which is probably true. But the good analysis—as so often is the case with good analysis—is not the first step towards solving the problem but the rationalization for pretty bad news to come. These Black youths are not about to be pushed around by a gang of white punks. They too promise to "get even." They also speak of weapons. Of the Heritage Front believers and their allies, one young man says, "Those guys want us to be afraid. Well, we're not afraid. Not at all."

He's not afraid because he believes—you can see it in his face, watch in the way he throws his powerful pose—his muscle and rage is stronger than the white kids' muscle and rage. It's Serbia. It's Somalia. It's west Los Angeles. It's wherever the delicate web of civilization, the restraints and tradeoffs and genial mendacity that ensure peace among the unlike, has come unravelled, or is about to.

It's also a kind of almost-violent adolescent posturing that Canadian multicultural education has been committed to eliminating for more than a decade. These are the kids who have been taught to celebrate Kwanzaa, the Afrocentrist holiday invented about twenty-five years ago in California to replace Christmas, and now a fixture in the multicultural classroom. Heritage languages abound, everything from Mandarin to Estonian. Toronto's students have a curriculum enriched with literature, history, art, and music from cultures outside the traditional white European mainstream. At one downtown grade school, Huron Street, a multicultural fair brought out displays from more than fifty countries. At my preteen daughter's private school, once solidly WASP, a Celebration of Our Roots food festival for forty second-graders brought out family recipes from twenty countries outside Canada, including Iraq, Israel, Hong Kong, Kenya, and Brazil.

But, in its most idealistic formulation, Canadian multicultural education was never merely about food and crafts and costumes, or "celebrating" colourful old country customs in public for the benefit of outsiders. It was about training our children "out" of racism, by patiently liquidating stereotypes and transforming the classroom into a tiny model for behaviour in a pluralistic society. It is an idea of mass education that did not originate in Canada. Versions of it have been tried in Lebanon, India, the former Yugoslavia. It always seemed to work in such places, as long as the police or some form of powerful social will was there to enforce its idealism. But in all those places, the social will fell apart. And in Canada something, everywhere, is going terribly wrong in the officially multicultural education system.

Even as Education Minister Dave Cooke was pronouncing his new policies, school boards across the province were faced with reduced budgets. Immigration has brought thousands of children who do not speak English or French into urban school systems where second-language classes were already overburdened. Teachers continue to report grim statistics about kids in trouble, kids who work full time and attend school, kids who are abused, neglected, abandoned, kids who have learning disabilities, behaviour problems, psychological problems, family problems. How are the schools to cope with all this, and more, at a time when taxpayers are demanding a moratorium on property taxes, when the federal and provincial governments are reducing the education budget, when parents and potential employers are demanding more emphasis on skills-building? The forces of education are in disarray—a fact that the ever-quickminded racists have not lost any time exploiting.

The teachers of the young racist interviewees, according to the CBC newscast, seem to be in denial of their own trauma. They preferred not to speak on the issue of race. The kids say that's just because their teachers want to pretend nothing is happening. One principal said flatly that joining the Heritage Front was just another adolescent phase for most kids, something they'd grow out of, like acne. Yet a handful of kids, he admits, don't outgrow extremist groups. "I don't know what takes them over the edge," he says, slowly and thoughtfully. But, in the next breath, the old optimism comes back: Not to worry, says he; things like the Heritage Front are, after all, just "small isolated groups."

What's impressive is the racist rhetoric so handily bandied around by the young people interviewed—the rhetorical stock expressions of attitudes that have not changed in the exchange of stereotypes between Blacks and whites in two hundred years. For these kids, the ideologically driven education system has failed and, worse yet, become the staging ground for a renewal of the old, deadly ideologies of race that many educators thought dead once and for all.

These children may never join the Heritage Front. They don't have to. They are already well on the way to constructing adult lives based on the premises of race hate, the belief that life in Pickering is destined to be a war, sometimes violent, between the races that have settled there. Even without extremism in the curriculum, extremism is insidiously spreading in the culture of secondary education.

Until quite recently, Canadians have been inclined to believe that racist extremism in the schools was merely a matter of a few isolated crazies in remote backwaters. Mention racism and immediately the name Jim Keegstra comes up. He's convenient, the stereotypical backwoods guy who passes as icon of the hick white supremacist. He can't have any redeeming qualities. Somehow, by a fluke, he manages to slip through one of those very rare chinks in the liberal Canadian educational system and get a position of authority over young expanding minds. And, the same urban reasoning goes, Eckville, Alberta, with its tiny population of just 879, and its funny name, has always been just the kind of place you'd find a Jim Keegstra. Somewhere remote, off the beaten educational path, a place where the intelligentsia don't end up.

Because of the attention paid by the media to his judicial trials, virtually every Canadian knows that Keegstra, Eckville's mayor, was a high-school history teacher who denied the existence of the Holocaust, was convicted in 1985 of promoting hatred, banished from his classroom, and has been involved in appeals of his case ever since. He usually loses, but he perseveres. For most observers, Keegstra is the classic self-blinded crank who just doesn't know when to call it quits. To the hard right, he is yet another case of an isolated revisionist visionary under siege by Jews, communists, and their numberless dupes in the stupefied, liberal land called Canada.

At each of Keegstra's trials, students have come forward to testify that he was a good teacher and to admit that they liked his brand of history. For ten years, Jim Keegstra sat in his social studies classroom in Eckville, teaching students the secret history of the Second

World War. This secret history was the standard mix of Jewish conspiracy theory with Holocaust denial. He taught them "facts" known only to the enlightened, hidden from common folk, but which he had learned during years secretly studying the vast literature of the anti-Semitic invisible empire—researching, comparing texts, delving into arcane interpretations of Holy Scripture. The result of this project was his conviction that the basic truth of our century is the Jewish menace and the Great Lie of the Holocaust.

Keegstra's mission, he believes, is to reveal the hidden facts of the real world to young people. Among these facts: the lie of the Holocaust, the essential purity of fundamentalist Christianity, the historic worldwide conspiracy of Jewry to wipe Christianity from human memory. One can understand the appeal of such thought to children raised on the black-white, good-bad simplicity of television and its version of history and "news." The real fact, of course, is that we do live in a fallen world, marred with conflict, horror, and seemingly insoluble problems, and disrupted everywhere by bloodlust and greed. Keegstra's worldview explained everything, or so it must have appeared to the typically melodramatic adolescent mind.

Kids also love to be "in" on secrets. And Keegstra gave them wondrous, mind-boggling secrets to be in on. He was a teacher of secrets who also inspired enduring trust. It took ten years of Keegstra's teaching before a parent questioned what her child was being taught. During those ten years, Keegstra was the only social studies teacher at Eckville High. He was also a highly respected mayor. Even after his trial, Eckville residents were still confused about his crime. One local admitted that he didn't like what Keegstra stood for, but added: "I don't think it was right that he was charged, either."

Keegstra's 1985 trial for wilfully promoting hatred against the Jewish people lasted more than seventy days, cost the taxpayers of Alberta more than $1 million, was given coast-to-coast media coverage, and spawned at least two books on the trial and the history of Keegstra, Eckville, and white supremacy, anti-Semitism, and racial tensions in Alberta.

Well-known civil libertarians, including Alan Borovoy of the

Canadian Civil Liberties Association, found themselves holding their noses in the name of freedom of speech while defending Keegstra's right to spew whatever ideological cant he chose.

Other voices, most notably those of the Canadian Jewish community, declared that there was a difference between freedom of speech and advancing hatred. At the end of the first trial, Keegstra was found guilty, fined $5,000, and his licence to teach was suspended. In a bizarre twist, Dwight Arthur, the twenty-six-year-old jury foreman who brought in the guilty verdict, appealed to the community to donate to a fund to pay the fine, calling such donations "gifts for the furthering of God's work."

In 1987, while his case was being appealed and re-appealed, Keegstra was named interim leader of the federal Social Credit Party at a meeting in Kelowna, B.C. When his house was burned down in 1990, police confirmed that arson was involved. Keegstra said: "I speak only the truth," and continued his crusade.

At the time of his trial, Jim Keegstra was fifty-one. He'd spent most of his life in Eckville, and there had been no indication that he was in touch with the white supremacists, Klan members, or swastika painters elsewhere in Canada. He appeared to be an isolated man with a personal obsession, which he fed by ferreting out presumably lost documents, books, alternative histories, "hidden" truths. Even the judge at his trial called him "a dupe of his own fanaticism, not unlike a drug addict."

That was an opinion shared by a few townsfolk, but not very deeply. "Every town has its kooks," sniffed Lorne Grummett, of nearby Red Deer. Like most other locals, Grummett believes Keegstra, and Alberta, got a raw deal. Sure, the headquarters of the local Aryan Supremacy sect is in Caroline, less than half an hour's drive from Eckville, and it's just possible that Keegstra's classes might have netted the Aryans a recruit or three. But, heck, nobody in God's Country takes that stuff seriously. As Dale Baxter, twenty-two, a former student of Keegstra's, put it: "It's one man's opinion, and if Jim believes that's how it happened, let him. I don't believe it myself. I know the Jewish people suffered very much in the Holocaust. I would only say that a lot of others suffered and were killed too, such as the Ukrainians. That should also never be forgotten."

Unlike most addicts and village oddities, however, this auto mechanic turned schoolteacher was remarkably well liked and widely respected in the community. And if all Keegstra had done was gather data, perhaps sharing it with a few friends, he might well still be mayor of Eckville and planning his retirement on his teacher's pension. But he wanted to share his discoveries with others. His chance came when he got a chance to teach social studies, after the job had been turned down by everyone else. At his trial, he insisted: "I did nothing wrong....I have been spreading truth, facts, and everything. I will never agree that I have been promoting hatred."

The charges, the school board hearing, and the trial changed Keegstra's life. From being a country teacher, he was suddenly an international media presence, rating notice in publications ranging from the world's establishment press to German neo-Nazi journals. Other true believers came to his door. Zundel came from Toronto to cheer and to watch the style of defence lawyer Douglas Christie. Keegstra supporters, some of them ex-students, others Bible-sporting members of Keegstra's Christian congregation, arrived in court each day wearing buttons that proclaimed "Freedom of Expression" or "Truth, the Final Solution."

But if many people dismissed him as an obsessed, self-deluded fanatic, Keegstra was unmoved and reborn. After his dismissal from his teaching post, he returned to work as a mechanic, continuing his research, and through the Christian Defence League of Canada, continued to raise funds for his appeals against his conviction, and to get the message of free speech out to the unenlightened.

None of his ideas has changed, and he remains convinced that he is the victim, not of his beliefs, but of a conspiracy to prevent him from telling the truth as he knows it to be. Former school trustee Kevin McEntee, a member of the school board that fired Keegstra and who believes that the matter should have ended there, believes him to be one of many "secret scholars" hiding in the educational system. "The only difference between Eckville and anywhere else," McEntee has said, "is that we found our Keegstra and they have not."

The confusion of the people of Eckville about their mayor-school-teacher is akin to the confusion of many who have a brush with devout believers of the inner doctrines of the invisible empire, with its peculiar self-righteousness, its alluring simplicity and cleanliness. Jim Keegstra never was a wild-eyed Nazi ideologue, but the sort of man we would want to have living next door, if good manners and kindliness to dogs and children were the only issue. Most of us would have rated him a good teacher, before finding out just what he was teaching—if being a good teacher still means persistence, loyalty to learning, passionate conviction, and an ability to keep teenagers listening and learning.

We'd have probably thought the same thing about Malcolm Ross, another schoolteacher, in Moncton, New Brunswick. Ross was also a respected member of the local teaching profession. But while no one would have made a case for Jim Keegstra's academic respectability, Ross was the very picture of the traditional gentleman-scholar, poring over his notes in the night after grading his tests. As a published author and natty in dress, he taught language arts and mathematics, and he didn't make Keegstra's mistakes. According to him and to everyone who knew him, he kept his beliefs out of the classroom.

Those beliefs, like the ones held by Keegstra, are part of the creed of the invisible empire. Ross believes in an international Jewish conspiracy to take over the world. The Holocaust was an invention to get sympathy for the Jews and abet their causes. While Keegstra was researching the secret history of the Holocaust, Ross was fighting the battle for Jesus Christ, comparing the Jews to Satan.

Unlike Keegstra in so many other ways, Ross followed an almost identical educational path: years of obsessive study in the "underground" literature of the invisible empire—everything from the secrets of the Rosicrucians to the "Protocols of the Elders of Zion" and the works of David Irving. To this he added an extensive analysis of the Bible, which, like many other Christian fundamentalists, he considered revealed truth. This study culminated in an intense desire to share the profound, suppressed truth he had discovered. His first two books bore titles—*Web of Deceit* and *Spectre of Power*—that have the same B-movie ring to them that so much of the "suppressed" literature of the empire sports on its covers.

As early as 1978, when Ross published his first book, the Moncton School Board and Moncton officials sensed that there might be a problem. But the problem was slow in surfacing, and in the meantime, the board did nothing. Julius Israeli, a former chemistry professor from Newcastle, New Brunswick, and a Jew who had immigrated to Canada from Romania, began lodging complaints against Ross, to no avail. "I made five or six attempts from 1978 to 1986 to have something done," said Israeli. "I went to the Department of Justice, the RCMP, and the Moncton police, but nothing was done."

This is not completely true. The Moncton Board of Education did look into the background and works of Malcolm Ross but, while they might have found his theories unsavoury, there was no reason to relieve him of his post. On the contrary, Ross enjoyed considerable support from his students and their parents, as well as his colleagues. He might have a weird hobby, but he kept his views, so it seemed, out of his classroom.

Israeli also took the information to leaders in the Moncton Jewish community. He claims they stabbed him in the back and didn't proceed with his complaint. He wanted a criminal charge laid against Ross, but the authorities, confused by the conflicting reports of Ross's capabilities and swamped with hundreds of letters from Ross supporters across Canada, opted for a more traditional Canadian solution to such problems: they put the matter in the lap of the provincial human rights commission.

In 1988, David Attis, another leader in the Moncton Jewish community and parent of four children in the school district where Ross taught, filed a complaint with the New Brunswick Human Rights Commission. Attis alleged that the school board was fostering anti-Semitism by continuing to employ Ross as a teacher. It had been eight years since the first complaints about Ross's views. There had been at least four investigations of his conduct and he was still teaching. In his complaint, Attis stated: "By its own statements and its inaction...the school board has condoned his views, has thus fostered a climate where students feel more at ease expressing anti-Jewish views."

The hope was that the commission, through the mediating talents of one of its officers, could effect a settlement in the case. The hope was dashed when the commission recommended an inquiry into Attis's complaint. Ross immediately hired Doug Christie, since the Keegstra case the ultra-right's attorney of choice.

The hearing began in December 1990, in an atmosphere of rancour and insult. Ross and Christie, in a series of legal manoeuvres, had managed to delay and delay again. A critique of Ross's work by James A. Beverley, a respected professor of theology and ethics at Mount Allison University, had been dismal news for the Ross supporters. At the same time, the anti-Ross forces were hit by legal changes. The tide was running against convictions on hate-literature charges, and the courts knew it. The Keegstra conviction had been overturned just months before by the Supreme Court of Alberta.

At first glance, it's difficult to see how any inquiry could go against Attis. He was fighting for his children's rights. He told of his daughter's reaction when she found out that the gym meet she was attending was being held at the junior high school where Malcolm Ross taught. She was terrified. "I didn't know where he was. I was afraid he'd pull me into the bushes or something." Attis saw this as an infringement on his and his children's rights. "If that's not discrimination—the fear of a child to enter a District 15 public school building in 1988—I don't know what is."

Attis also found it dangerous that Ross and people like him could fit right in at the PTA tea and then go home and write anti-Semitic tracts. Can a teacher harbour extremist beliefs and not convey them—by gesture or act, if not in words—to his students? "Teachers are put on pedestals," says Attis. "Children look to them as role models. We've all said to our children, 'Listen to your teacher. Your teacher is right.'"

Christie's tactics to discredit Attis were the same ones he used in the Zundel and Keegstra hearings. The inquiry degenerated into arguments over who and how many died in what death camp and when. Attis described Ross as "a virulent anti-Semite" and a "cancer" who should not be allowed near children. *Web of Deceit*, Attis declared, was "the height of obscenity, perhaps the most anti-Semitic, bigoted piece of material I have ever picked up."

Through it all, Ross listened, smiled, and kept respectfully quiet. His defence was that he was on trial for his religious beliefs, which he had never advanced in the classroom. The issues were free speech and the right of the Christian faith to exist.

Teachers and counsellors spoke movingly of Ross's rapport with students. Other children testified about facing anti-Semitic comments every day, told of being tagged with such obscenities as "Jew bitches," "Jew bags," "damned Jew." Attis said his own daughter had walked into a classroom with swastikas on the blackboard, and further claimed that white supremacists had left a Halloween pumpkin on his doorstep with swastikas on it as well as defaced the doors of the synagogue where he worshipped.

Christie fought back by demanding more and more minutiae from the children, driving some to tears during his cross-examinations. As had happened in the Keegstra trial, members of other ultra-rightist groups converged on Moncton to demonstrate support for Ross.

One local Jewish leader claimed to have seen Ernst Zundel in a crowd by the courthouse. Terry Long, leader of the Alberta-based Aryan Nations group, appeared on a Saint John radio station to discuss his "basic belief that communism is Jewish and the Holocaust is a farce." During the two-hour program he also said there was a conspiracy to prosecute and silence dissident voices like those of Keegstra and Ross. Afterwards, the station was charged with unlawfully broadcasting abusive comments.

The hearing continued until Christmas and then recessed until April. There were more testimonials to Ross. The hearing ground down under the weight of line-by-line readings and analyses of his written works. Testimony ended in May 1991, and in August Ross was placed on an eighteen-month leave of absence. The Moncton Board of Education was to find him a non-teaching position or he would be fired. During that time he was not to publish or speak his views on Jews or the Holocaust. Christie and Ross promptly launched an appeal.

The Moncton Board of Education found Ross a job as a curriculum planner. Meanwhile, he made speeches, in Toronto and Moncton. The theme of these speeches was the Jewish plot against freedom.

Ross has never officially joined any white supremacist group or organization, although he is considered a hero of the struggle by all of them. He maintains that he is a victim of hatemongering and that his twelve-year struggle has simply been his way of defending himself against the libels of the Moncton Jewish community.

On December 20, 1993, the New Brunswick Court of Appeal overturned Ross's removal from the classroom. He could teach, as long as he refrained from passing his views to his students in class; he was free to do and say what he liked outside school so long as he discontinued his publication. Despite public outcry, Ross could return to his classroom. This decision is being appealed currently and Ross is suspended from teaching until all court proceedings are complete.

He surfaced just once more, as a footnote in the case of Matin Yaqzan, assistant professor of mathematics at the University of New Brunswick. Professor Yaqzan's views on date rape—that adolescent boys need sex and that "promiscuous" girls get what they deserve— made headlines nationwide after they were published in the campus newspaper. Almost lost in the furore over Yaqzan's ideas was the casual comment that his wife was a friend and disciple of Ross's, selling his books and pamphlets on the streets of Moncton and Fredericton.

Unlike Malcolm Ross and Jim Keegstra, Paul Fromm, of Mississauga, Ontario, seldom mentions Jews or other races in his published works. He lets other people, like his hero Philippe Rushton, do it for him. Take a look at the pamphlet entitled "Race, Evolution and AIDS: What Rushton Really Said." The pamphlet is one of two dozen in the respectable-sounding "Issues Series" put out by Canadians for Foreign Aid Review (C-FAR), edited and introduced by C-FAR Research Director Fromm, whose day job was teaching

English at the Applewood Heights Secondary School in suburban Mississauga.

The pamphlet is a reprint of some work on race by Professor Rushton, of the Department of Psychology at the University of Western Ontario. Rushton claims that Orientals have larger brains and smaller penises than whites or Blacks and are hence less aggressive and more cautious. Blacks, scoring large on penises and aggression and small on brains and caution, are the reason for violent crime and the rapid spread of lethal diseases in Africa. The "study" by Rushton is heavily footnoted, though a glance at the documentation reveals that many of the cited works are by Rushton himself.

Rushton has become a cause célèbre in academic and antiracist circles. Former Ontario premier David Peterson went on record saying he should be fired. Academics, many of whom question his scholarship and dodgy views, refuse to permit him to be dismissed from his post, citing the sanctity of tenure and the rights of free expression in university circles. Students, particularly those of colour, want Rushton fired, and they want his views on race officially disavowed by the university officials. There have been pickets, demonstrations, letters in the newspapers, and articles from both sides of the divide.

Rushton, for his part, has fought back, citing his string of academic publications and his academic rights. In at least one case, he threatened the Toronto *Star* with a libel action and then took his complaint to the Ontario Press Council, after the *Star* referred to him as a "charlatan" and a cartoon depicted him as a member of the Ku Klux Klan talking with Hitler. It was Rushton's claim that the *Star* was engaged in "a vindictive attempt" to belittle him in a series of stories on his work. The press council rejected the complaints but did urge the *Star* to be more circumspect when dealing with controversial issues. Rushton professed to be satisfied with the decision but, since then, he has repeatedly stated that he is a victim of media manipulation and that the media has a vendetta against him.

Fromm, Rushton's self-appointed defender, is a teacher from a *Leave It to Beaver* episode. He's of medium height, fortyish, with just a touch of grey in his hair, and with the kind of disingenuous expression that invites trust. If you met him at your child's school and knew nothing about him beyond what you saw, you would almost certainly leave with a safe feeling inside.

As it happens, Fromm is dedicated to making Philippe Rushton, among others, feel safe, and be safe, in the midst of howling anti-Rushton forces. Fromm introduces the pamphlet on his hero with a horrific picture of the personal and professional trauma that beset Rushton when his work was made public. According to Fromm, Rushton was the victim of a ferocious campaign in the press. Articles had denounced him as an academic fraud. Fromm reports that when Rushton hired "a prestigious Toronto law firm to launch a libel action, the press attacks immediately stopped." The implication is clear: they stopped because they were untrue.

All this leads Fromm to conclude that, in Rushton's works, he has a genuine piece of rejected scientific knowledge, rejected, he writes, because "Canadian media and political elite cling with near religious fervour to certain articles of faith. One of these articles of secular humanist faith is an almost fanatical belief in 'equality.' This is not the equality of religion—that all men are equal in the sight of God— or the equality of law—that all men will be judged by the courts without fear or favour—but the concept of equality that holds that all men are equal and, therefore, there must be equal outcomes or results for them in any society. Any failure to produce equality of outcome must, the liberal extremists argue, mean some hidden agenda of prejudice or discrimination. Rushton has collected data that strongly argue that all men are not equal in the sense of the same and that this inequality of difference stems significantly from genetic causes."

Shorn of rhetoric, what Mr. Fromm is saying is that biology is destiny. If Black Canadians are poor, it is genetic, not social. What is remarkable is that he can get away with saying this while teaching in a school system that is completely committed to levelling the playing field for disadvantaged children and particularly those from visible minorities.

Rushton's works are thin camouflage for the same old hatred. Blacks, so this argument goes, with their innate predisposition to aggression, their increased libido, their larger organs, are prone to criminal behaviour. You don't have to go very far to see that the criminal behaviour that involves sex and aggression is rape—a charge against Black men since the first slave ship landed in North America. Orientals, with their larger brains and punier penises, can spend more time planning world domination. Whites, caught in the middle, are in the classic squeeze, not smart enough to overtake the Oriental wizards and fair game for the Black criminals. A perfect description of what a good many beleaguered citizens in various Canadian suburbs believe is happening every day, and that's the real danger with Rushton, the point that Fromm understands. Rushton's work is spurious, his research suspect, and his thesis—that you can somehow extrapolate from the physical to the psychological—is downright ludicrous. His importance is as a scientific authority to back up entrenched racist thought.

I purchased the C-FAR pamphlet, and two others. "The Vietcong Front in Quebec" is by Gilbert Gendron, identified as a graduate in history of the Université du Québec à Montréal, a member of the Research Group on the History of the Port of Montreal, and author of "L'histoire des élévateurs à grain du Port de Montréal 1885–1970." He is listed in the C-FAR pamphlet as a regular contributor to "Canadian and European periodicals," but his name does not appear in the *Index of Canadian Periodicals*.

The other pamphlet, "Over-population and Third World Immigration," is a pair of essays by South African–born W. Harding LeRiche, M.D., a retired professor of epidemiology at the University of Toronto Medical School. In the second essay, LeRiche writes that "Canadians are a generous people....But they do not wish to become a minority within their own country. They want Canada to remain a Western European community. They prefer the philosophies, religions, and customs which originate in Europe. They know that most of the world's few democratic societies are in Europe and North America and not anywhere else. Thus, most people from 'anywhere else' do not understand how democracy works."

I purchased these works, as well as several copies of the *Canadian Immigration Hotline*, a monthly C-FAR publication, at a

Heritage Front rally at the Latvian Hall where Paul Fromm was a featured speaker. They are also available from C-FAR, along with a subscription to the newsletter, and that night they were in short supply. After Fromm's lecture, they were snapped up like popcorn.

His topic that night was immigration.

Fromm's presentation is to be an almost perfect example of the newest face of North American racism. What Wolfgang Droege's smart suits are to the brass knuckles and cudgels of anti-Semitic thugs, Fromm's seemingly intellectually respectable pamphlets and suave, intelligent manner are to traditional vicious Jew-baiting: spiffy new packaging for the same old bucket of bile. Fromm comes armed with the new media savvy of David Duke, laden with thick files of numbers and statistics from the Canadian government and clips from reputable daily newspapers, such as the *Globe and Mail* and the liberal Toronto *Star*. He makes a point of excluding the tabloid Toronto *Sun*, even though it's the newspaper most often quoted by his audience and its pro-police, anti-immigration stands on many issues might be construed as support for his views. But Fromm wants to impress upon his audience that he's serious, scholarly, to be respected. Right off the top, he wants people to understand that the issue for him and his followers isn't race, it's immigration and foreign aid. He's a self-taught authority on foreign aid, and what he's learned, he doesn't like.

"I'm opposed to the foreign aid giveaway," he begins, reasonably setting forth an argument that many thoughtful people might find time to mull over. But the point isn't to convince. This crowd is convinced. The point is the immediate establishment of intellectual respectability, of a certain calm, that puts the Aryan Nations lads in the back of the hall firmly in their place. He whips through his curriculum vitae, lightly peppering his comments with a phrase or two in decently accented and perfectly understandable French. He comments that the owners of the Latvian Hall were under "intense pressure" to cancel tonight's meeting. Who pressured? "The agents of human rights and Stalinists who are taking over with their miserable doctrine of political correctness."

Majority rule is his byword. "Our government gave Nelson Mandela $25 million for majority rule in Africa," he says. "How about majority rule in Canada?" There are a few thin cheers. This isn't the message these people have come to hear. It's almost too tame. One gets the impression that Fromm is a racist whose time has not quite come—someone the white Pickering young people will be happy to know when they take their place in the technocracy around the turn of the century.

Undaunted, Fromm continues his measured talk. Before 1967, he says, every political party in Canada saw Canada as a European country. He cites the book *Strangers in Our Midst*, by J. S. Woodsworth, a founder of the CCF party, as one example of this universal truth. He goes on with his little potted history of Canada, augmenting the dry facts with little jokes and funny stories. Fromm is a good speaker, witty and precise and, as he heads into the heart of his address, laden with statistical facts.

Now Fromm is ready to start connecting with the audience he's finally impressed. This is what they've been waiting for. For decades, he tells us, the Canadian government has been selling the public a bill of goods about the usefulness of immigration. One: Because Canada is a big country, it needs more settlers. Two: As our population ages, we need more people because our birthrate is low. Three: Immigrants create jobs. This last brings a howl from a young man in the audience: "If that's so, why can't I find one?"

Fromm nods and smiles. These are the folks he's come to reach. It's working. "How do you like being mushrooms?" he asks, grinning. When the audience looks mystified, he answers his own question. "Mushrooms are kept in the dark and fed doo-doo." There are giggles and guffaws.

Deftly, and using reams of figures from Statistics Canada, he launches into his rebuttals of each of the arguments. "If prosperity came with population," he says, "why aren't India and Red China rich? Switzerland, with a very small population, is rich."

He goes on to show that Canadians of colour are just as opposed to these myths as he is. He's at pains to point out that he's not biased against any race, just immigration policy per se, which favours

Orientals, Blacks, and East Indians. On the subject of jobs for Canadians, he quotes from *Share*, a newspaper published by the Black community, that he claims supports his views.

Fromm's reasonableness, his indirect, subtle calls to the discontent simmering inside anyone who's lived in Toronto more than ten years works. It's easy to fall prey to the idea that "they" are the problem. Things are not the way they were. The city is changing, and we hate what it's turning into. Compared to the good old days, crime and clutter are up and civic responsibility is down.

There are a lot of reasons for this change, but Fromm homes in on the one that's easiest to understand, that seems to explain most of what a good many middle-aged white people don't like about what's happening to us: increased immigration. Immigration means more crime, dirtier streets, noisy protests, more drugs—every urban evil that haunts the minds of those of us who are growing older in Toronto and not liking the feel of it.

But there's salvation, says Fromm. Turn off the taps. When the dirty flood of immigration recedes, we'll have our safe, calm, Canadian streets back again.

Fromm's audience is nodding, believing. He denounces the notion that new immigrants are more law-abiding than "old" Canadians. "If that's so, why are crack sales up? Why are there gang wars in Asian districts?" He uses the example of Sgt. Ben Eng of the Toronto Police Department, who was censured by the department for releasing statistics on race and crime to the local media. Fromm defends Eng's actions, calling this a case of "shooting the messenger."

Eng, that is, is another martyr to the cause of truth, and a friend to us "mushrooms." Listen to this respected police officer, says Fromm, and you find out the truth about the dusky folks hopping off planes at Pearson and setting up housekeeping—along with crime rings, drug operations, and the groundwork for urban decline—across Metro. He cites a story by the well-known journalist Diane Francis in the *Financial Post*, claiming that it costs Canada $2 billion a year to service illegal refugees. He mentions the RCMP's "notorious Singh decision," which permitted Sikh members of the force to wear turbans with their uniforms.

The crowd is with Fromm now. He's articulate and persuasive and, if you don't know the numbers game extremely well, completely plausible.

Then Fromm begins discussing government statistics, those provided free of charge by Statistics Canada and Employment and Immigration. This is the real authority, not some fly-by-night researcher or lib-left reporter, but the Government of Canada. It so happens that I've been working for three years with those same immigration statistics for a book on the Hong Kong Chinese. They are easy to get and astonishingly thorough. They tell who's coming, from where, bringing how much, and in what job categories. What I know, because I know the numbers, is how Fromm is interpreting them to support his argument. Indeed, non-white immigration is up since 1975. Most of our new Canadians are coming from Asia, the Indian subcontinent, the Caribbean, and South America. Our immigration policy, which favours the reunification of families, does encourage this migration, and, since those coming are wives, children, and older parents, the skills levels of these migrants are lower than the immigrants who come on their own and who must pass a rigorous point system to be admitted.

But such things are outside Fromm's horizon of interest. His trajectory is from facts to a wind-up fantasia horrifying enough to scare anyone. A man Fromm names as Robert Blackwood is described as "paradigm immigration client." Fromm says that Blackwood, "a Jamaican reggae singer," tried to shoot a Jamaican policeman. He fled to the U.S., was deported and fled to England. England deported him to Canada. At this point, Blackwood claimed refugee status and then, while awaiting his refugee hearing, commenced a life of crime in Canada. According to Fromm, Blackwood was charged with handgun and drug offences and then just "last month" was charged with assault after a fistfight. He was sentenced to a year in jail, "but his immigration hearing continues." QED: the mushrooms in the room had better come out of the dark and see how government is conspiring to destroy everything good, hard-working Canadians have created, by its kid-gloves handling of one dangerous immigrant after another.

There is no point arguing the errors of law or information in this sorry saga. If any of it is true (and given Fromm's record of meticulous research, some of it must be), the Blackwood incident is evidence of gross abuse in the Canadian refugee system, but something that must have happened almost by accident. The story does its work, however. It becomes what you remember: the scare, not the statistics; the worry, not the tedious schoolmasterish method by which Fromm works up to his final point.

All racist hysteria is based on fact, or half-fact, and, just as predictably it abandons the facts when they become inconvenient or difficult to fit in to the emotional charge, the pleasure of hitting back hard. That's the real aim of all such demagoguery. Tonight is a sedate feeding of the grievances that have made people come out to hear Paul Fromm. He's fed their stored-up sense of loss and failure accumulated over years of frustrations. There is intoxicating magic in the air. Even if one knows better, it's hard to remember the truth that's being left out. Memories of menacing black youths hanging around a subway station trading drugs spring to mind, with ease and with a kind of immoral pleasure. We forget that Unionville and Thornhill and even the outer reaches of Paul Fromm's own bailiwick of Mississauga, once farmland and little villages, have been far more radically transformed by the great white influx from Calgary and Halifax and Kamloops and downtown Toronto than by anyone from another land. Whites have been lured here by jobs and money and all the things middle-class Canadians want to preserve.

I make myself remember that I have been in those suburbs, partied, and talked, and walked along the streets. There are some enclaves of wealthy East Indians, some very wealthy Asians, and a smattering of middle-to-rich Blacks. Mostly, however, there are upper-crust or upwardly mobile white people with nice houses, good cars, and lots of disposable income.

It is this white migration that has doubled and tripled the size of Toronto and led to the increased crime, dirt, and pollution. According to Statistics Canada, immigrants of all hues and languages account for sixteen percent of the Canadian population. That figure remains essentially unchanged since 1951. If the Emerald City is becoming ever more grey, it is size and numbers that are the reason. Every study done on crime and urban blight reinforces that simple truth. But Fromm, speaking to a crowd of young adults, most of them under thirty, is not interested in such studies. He is interested in feeding the anxiety that is almost palpable around me. Dave from Brantford, who is sitting next to me, is absolutely convinced. "Ya can't argue with Stats Can," he says.

After this meeting, some members of a Jewish group launched an attempt to have the Peel Board of Education dismiss Paul Fromm. It appears they were unaware of the topic of his talk, but the fact that he delivered it at a Heritage Front rally was enough to get them moving.

As with other cases of teachers accused of supporting ultra-rightist causes, Fromm's colleagues in teachers' organizations found themselves in the distasteful position of having to publicly defend his actions in the name of freedom of speech. Compared to Keegstra and Ross, Fromm appears to be gentle. The Alberta and New Brunswick teachers advanced hatred, anti-Semitism, and Nazi propaganda. In Alberta, the teachers union had to pay Jim Keegstra's legal bills as he fought against his dismissal. Fromm merely trots out his little facts and stats and lets his listeners read between the lines.

Of the three, Fromm is infinitely the more dangerous because he is plausible. He has spent twenty years in the trenches of ultra-right thinking. He's founded the Edmund Burke Society and the Canadian Association for Free Expression. His pamphlets supported Ross's "struggle," and when Ross was awaiting the outcome of his appeal, Fromm arranged a public lecture for him in Toronto.

All that, and he managed to remain quietly at his teaching post. Had he not appeared at the Heritage Front meeting, no one, except for his followers (and he claims they number several thousand), would have known that the nice schoolteacher was the same man as the publisher of the *Canadian Immigration Hotline* information sheet that proclaims war crimes trials to be "Ethnic Vengeance."

In the June 1991 issue of the *Canadian Immigration Hotline*, under the headline "P.M. Promises More Ethnic Vengeance War Crimes Trials," Fromm writes: "The Prime Minister who has allowed our immigration screening to deteriorate to the point where large numbers of violent criminals are flocking to our shores and whose policies do not permit officials to screen out people with the deadly AIDS virus, will continue to drag 80-year-old men out of retirement homes and put them through immensely costly trials to replay World War II, all in the name of highly selective, one-sided ethnic vengeance."

To date, the only action taken against Fromm has been to remove him from his highschool classroom. He is currently teaching evening courses in adult education in Peel region. There have been, as with Malcolm Ross, several inquiries into his teaching practices. Despite repeated attempts by the Jewish community, Fromm continues to teach and to publish his C-FAR pamphlets and the *Canadian Immigration Hotline*. He has not, however, appeared at recent Heritage Front meetings.

Paul Fromm would seem, at first glance, to be a light year away from Louise and Emily, educators who have no sympathy for the likes of Keegstra, Fromm, or Ross. But if the invisible empire has a centre, it also has far horizons, where the weather is more congenial to the natures of Louise and Emily. They're teachers in the old style, white and crisp, insisting on good manners and neat papers. I met Louise and Emily at a conference where I was to speak on the problems of Hong Kong immigration. Louise had just retired—"I couldn't carry on any more"—but Emily still has seven years to go to reach her pension. She's already counting the days.

"I don't know what people expect of teachers any more," she says briskly. "We ought to be the ones who say what the curriculum will be and what the children will learn. Instead, it's the parents or the school board or the consultants. Anybody but the teacher."

What has Emily's dander up, and what impelled Louise to take an early retirement, is multiculturalism and its handmaiden, political correctness. The situations they describe, in extreme detail, are the teachers' version of the kids' complaints. "You don't dare say a word to a child who's coloured. I've had children who couldn't read, couldn't write, couldn't spell, and because they were from the

Islands, they were just passed along." Furthermore, children who are bored because they don't understand the classwork are disruptive, says Louise. "They end up agitating the other children, so nobody learns anything that day."

Are the only "disruptive" elements children of colour? I ask. Louise and Emily recognize a loaded question from a nosy reporter and backpedal. It's not race, it's people who are different: "No. There are children who don't speak English, and they're lost in the classes too." Louise and Emily are also distressed by the lack of facilities for these kids. "We used to have special-education classes for kids who needed it, but now it's all taken up with the retarded kids."

"Who don't belong in a public school at all," barks Emily. "You have no idea how much time is consumed in a class with one or two multiply handicapped children, even with keepers."

Louise is more cutting. "These are just parents who can't accept the truth that their children are not normal and are never going to be normal, and pretending that they're normal doesn't help them or anyone else."

But it wasn't the physically or the mentally challenged who caused Louise to leave. It was race. "In our department, we'd always been a real team, working together. The day came when I didn't feel that way any more. I felt outside." Louise questioned a decision on curriculum, the inclusion of so-called multicultural materials. "I didn't think they were appropriate," she says. "I said so, and the chairman of the department, a man I'd worked with for ten years, told me that I had a racist attitude. Just because I questioned adding materials just because they were racially and politically correct. We were supposed to be in charge and here we were kowtowing to some idea that no one, not even the person who told me I was a racist, believed in. I had my years in and I took my retirement. I miss teaching and I miss the kids, but I don't miss that."

Louise is deeply offended and angry about what happened to her, and those who say "good riddance, she probably needed to go" shouldn't be cheering just yet. Throughout Canada, political correctness is becoming a synonym for unwanted change in the schools, and the backlash has begun. Heritage programs, heritage languages, separate race schools, all are possible when there's plenty of money for education. But today's school boards are strapped, cash is getting shorter, and when the crunch comes, there's going to be a battle between "us" and "them" for whose programs get scarce dollars.

I thought of Louise when I went to curriculum night at my daughter's school. The place was packed with parents poring over their kids' work. It is a private school, expensive and exclusive, with none of the problems that teachers like Emily complain about in the Toronto public school system. There are no heritage language classes, no irate parents demanding a purge of the library, no physically or intellectually challenged children. There are also no boys. (I support single-sex education for women. It means they get all the breaks, and they'll need them when they discover that the road to full employment equity is long and hard.)

Once, this school was reserved for the pretty blond daughters of the Toronto Establishment. In many ways it still is, but there are as many kids celebrating Passover as cheering for the Easter Bunny. Muslims, some wearing traditional headcoverings, share classes with Hindus, Sikhs, and agnostics. There are plenty of Chinese, Japanese, and a small but growing group of Blacks. All of them get a thorough grounding in Canadian and European history and literature, Greek philosophy, English games, and Western art and music. The ambience is Church of England and Protestant Christian, all of which is usually referred to as the Canadian Establishment. While the public schools are under pressure to become all things to all people, Bishop Strachan School has no such dilemma. It is what it has always been, the training ground for the next generation of establishment power. What has changed is the Establishment. Power is passing, and, in the places where power is taught, race and religion are no longer barriers to entry.

I have a particular interest in and regard for teachers. I happen to be one. In thirty years, I've taught everything from fifth-grade social studies to first-year university humanities. I know firsthand the power teachers have and the responsibilities they accept. I know how much damage a bad teacher can do and how much good can come from one who cares.

For the past fifteen years, I have taught first-year courses at York University. Currently, I teach classes in literary analysis and in media criticism. My students are typical York youngsters, not the products of privilege but the children of first- or second-generation immigrants. Most of them have jobs and a surprising number work full time either in family-owned businesses or at the kinds of jobs students always seem to have—retail, waitressing, busboys. They tend to be intelligent and, at the same time, profoundly ignorant. They are critical without having a shred of political savvy. They are highly moralistic and cover it with a veneer of false sophistication and cynicism. In short, they are like most nineteen-year-olds. They believe in the future.

My classes are small, and so I have the luxury of knowing my students' names, reading their essays myself, listening to them in class. Our seminars range over many topics, but at some point we always seem to include racism, sexism, anti-Semitism, feminism, the new masculinity, and the important (to them) but regretfully named ageism, lookism, and speciesism.

I believe my students, over the years constitute as representative a sample as Philippe Rushton's. I've had my share of smart and capable Black students and a few not-so-bright and lazy Orientals, as well as white kids from every ethnic heritage and religion. I took Professor Rushton's conclusions to my media-criticism class and let them compare them with their own experiences.

My students were, in a word, appalled. They pointed out Rushton's spurious research, which had few sources beyond himself. Cam, a Chinese Canadian, and Jason, a Korean, pointed out that Oriental academic excellence has far more to do with family demands and the long tradition of Confucian respect for scholarship than brain power, and yet this important variable wasn't factored into Rushton's research.

There were other comments, including white students who pointed out that, despite years of antiracist education in schools, they still saw racist incidents on a regular basis. Danny Knowles, a bright and articulate Black student, said that in his entire educational career in Mississauga, he had never had a Black teacher or principal. "I didn't think much about it," he admits. "But it would have been good, once in a while, to see someone who was like me."

No one wanted to bring up the penis-size research; my students are still young enough to be embarrassed by open discussions of body parts. But Raymond Grant, who is over thirty, and white, went straight to the heart of Rushton's work. "All this business about aggression and crime and race is really bad," he said. "What it means is that Blacks are sexually and mentally predisposed to violent crime. It means when you kill one, it's okay."

It was so simple that I wondered why it hadn't struck me before. Maybe it's because I really don't want to believe that the evil equation of race and legalized murder can exist here in Canada. But Ray was right. I know all about the myth that Black men are oversexed predators bent on rape and criminal intent. I know about lynchings and why they happen. I know about justice perverted to meet a racist demand. I know because I was taught it in school and the people who taught me—decent, God-fearing, kind—were teachers just like Malcolm Ross and Jim Keegstra, people who believed to the racist marrow of their bones that when you kill a Black, it's okay.

4
WORDS AND MUSIC

IN THE SPRING OF 1992, talk show host Dini Petty was interviewing women on nationwide television. The subject of the day was husbands who keep their wives short of money. Most people think of such men as cheapskates. This day Petty referred to them as "Hymies." The show wasn't off the air before the calls started rolling in. Derogatory, defamatory, disgusting. Petty, bemused, pointed out that she had no idea that "Hymie" meant Jew. It was a word in common parlance where she grew up, one that many people used to mean cheapskate. She was genuinely apologetic both on and off the air. It went without saying that she promised never to say it again.

Petty isn't alone in using derogatory or racist words and having no idea of their meaning. I know any number of people who talk, especially in these recessionary times, about "Jewing down" the price of an item. When I point out that phrases like "Jewing down" or "gypping" are derogatory to Jews and gypsies, they haven't a clue what I mean. The origin of the phrase is lost but the unpleasant meaning lives on, transmitted from generation to generation in the casual language of everyday life.

Like most people, I don't give much thought to language in private. It's what I say, how I live, how I make my living, so I worry about being precise when I speak in public or when I go into print. But in my everyday life, removed from the scrutiny of readers or editors, I don't think about the words I utter. I use catchphrases like "the dark night of the soul" or "Chinese water torture" with abandon. I speak of "white knights" who save companies and "the darkest depths" to which one can sink. I know that an "Indian giver" is someone who takes back a gift and that nasty people are "black-hearted."

I was chatting one day with my friend Althea. I referred somewhat idly to my most recent bad day as "Black Monday." Althea, who is Black, stopped me: "Please don't use that phrase. I find it offensive."

Offensive? That innocuous little cliché? A phrase that everyone uses? My first reaction was that Althea, who, I hasten to add, is a woman of wit and humour, had lost her mind. My second was to think about what she had said. Words can wound and they also reinforce powerful cultural stereotypes. The image of Black people as bad, mad, and sad is tied in with phrases like the one I had used. Little Black Sambo does form an idea in a childish mind about Blacks and Africa, just as Ming the Merciless in the old Flash Gordon comics created a stereotype of Asians and just as Hymie the cheap insults Jews. An Asian friend once confessed, rather sheepishly, that she hates to hear "Confucius say" jokes. Another loathes references to "China doll" with the implications of passivity and mindlessness.

"The only way to get people to stop using these phrases is to make them think about them," Althea told me. "The only way to do that is to say at the time that they are offensive, that they shouldn't be spoken."

This implies, of course, that we want to change. Certainly in the current climate, as Dini Petty learned, one should think before one speaks in public. But what about private life? The difference between what we say in public—to enhance our image, to maintain a certain view of ourselves as respectable citizens—and what we practise, or say in private when no one can hear but us, is the measure of how deeply the roots of racism extend into our hearts and into the heart of society. Breaking open that difference, so carefully camouflaged in modern culture—looking into the gap between ideology and practice, public images and private ideals—is essential to any understanding of racist thought. That is what happens when the Other, just as Althea did to me, calls us to account for our unwitting acceptance or utterance of racial slurs that are invisible because they are accepted.

These are peculiarly difficult topics, simply because freedom of expression is fundamental to human freedom itself. Yet restraint in self-expression is very likely just as crucial to the existence and continuity of pluralistic civilization; and that civilization requires that we have a polite language to speak of the Other—the person or persons outside our tribe—no matter how uncomfortable we may be with this fact of any group as outsider. Our entire legal system of protecting human and civil rights is based on a notion of law as enforcer only until it can become educator: as Martin Luther King Jr. once remarked, civil rights laws cannot change hearts, but they can defend the defenceless until hearts change.

Because a measure of restraint is necessary if the weak are to be defended, we should not find it surprising that the radical racist right is perhaps the greatest foe of what they deem the hypocrisy in our midst, perhaps because they have the most to gain and the least to lose by such self-righteousness.

"I'm just saying out loud what most Euro-Canadians believe in their hearts," says Wolfgang Droege, head of the Heritage Front, referring to his views on non-whites. "Most people are afraid to speak out publicly. But when you speak out, it's surprising how many people agree with you."

For most of us, benign duplicity is preferable to this malicious realism. Hence, our expectation that the traditional guardians of our highest moral and cultural values will be, if not thoroughly good—

that's a lot to ask in a society as imperfect as this one—then at least consistently duplicitous; and hence our shock when they drop that mask we ask them to wear for civilization's sake and publicly air their private views.

The public spokesmen of the modern Roman Catholic Church have always proclaimed the love of God for all and the grace of tolerance, understanding, and human love. That's not a bad thing, and is a positively good one. We would be disappointed if any organization of such vast prominence, and with such powers of moral persuasion at its disposal, were to renounce its historic teaching on mercy and the plain necessity of a measure of grace in human relationships.

Privately and tacitly, however, the church has traditionally sanctioned a range of practices it would never advocate publicly, thus compromising its highest understanding of the human in quick-fix rapprochements with the powers that be. All peoples might be considered equal in the sight of God, but for decades racial segregation was the rule in Catholic schools and churches in segregated societies, just as in Protestant schools in the pre–civil rights South. But the discrimination was not confined merely to people of colour; it cut across numerous other lines. Non-Christians were seen as deeply inferior at best and non-believers and non-persons at worst.

Unlike the Catholic churches of Europe, Catholicism in North America—traditionally a church of uprooted immigrants, shut out socially by a Protestant majority, so all the more likely to remain staunchly wedded to Old World tribal customs and meek attitudes towards authority and obsolete gender differences—has been dominated by elderly white European men much given to insistence that a Catholic woman's place was in the kitchen or the convent, a Catholic man's place was in the Knights of Columbus, and all other peoples' place would be, if they were not fortunate enough to find the truth, in Hell.

As modern Catholics are quick to point out, this is, and perhaps always was, something of a caricature and, anyway, didn't differ substantially from the sexist and racist practices of most Protestant sects. But it was more true than not, and more true then than it is now. We are past those bad old days. There is at least marginal acceptance by the hierarchy of Liberation Theology, and women have been given some access to church power—though nothing approaching what the most vociferous of Catholic women's rights advocates want. Nevertheless, change is change, even if it's only a little.

Then along comes Aloysius M. Ambrozic, archbishop of Toronto, to remind us how really little, if at all, times have changed, despite the window-dressing, despite the public rhetoric of inclusion and acceptance. Even for a lapsed Catholic like me, who long ago gave up on the church and its various posturings and trims, it came as something of a shock to see, in print, this Successor to the Apostles chatting amiably about how Spanish dictator Francisco Franco wasn't such a bad fellow, and going on, in full racist bellow, about the impending "extinction" of the white race in Europe by floods of fecund Arabs, Turks, and Africans. It's the kind of thing we might expect to hear from a shaven-headed Dresden Nazi, or a member of Mr. LePen's French neo-fascist party, not from a grandee of the Universal Church, even if these were his private beliefs.

So why did the archbishop of Toronto, the richest and most influential English-speaking diocese in Canada and a city chock-full of minority groups, feel free to air these unpleasant attitudes? One reason seems to be that he felt safe. He was with author Michael Coren, who was interviewing him for a profile in *Toronto Life* magazine. Coren, a British-born convert to Catholicism, is the associate editor of *Canadian Catholic Review*, a respected literary magazine. The archbishop felt safe, we can only assume, being interviewed by one of the saved. Perhaps he confused Coren with Malcolm Muggeridge, another English Catholic author much more inclined to share, or at least jocularly tolerate, such cranky views.

Whatever his reasons, the archbishop's crude language and cruder ideas shocked Coren. "I simply couldn't believe my ears," he told a television reporter a few days after his article hit the stands. "He obviously thought because I was one of the flock I was doing a puff piece and I wouldn't print these quotes."

It's not the first time Archbishop Ambrozic has jammed his foot in his mouth. His hardline stands on issues ranging from women serving Communion to the use of church venues for meetings by liberal Catholics have made him a controversial figure from the day of his appointment. Joanna Manning, a teacher in a Catholic school and a longtime feminist and social activist, is a pet hate. In the interview with Coren he refers to her as "the bitch" and says that Toronto *Star* reporter Judy Steed "sicced" her on him.

The problem of what to do with errant or incompetent clergy dogs most religions. As a Catholic child I was accustomed to priests with "problems"—usually ones with alcohol. In those days, we were taught to honour the cassock and ignore the man inside it. The strategy faithful Catholics have chosen to deal with the archbishop's twaddle is to attribute his comments to his past. Ambrozic was born in Yugoslavia, grew up during wartime and the Nazi occupation, then saw the communist takeover of his homeland. He entered the seminary shortly after his family's immigration to Canada in 1948, and even his staunchest supporters don't deny that he's hardly at the cutting edge of Catholic theology and action. They describe his position on most issues as one of "us" and "them." He is, by all accounts, deeply suspicious of the media. Like many old-style Catholic prelates, he believes the press should act as good-news reporters, printing up glowing press releases from church officials. Investigative reporting is despised and discouraged.

In past years, investigative reporting has turned up a lot of uncharitable and unchristian news about Holy Mother Church. There was the Mount Cashel affair, in which Christian Brothers were convicted of sexually assaulting boys in their care. There have been similar scandals in schools for Natives, charges of assault in institutions in Alberta.

What all these squalid scandals have in common is silence—not the saving silence necessary to have an ordered civil society, not even the language of the Other we need to explain what has happened to us and to our institutions, but the corrosive silence that maims and destroys. The victims, the perpetrators, and the persons in charge all kept quiet. The excuse was protection of privacy, keeping the dirty secret within the family. So in this private world, evil is allowed to coexist with good, in a relationship that becomes more and more incredible. Where is there any redeeming virtue in Archbishop Ambrozic's ability to speak a half dozen languages—a key element in his self-image as representative of Toronto's multicultural Catholic mix—if he doesn't have the good taste and good sense to refrain from calling Joanna Manning "the bitch" and describing Arabs as infidels, conquering Europe with babies instead of swords?

It could be argued that, prelates being prelates—that is, irrelevant to a very large section of influential contemporary culture—the archbishop of Toronto's comments are best forgotten. But it would be a feeble argument. No matter what one thinks of the Catholic Church, and no matter how far one stands from it, the things institutional leaders say count, if not as outright injunctions, then as licences to those among us who are always advocating greater "realism" and "frankness" about the racial vexations no one can avoid feeling. The idea that an archbishop's gaffe doesn't matter because the archbishop is irrelevant also rationalizes the actions of those secret racists who have the most to gain by keeping their views private, expressing them in demands for "Canadian experience" on the job and reductions in the numbers of immigrants and refugees allowed into Canada.

One of the fruits of private racism is the so-called glass ceiling. It kept women out of management for decades and still keeps them out of the boardrooms. It works against new Canadians of all creeds and colours and its power is its invisibility and its prevalence.

"I grew up in Halifax," says Harriet (not her real name). "I hated it there. The poor called us niggers and beat us up. The rest just pretended we weren't alive. I came to Vancouver fifteen years ago. I wanted to get as far away from Halifax as I could. At first, it was strange because there weren't too many Black people in Vancouver. I went to work for the bank and there were no problems. People just accepted me as me. Oh, there were some bigots and racists, but they kept their mouths shut. I could tell they didn't like me working with them, but they couldn't say anything because of the human rights legislation.

"After a while I began to realize that I just wasn't moving ahead.

Women I worked with were being promoted, to head teller and so on. I got regular incentive raises, but I just didn't move up. I checked around. The Chinese women got promoted and the white women got promoted. The South Asians and myself didn't get promoted. I didn't do anything about it because I have kids and a husband and I couldn't afford to lose my job and my seniority. The South Asians, they fought back, and things are changing for all of us. But there's a glass ceiling for women of colour, you bet there is, and I'm sitting under it."

The glass ceiling has probably existed in business and the professions since the first Phoenician trader scrawled the first receipt on a clay tablet. There is a tendency in any profession to pass "our" jobs, businesses, professions along to "our" kids. I get regular calls from friends and acquaintances, as well as from my students at York University, asking about summer internships at newspapers and magazines. I pass along the information I have without thinking. When I hear of a job, what's more natural than that I should call my friend and tell her son or daughter about it? These are kids I know and, when the time comes, their parents will do the same for my child.

It is this informal private network, this cosy sharing of jobs and wealth and information and power, that ensures the survival of my group, even if it comes at the expense of another. We are, whether we like it or not, tribal by nature. We cling to our own kinds, our own ways, our own people. "They"—the Other, be it Jews or Chinese or Blacks—are encroaching on "our" privileges and place. White British Columbians complain that Chinese students are "taking over" the University of British Columbia, keeping "our" kids out. In Ontario, there are complaints about too many Orientals in the medical and pharmacy schools. Thirty years ago, there were the same complaints about too many Jews.

Foes of affirmative action programs and employment equity speak darkly of reverse discrimination and an opening of doors to the unqualified, the less deserving, simply to meet some form of racial or gender quota. A doctor, a woman who benefited substantially from equity programs for women in medical school, is unalterably opposed to the licensing of immigrant physicians, even those whose credentials are as good as or better than her own. "There aren't enough hospital spaces for graduates of Canadian universities," she says. "We don't need foreign doctors taking up our spaces."

Foreigners taking our places. For Archbishop Ambrozic, it's Turks and Arabs overrunning eastern Europe and taking over good Catholic countries. For others, it's cultural domination, the fear that the culture that defines us, makes us unique, is being eroded, changed, destroyed.

Culture and language are inextricable. (Québécois are absolutely correct about that one.) They're the glue in the tribal cement determining who and what we are, how we think and act. It can be argued endlessly that strict language laws like those in Quebec are not necessary to ensure the survival of culture. After all, Welsh survived three hundred years of suppression by the English and continued to flourish in private. Welsh people who wanted to succeed spoke English in public and, if they chose, Welsh at home.

So French survived in Quebec. For centuries, the language of business, of commerce, of wealth and power was English. When René Vaillancourt titled his 1971 call to arms "White Niggers of America," he knew what he was saying, in both official languages. For the Québécois to survive economically, they had to know English. The English, on the other hand, did not need to learn French and so, eventually, French would become the language of the poor and the dispossessed. It might survive in private but, as a cultural force, it would begin to die.

No group understands the relationship of language to culture better than the Native peoples of North America. They have seen whole religions and cultures diminished and, ultimately, ended when language died. Their battles against Canadian constitutional settlements, such as the Meech Lake accord, are all attempts to ensure some protection for their beleaguered cultures. If Quebec can have status as a distinct society, so can the Sandy Lake Cree, the James Bay Cree, the Inuit, and all the other tribes and peoples. If the Québécois can be *"maître chez nous,"* why can't all the other tribes have the same? We share a country, but we do not share a culture.

If the bedrock of culture is language, its essence is shared knowledge. I went to a sedate girls' school in Arkansas and graduated in 1959. My friend Anne grew up in Whitby, Ontario, attended a large suburban secondary school and graduated a decade later. When we hit university, however, the requisite readings for both of us were Poe, Dickens, and Shakespeare.

In university, we bit into Greek philosophy, modern art, and Russian, French, and English literature. We know that the Transcendental Movement is not a meditation centre. We may not reread all thirty thousand pages of Proust, but Proust and his madeleines are there, at the edge of our consciousness, occasionally dropped into conversation. Those same cultural flags link me with English-speaking peoples from Great Britain, the Caribbean, South Africa. We may not share music or drama or dress, but we do have a common language of understanding. This is our public educational unity. In private, we are divided by history, by our relationships to capitalism or to imperialism, by sex. This private world is, in the language of the critics, our context.

When I first came to Canada in 1971, I knew very little about its history and cultural development. I asked a friend, a professor of English, to recommend what he considered essential reading. The books were *The Journals of Susanna Moodie* by Margaret Atwood, *As For Me and My House* by Sinclair Ross, *Two Solitudes* by Hugh MacLennan, and a collection of essays on Canada by Northrop Frye. Years later, I can still marvel at his ingenuity at selecting that group. He managed to put together the problems of Quebec, prairie alienation, the British colonial experience, and a historical context for it all in one carryall bag. Were I to attempt to put together that package now, I don't know what I'd do. Where to put Neil Bissoondath and M.G. Vassanji? Paul Yee and Austin Clarke? The country I came to in 1971 no longer exists except in my library.

But it continues to have an existence in the minds of certain Canadians for whom it is the very source of the oppression they feel in their bones. They have an entirely different context. To them, that Canada, marked by British colonialism and, by implication, British racism, is alive and well. It is there when they don't see books by Black or Chinese or Arab authors on school reading lists. It's there when they study European but not Asian or African history. It rears its head when they read the great works of European literature, ones that I take for granted as being essential to an educated person, and don't hear a word about Zora Neale Hurston or Jamaica Kincaid, or even Nobel laureate Toni Morrison.

It is there when they go the the Royal Ontario Museum, a publicly financed entity that supposedly represents all the cultures of Ontario and Canada, and find images and words that are deeply offensive to them. Like my "Black Monday," the curators and professors and marketers at the ROM assumed that their cultural context and their language were perfectly understandable to anyone speaking English. And in so doing, they opened themselves up to one of the nastiest cultural confrontations in Toronto's recent memory.

I don't know Prof. Jeanne Cannizzo of the Department of Anthropology of the University of Toronto and a former curator at the Royal Ontario Museum. I've never met her, because she will not talk to reporters. But, were our paths to cross at a faculty lunch or a seminar, I would probably enjoy her company. We come from the same world—white women of a certain age who have fought the academic wars—which is why I found her plight, in the summer of 1990, excruciating.

In late July that year I went down to the ROM to watch a full-blown media circus. Each day, the Coalition for the Truth About Africa, a gaily dressed crew of attractive young people, mostly university and high-school students, would gather at the museum's imposing entrance. They would hoist their signs, which read "Racist Ontario Museum," and shuffle their leaflets and prepare to stop people entering the museum. "This is a racist institution," one told me solemnly as I arrived at the front steps. "Boycott this museum and tell them why."

"I don't know why," I told the young woman.

"This museum is scapegoating Africa," she said. "This show, 'Into the Heart of Africa,' is racist." For proof, the woman, who preferred not to give me her name ("I'm not here for publicity. I'm here to stop racism"), listed a number of offences that the exhibition committed. These included false representation of African people, denigrating language and images, perpetuation of colonialist and imperialist thinking about Africa, perpetuation of stereotypical images of African people, and failure to celebrate the contributions of Africa to world culture. "It's this kind of thing that teaches people that it's all right to go out and shoot African people on the street," she told me. "This show is making police brutality and murder legitimate."

The exhibition, and the attendant publicity, had been a nightly news affair since its opening in March. I had a fat file of newspaper articles about the controversy and I'd talked with several people who had seen it. Some reacted positively, some negatively. By the time I arrived, the show was scheduled to close in less than two weeks. The demonstrators were down to fewer than thirty from a high of nearly a hundred in the early days of police confrontation. A restraining order prevented the demonstrators from going within 50 feet of the doors, and a wary security guard drifted at the edge, just in case of any trouble. The demonstrators were not about to pass the boundaries. "We got people to listen," the young woman told me. "The rest of the museums that were supposed to show this all cancelled. We stopped it."

I explained that, even though I might agree with the demonstrators, I was going to see the exhibition for myself. That was okay. "Just tell them that you didn't approve of it," said one. "Let them know that racism isn't acceptable."

I didn't let on to the kids, but their bright show of solidarity had moved me. I hate crossing picket lines. Even more, I hate being classed as the right-wing oppressor, imperialist, capitalist, WASP woman of white privilege—the group against which all others must fight. I entered the museum in a nasty mood, ready to take the exhibition apart.

"Into the Heart of Africa" is the most controversial show the ROM has ever mounted. It started, simply enough, in the bowels of the museum. Jeanne Cannizzo, a research associate at the museum, was a well-respected anthropologist who did her field work in Sierra Leone and had taught at the University of Western Ontario. She looked at the African collection in the museum's vaults and saw something new and different. Old museum shows simply displayed a batch of objects in a case and told the public what the objects were. New thinking, laden with the ideas of context, proposes that the objects are part of a historical continuum, a dialogue with the past. This, according to all sources, was what Jeanne Cannizzo intended to present. Margo Welsh, head of exhibitions, told journalist Robert Fulford in an article for the museum's *Rotunda* magazine: "The idea evolved into something that was more and more exciting. It was clear that it was going to involve the attitudes of people in Canada in the late nineteenth and early twentieth centuries. It was extremely original. No other museum was producing an exhibition that showed how material came into the museum's collection."

The ROM's African collection isn't particularly distinguished. There is nothing in it to compare with Bishop White's magnificent collection of Oriental works, which occupy pride of place in their own galleries. It can be argued that Cannizzo was making a large visual irony, a clever didactic use of inferior museum material, much of it shot through with the visual and verbal racial stereotypes that grease the wheels and gears of all forms of imperialism. Most of the African collection was provided by missionaries of a lower social and economic order than the bishop, and their pictures, drawings, photos, and letters—the private revelations—are of far more importance than the souvenir masks, carvings, and baskets they collected and donated. What Cannizzo proposed was to make the missionaries part of the show. Their attitudes, reflected in their letters, notes, and books, would be presented alongside the objects. There was no attempt to disguise the racist overtones in the missionaries' hearts and minds. Their belief in their own religious and racial superiority was enhanced, presented in its unvarnished Victorian and Edwardian extremity and banality. No one ever expected the missionaries to be taken seriously.

"Don't those people have any understanding of irony?" was a

recurring cry from the day the exhibition opened. The demonstrators were seen as small-minded moralists blinkered by the new puritanism of political correctness. This was a show about irony. The juxtaposition of the missionaries' visions of themselves as courageous purveyors of salvation against our own knowledge of their roles as agents of imperialist rule was clear—to us.

As I walked into the exhibit, the first thing I saw was the larger-than-life blowup of a drawing of a British soldier stabbing a Zulu warrior. My response was that the drawing wasn't bad for an amateur artist. That same image shocked some unprepared Black schoolchildren nearly to tears. The slide show—a mockup of the old-fashioned magic lantern evening—had an audio track of a "Canadian missionary" telling the folks back home about the heathen, accompanying the talk with original photographs. It was slick and ironic and, to me, a bit arch. Black schoolchildren found it condescending and insulting. "Why don't you want to see Africa as it is?" asked a young man from the Coalition for the Truth About Africa (CFTA). "It is a great continent with history and culture. Africans built the pyramids, the temples of Egypt. They had science, mathematics. Have you heard about the Great Library at Alexandria?"

The young man had it a bit muddled. The Egyptians who built the temples and pyramids were one race and the Ptolemaic Greeks who built the Great Library were another, but he was right about the history. The Empire of Mali flourished at the time of Prince Henry the Navigator. Venetian dukes and Turkish sultans sailed down the coast of Africa to trade with the great chiefs and princes. I also agree that we know far too little of the literature and culture of Africa. But I also know that if there had been no show of African masks in Paris in 1905, then Pablo Picasso wouldn't have seen them, been profoundly moved, and then gone out to paint the *Portrait of Gertrude Stein* and then *Les Demoiselles d'Avignon*, the first masterpieces of cubism.

The dilemma of "Into the Heart of Africa" was that it was about the white missionaries, not the Black Africans. It was Africa as it was perceived by a specific group of provincial religious folk at a time when racial superiority was openly expressed. "Why don't they have a show of Africa from the vantage point of the slave traders?" asked one CFTA member. "Or one about women from the vantage point of men?"

The rage of the group increased with each chant. I want to know how the show leads to murder. "That show is about how African people are subhuman, savages, barbarians," says coalition spokesman Ras Rico. "This exhibit and racism are inextricable. The behaviour of the police in this city is directly connected with misrepresentation and propagated in institutions like the Royal Ontario Museum."

Rico was referring to the unrelated shootings, in 1990, of three Black people by the Metro police. Wade Lawson was shot in the back while driving away from police in a stolen car. Sophia Cook was a passenger in a car stopped by police. Lester Donaldson, who had a long history of mental illness, was shot while allegedly coming towards officers with a knife. The ROM exhibit, full of irony and images, became the symbol of racist thinking in Toronto today. The words of missionaries long dead were suddenly the words of people today. It was all right for a British soldier to kill a Zulu warrior in 1890, so the ROM was telling the world that it was fine for a Toronto police officer to shoot an unarmed Black youth today.

"What did you see?" asked the young woman who had first spoken to me.

I told her the truth. I had seen an ironic look at a lot of dead white people who thought they were doing the right thing. She left me, shaking her head. I had failed the perception test. I didn't get a chance to say that I also saw what offended her, deeply and truly. I have never been on the margins of culture, but I have some idea of what it must be like to never see yourself portrayed in those paintings or books or ballets or sculpture. When you do see yourself, it's on the receiving end of a white man's bayonet.

In all the hype and hysteria that accompanied the exhibit, the focus of the CFTA's rage became Professor Cannizzo. She was roundly condemned, her privacy invaded. Demonstrators went to her home and, not content with shouted insults, left obscene graffiti on the walls. When I mentioned this to a CFTA member, I was told,

"Now she knows how it feels to be insulted. To have everyone read it out." Tit for tat.

In September, when Cannizzo began teaching a class in African anthropology at Scarborough College, students from a variety of self-described antiracist organizations packed the classroom and screamed insults to prevent her teaching. When she left the classroom, one student followed her down the hall, calling her, among other epithets, a "racist bitch." She was unable to continue the class and it was cancelled, the first time in the history of the University of Toronto that students had prevented a professor's teaching. There were dark comments from academics about censorship and the demise of free speech. Academics dislike having their credentials questioned or their classes challenged. Students are encouraged to air dissenting views but not to take over the classroom.

The CFTA, for its part, already on to other issues, simply said "good riddance" and commented that African courses should be taught by persons of African heritage. Cannizzo, as a white woman, had proved in public that, despite her years of study of language and culture, she didn't understand the minds or the feelings of Africans or African Canadians.

In all the hue and cry, though, one still fails to understand how the ROM could so misunderstand the audience. Or did they? There are no Black curators at the Royal Ontario Museum. In fact, there are no persons of colour in any position of authority in any museum or major gallery in Canada. Could an African Canadian curator have seen the problems with "Into the Heart of Africa"? The museum did consult with a group of prominent Black Canadians before the opening and made a few changes in the show based on their recommendations. (It was originally titled "Into the Heart of Darkness.")

In the final analysis, the best explanation of what went wrong comes from a ROM security guard, Tony Hanik. According to Robert Fulford's account in *Rotunda* (the best of a lengthy bunch of articles on the show), Hanik asked to speak to the board of trustees to give them his views on the whole controversy. "I saw it at least three times a week," he told them, "and it took me ten months to figure out what they were doing and why it didn't work."

What he saw was a specialist show, designed for the sensibilities of academics. Everyone else could interpret it in various ways. He also pointed out that a previous ROM article quoted studies of museumgoers that showed they usually take away no new knowledge as a result of the exhibition because they don't read the captions. They look at the pictures and the artifacts, and leave.

According to Hanik, visitors to "Into the Heart of Africa" had to pay attention to the texts as well as the artifacts. The viewer had not only to read the texts carefully, he or she had to judge them false. But if most people didn't read the texts but just looked at the objects, then, Hanik said, they would go away with a powerful image of white racial superiority. "Walk through the exhibit and pretend you can't read. You will find image after image of superiority: the mounted swordsman over the spear carrier, the military leader over his troops, the missionary over the convert."

It wasn't just the protesters who didn't get the ironic content; the ordinary viewer couldn't "get" it. The missed perceptions were real. As Fulford puts it: "The liberal view of the texts was simply overwhelmed by the much more powerful imagery."

But there's another side to those texts and to that irony. It is the irony of academics, the kind of irony that flourishes in the Senior Common Room and the faculty club. It is the irony born in the shared knowledge, the common culture that binds us. Just as Archbishop Ambrozic felt safe in revealing his private thoughts to his coreligionist, Mr. Coren, Professor Cannizzo and the curators at the ROM felt safe exposing the racist thoughts of a handful of dead white Canadians to other Canadians who could understand that irony. Where they made their mistake was in presuming that, because the missionaries' racist ideas are no longer permissible in public, they have been eradicated as a painful, degrading force within the social fabric. What the protestors showed them was that racism is unconscious, just as unconscious of itself as it was a hundred years ago on the African plain.

In its collective wisdom, the ROM didn't understand that what is ironic in one culture can be read as barbaric by another.

A year later, the museum mounted a splendid show of Caribbean carnival costumes, celebrating the history of the carnival and, particularly, its contribution to summertime in Toronto, with the ten-day Caribana fête with its parties, dances, five-hour parade, and two million tourists who flock in to join the fun. The Caribana show was perceived in some Black circles as a sop, a gesture from the ROM to the community, but even the most irate Black Canadians agreed that it was an acceptable sop. It appeared that the ROM had learned its lesson. A message had gone out to white Canadians to think before they speak.

And then came *Show Boat*.

Marlene Nourbese Philip, in her collection of essays *Showing Grit: Showboating North of the 44th Parallel*, refers to the mounting of a new production of the musical *Show Boat* as "The ROM Revisited." She went on to point out that the problems with "Into the Heart of Africa" dealt with fundamental differences of perception between Black and white Canadians. "Central to the ROM dispute was the issue of who had the power to make images—who, in fact, controlled and controls the image making potential in society and about whom those images are made. Those who objected to 'Into the Heart...'—primarily African Canadians—argued that certain images about Africa and African peoples were offensive, painful and inaccurate; they demanded some say in how those images—images about themselves, their culture and their history—were being represented."

For Philip, the ROM protest achieved a pyrrhic victory. The protestors were able to keep the show from travelling to other museums but they were unsuccessful in getting it to change or be closed in Toronto. For Philip, and a good many other Black Torontonians, outright closure was the only route for *Show Boat*.

Long after the controversy was boiling, I learned—from a Black actress—that *Show Boat* was the first American musical to have a real plot, the first to incorporate the music into the story, the first to deal with serious social issues. Until then, she told me, musicals were just fluffy collections of tunes and dances. She still didn't want it produced in North York.

When it first hit the news, the *Show Boat* controversy seemed incomprehensible to a good many people. Stephnie Payne, a trustee of the North York Board of Education, was protesting the presentation of the musical as the inaugural event of the brand-new North York Performing Arts Centre. More specifically, Payne wanted to have the North York Board of Education keep *Show Boat's* producer from distributing educational kits in classrooms and organizing school trips to see the show.

Racist was the mildest word Payne used to describe the venerable musical. She called it a "form of hate literature" and said it portrayed Black people as "subhuman savages, dimwitted, childlike, lazy, drunk, irresponsible, and devoid of any human characteristics."

That doesn't seem like the same play that was banned in parts of the Southern U.S. because of its indictment of the Mississippi antimiscegenation laws and its sympathetic portrayal of Black oppression. As I understand it, *Show Boat* also portrays women (Black and white) as loud-mouthed harpies, irresponsible children, or spineless wimps living only for a caress from their worthless men. "Fish gotta swim, birds gotta fly, I gotta love one man till I die." The National Action Committee on the Status of Women, however, wasn't calling for a boycott.

Just what was going on? I tried to track down trustee Payne, but she was avoiding the media, having made a major gaffe on a CTV interview. Ruminating on the meanness of it all, she mused that when "most of the plays that portray Blacks and any other ethnic group in a negative way is always done by a white man, and usually a Jewish person."

In the twinkling of an eye, Trustee Payne had moved out of the realm of victim and into the role of victimizer. Whether she meant it or not, it appeared that she had, for an instant, allowed her private thoughts to become public. In so doing, she had shifted the issue from a protest about *Show Boat* to a fight between Blacks and Jews. The next day, urged by Black leaders from the likes of former provincial cabinet minister and MPP Zanana Akande and MP Alvin Curling, Payne apologized. Her remarks, she said, "can be correctly characterized as anti-Semitic."

There were plenty of Jews behind *Show Boat*. Edna Ferber

wrote the novel in 1926. Jerome Kern composed the music, and Oscar Hammerstein wrote the script and most of the lyrics. Florenz Ziegfeld staged the first New York production in 1927. The current incarnation in North York is being staged by Garth Drabinsky of Live Entertainment Corp. (LIVENT), the successful producers of *Phantom of the Opera* and *Kiss of the Spider Woman*. The stage director is Hal Prince. Mel Lastman, North York's mayor and inveterate booster, has moved heaven and earth to get the Performing Arts Centre built and opened and to get a major (read Broadway) production in it. No question. There are Jews behind *Show Boat*. And all of them thought they were bringing to the stage a good story, great music, and a message that racial intolerance is a bad thing. How on earth did "Ol' Man River" get to be a racist jibe?

In the absence of Ms. Payne, I went to Sondra Carrick, a Black professional. "I've never seen the play, but I saw the movie on TV a few years back. Ava Gardner played Julie"—the half-Black star whose marriage to a white man causes her to have to leave the show boat and flee north —"and I thought she was a bit silly, lip-synching the music. I have the record of Helen Morgan singing 'Bill' and it's wonderful."

Sondra is aware of the controversy. "It's in all the Black papers." She hadn't planned to see the musical and so the boycott doesn't mean much. "I can see why Ms. Payne is upset," she says. "I don't see why they have to open the theatre with a play about race. The first line is, "Niggers all work on the Mississippi." That may not offend you, but it really does offend me."

But by the time I saw Sondra, all semblance of reason about *Show Boat* was gone. *Share*, a widely read Black community newspaper, entered the fray with an editorial published under the glaring headline "Tired of Being Your Niggers." The editorial said that *Show Boat* was written, scored, produced, and promoted by Jews. Like Professor Cannizzo's irony, it's clear that the writer intended his comments to be somewhat over the top. What he did was to express his dismay that "members of the Jewish community—who, if no one else, must know what it is like to be reviled, denigrated, and to suffer abuse because of race—were involved in such an insensitive work."

The editorial then condemned Drabinsky, Lastman, et al. as having "not so much as a second thought to the effect the words—and what the show represents—must mean to us....Maybe it is that the Jews are so consumed by their own memories, grief, and anguish over the Holocaust that they have little attention to spare for the suffering of anyone else." Just in case there was anyone the editorial hadn't offended yet, it attacked the United Way, which it claimed gave a disproportionate amount of its funds to Jewish groups.

Charges of racist theatre now became howls against Black perfidy. "Jews were marching and dying for civil rights for Blacks and all people before some of these people were born," sniffed my friend Louise.

As for references to the Holocaust, York student Aviva Kemper summed up Jewish response: "They're comparing a line of music in a play to six million people hauled off to concentration camps and murdered! Get a life!" Kemper, like a lot of Jews, had initially been sympathetic to the *Show Boat* protesters. "After all, we've had our protests over Shylock and *The Merchant of Venice*," she said. She also pointed out that when the first concerns were voiced to Drabinsky and LIVENT, Morley Wolfe of B'nai Brith went with Payne and supported her. For Kemper, however, and for many other Jews, the *Share* article ended the support. "The way to fight racism isn't to replace it with anti-Semitism," she said flatly.

Demands were made that Trustee Payne resign, that Drabinsky halt the show, the benefit, and the run. The United Way was urged to refuse to participate in a gala fundraising performance. When the United Way decided to proceed, the entire Black and Caribbean Fund Raising Committee resigned in protest. Black organizations that usually supported the United Way made public their disapproval and their intent to reduce or end their participation.

In April, a public forum on *Show Boat* drew more than a hundred mostly young, mostly Black, mostly angry citizens. I tried to poll the crowd on who had actually seen *Show Boat*, read the book, or even seen the awful movie. (There is an earlier film with Irene Dunne,

Paul Robeson, and Helen Morgan that is slightly better only because it's more true to the stage script and because Robeson is in it.) Most refused to answer, dismissing me as a white bitch connected to the media. The few who did respond told me that they didn't have to read, see, or reflect. Stephnie Payne or the Black Action Defence Committee or *Share* had told them what it was about and that was good enough. One young white man told me he wasn't interested in paying good money to "see racist pollution."

With all the howls of hate that people let fly that night, one thing was clear. Hardly anyone had seen the show. A few, including Trustee Payne, had read the book. Ferber's novel of outrage at the mistreatment of Blacks—admittedly dated and, by today's standards, written in repulsively racist language—was ignored. Kern's moving musical motifs and Hammerstein's powerful words weren't part of the discussion. Everyone was yelling but nobody was listening.

Show Boat opened to a packed house and a hundred chanting demonstrators outside with signs calling to "Sink Show Boat." By this time, it was clear that what was really at issue wasn't a musical but an exercise in community action. Unlike American Blacks, who have the ugly unifying history of slavery and segregation to bind them, Canadian Blacks come from many lands with many cultures and histories. Jamaicans don't always see eye-to-eye with Africans. Emigrés from Britain or the United States have little in common with immigrants from Trinidad or Guyana. There are middle-class Blacks and very wealthy Blacks and extremely poor Blacks.

What there isn't is a single group, focus, or entity that speaks authoritatively for the entire Black community. Even as seemingly simple an issue as the term Black takes on monumental proportions. Many Americans now prefer African American, which is also preferred by many African Canadians. "It is a reference to our roots," explains Sondra Carrick.

But immigrants from the Caribbean have their own culture, their own history, even their own distinct dialects. They prefer—as Nourbese Philip does—to be known as Afro-Caribbean Canadians. Some Guyanese, with a different racial mix, call themselves Indo-Afro-Caribbean Canadians. Africans, on the other hand, do not like to see the word *African* attached to people born away from Africa. "We are Africans," says Joseph Iwambe, a Nigerian. "It isn't proper for these people here to refer to themselves as Africans."

Even Black Canadians, many of them descendants of the Blacks who came north with the United Empire Loyalists or who travelled to freedom on the underground railroad, don't always agree. I found the term *Black* to be the most universally acceptable, but two women, both elderly and both descendants of early settlers in Halifax's Africville, informed me that they were "coloured" and that I'd better not call them Black under any circumstances.

All these disparate groups share skin colour. Many of them have a common language—English—but they don't share a history, and culturally, they are very diverse. Moreover, their history in North America—from service in His Majesty's Forces to fiction to drama to music—have been systematically ignored by the larger white culture.

Black, African Canadian, or African; those names are important. They delineate the lineage, dreams, hopes, histories, and cultures that came with them. When the Black community of Toronto needed to band together, those hopes and cultures got in the way. The one thing that everyone agreed upon, however, from the august presence of former lieutenant-governor Lincoln Alexander to radical Black Action Defence Committee founder Dudley Laws, was that the *Show Boat* protest brought the community together. For once, the backbiting and internal squabbling was halted. *Show Boat* had forged a bond.

After all the agony, after the name calling and the conflict between Jews and Blacks, I went back to Sondra for a bit of balance. "I'm not offended by *Show Boat*," she said. "I don't believe in any Jewish conspiracy. I know that, in its time, *Show Boat* was intended to be a good thing, but that was sixty years ago. I'm offended that the North York Performing Arts Centre, which was built supposedly for me, since I live in North York, and was built with my tax money, and is located in a city with one of the largest Black populations in Canada, has chosen to open its doors with the word *nigger*. I don't give a damn how well meant it is, it's still offensive."

Did it have to be *Show Boat?* Was there anyone in LIVENT who suggested, perhaps, that *Oklahoma!* might be a better choice? *Cabaret* could have been a winner. Martin Knelman in *Toronto Life* suggested *The Sound of Music* —"It's still okay to hate Nazis." Did anyone, anywhere consider the possibility of a Canadian musical? Did anyone think that it might be insensitive to open the people's new hall with the word *nigger?* (And make no mistake, substituting the words *Black folks* for the offending epithet doesn't work.) Just as Archbishop Ambrozic thought nothing about his comments on Turks and Arabs, just as the ROM didn't see the image of the Black man on the bayonet, just as I didn't understand the relevance of "Black Monday," so the LIVENT folks didn't see anything wrong with *Show Boat.* Those protesters—those others—just didn't get it.

But they did.

M. Nourbese Philip saw this clearly. In *Showing Grit*, she writes: "*Show Boat* is really about America's fear of the Other represented, in this instance, by the African; it is about America's desire to define itself and all its dreams in distinction to what they perceive as radically and fundamentally different—Blacks. As Toni Morrison argues, this explains why every group that comes to America has to define itself in opposition to the American Black, since the very freedom on which the American dream rests is in turn based on the absence of freedom—in all its manifestations—of its African population."

One of the many defences of *Show Boat* is that it is historically accurate. That may possibly be so, but it is not an accurate, or even remotely familiar, rendering of Canadian Black history. Racism is not only a matter of what we remember, or think we remember, about the Other. It's also what we say, what we forget, and what we ignore.

5
Jobs and Power

FEBRUARY 14, 1993. The prime minister has announced that he is leaving, and there's cheering in the York University Common Rooms. Like most of my teaching colleagues, I hated Mulroney and his merry band of backbiting bottom liners. His departure is proof positive that the 1980s are finally dead. Over a celebratory sherry in the Faculty Club with a couple of other profs, I mention that I'm looking around for new authors for my survey course on detective fiction. I have a number of women, one a lesbian, and finally a really good male African American, but I wish I could find a woman of colour.

One drinking companion, a genial senior professor of impeccable academic and political qualification (Oxbridge and NDP), teaches a course in British lit, one of those courses reviled as being full of works by dead white European males. He is a bloodied veteran of the academic wars. He sighs. "My goodness, Margaret. Don't tell me you're becoming one of those dreary little PC shits."

PC—Political Correctness—once the designation of choice for campus activists concerned with issues of sex, race, and peace, has become a despised generalization for everything trite, sophomoric, and silly. "PC" reduces my concerns about introducing race into my course (in a school where a substantial number of undergraduates are members of visible minorities) to the level of young fogies who dig around in course outlines for evidence of sin and who insist, without a shred of irony, that God be identified as "S/He/it." "PC" puts me in the same category of feminist as those who demand public floggings for men who ogle women in the campus pub. Calling me a dreary little PC shit is an attempt to shut me up completely.

Not me. I've spent the past thirty years working hard to be taken seriously as a writer and academic. I'm not about to be tossed onto the metaphorical ash heap of history embodied in "PC."

Later, when I have a chance to consider what I could have done or said, I wish I'd simply told the arrogant son-of-a-bitch to fuck off. That's a universal end to such discussions, a throwback to my rebellious twenties, when I first uttered the dread f-word in public as a defiant challenge to my white middle-class background. My parents had beggared themselves to send me to private schools, exclusive summer camps, art and music lessons, dancing and deportment classes, a fine university, but I was eager to reject all those trappings of civility. I said "fuck off" in public.

It all seems a tad silly now, believing that a word could change a world. But I did believe just that. So I shouted "fuck" for the same reasons my redheaded mother had lit her first cigarette in public and my elegant grandmother had bobbed her long dark hair. In a world of oppression directed against women, you do what you can. In later years, I tossed my brassiere into the campus garbage and joined a sit-in to salvage the reputation of a local poet who took refuge in a tree because the campus printer refused to set the words *red-assed monkey* into type. I dismissed my sorority sisters as elitist pawns of the military-industrial complex, fought over the wording of obscure manifestoes, and marched, marched, marched. In 1968, I joined the Students for a Democratic Society and fell madly in love with a Chicano political theorist named Tony Mares. I read books like *The*

Second Sex by Simone de Beauvoir and *Eros and Civilization* by Herbert Marcuse. I sat in serious little meetings with serious young people who demanded that anyone who smoked dope resign from political work. "Politics," we would intone, "is serious business. Dope and politics don't mix."

So, here I am in 1993, sitting in the mauve and grey tastefulness of the Faculty Club, wondering how the cutting edge of revolution became a dreary little PC shit. My generation's battlecry is this generation's comma, a word squawked by every boy and girl on every grade-school playground.

My female friends and I don't sail through the world dropping the f-word at every turn. We save it for the right time and place—the disgusting guy at the bar who simply won't take no for an answer or the oh-so-superior salesclerk who, having waited on everyone in the store, finally deigns to turn our way. It's reserved for the really bad day, the final fillip, the straw that breaks, etc. We are Nice Girls, well brought up, from Good Families and when we tell someone or something to fuck off, we want it to count. It is the ability to understand such nuances, we believe, that separates us from the yobbos on the streets.

Which brings me to reflect on the meaning of the June Callwood mess.

People whom I respect—on both sides of the June Callwood story, as it has come to be called—have challenged me to join one side or the other. Both sides—being well brought up, from good families, etc.—long to tell the other to fuck off. Both sides are represented by smart women with impeccable feminist credentials and plenty of zeal. One side (those who support the decision to oust Callwood from her position) believe they are the vanguard of change in a society that systematically excludes persons of colour, particularly women, even more particularly lesbians. The other side believes that these women are dreary little PC shits engaged in the systematic destruction of a genuine Canadian heroine.

The battle lines between these two camps indicate the complexity of the issues. Racism is the battlecry, but poverty, access to services, cultural differences, and sexual orientation are all part of the mix, confusing people as to just what the problems are. No one can deny that the majority of Canada's poor are women and children. If you're poor and non-white, you have a double burden. If you're poor, non-white, and an immigrant or refugee, you fall further down the ladder of discrimination. If you're poor, non-white, and a lesbian, you have few places to go and few resources to rely on. Nellie's is one of those few places.

The story of June Callwood and Nellie's revolves around a highly publicized incident in which Callwood, a Toronto journalist who has spent a lifetime organizing for good causes, was forced to resign from the board of Nellie's, a hostel for battered women that she founded, because she was a woman of white privilege who exercised that privilege. As board member Laura Coramai told journalist Adele Freedman in an article for *Saturday Night* magazine, "June Callwood told a Black woman to fuck off. She treats some people differently than others. It's not as though June thought about it and learned from it." What Coramai was saying is that Callwood wasn't reflecting on her role in the racist superstructure of Canadian society. A lot of people believed there was no need for Callwood, after a lifetime of work, to reflect on anything but her Order of Canada. As my friend Anne Collins put it: "If June Callwood is a racist, what does that make me?"

The June Callwood incident caused considerable consternation because Callwood has long been considered a dedicated activist. She is an award-winning journalist and book author with a career spanning fifty years. She is a founder of the Canadian Civil Liberties Union, a cofounder and past-president of the Canadian branch of PEN International, a member of the Writers' Union, and a spokesperson for the coalition to change Canada's outdated libel laws. Even a partial listing of her accomplishments takes several pages of small print. She is a member of the Order of Canada, a frequent candidate for the Governor General's Award for excellence in non-fiction. She appears regularly on radio and television lobbying for the rights of women or kids or Natives. As a fundraiser, she is a celebrity whose name on a masthead means money in the bank.

Throughout her career, Callwood has targeted the needy and the forgotten as her special subject for study. But she doesn't stop there. When Callwood sees a need, she does something about it. In the 1960s, she founded Digger House, a haven for drugged-out hippies. In 1976 she founded Nellie's, one of the first havens for battered wives in Canada. Hard on the heels of Nellie's came Jessie's, a drop-in centre for teenaged mothers, and in 1986 she founded Casey House, Canada's first hospice for people with AIDS. In addition to the tangible projects, Callwood wrote books and articles on controversial subjects. She chipped away at AIDS prejudice or the stigma of being a battered woman and made the causes respectable. She could get people like the Eatons to hand over the cash for the cause. Behind her back people might refer to her as "St. June" or "La Causista," but in public, they opened their wallets and joined the dance.

No single event in the wordy little world of Toronto charity and Toronto media has so enraged liberal Canadians as the verbal assault by Nellie's Women of Colour Caucus on June Callwood. All those people who sent in their dollars for Nellie's and Callwood's other worthy causes are bemused now, wondering how a woman so committed to doing good could possibly be tossed out on her keester, from a hostel she founded, for being "racist." If June Callwood is a racist, what does that make me?

The June Callwood incident demonstrates clearly the chasm between the perceptions of race held by the majority white society and by the minorities who are no longer willing to remain invisible. Louis Chan, president of the Canadian Ethnocultural Council, put it succinctly: "Multiculturalism isn't about eating and dancing any more. It's about jobs and power."

The battle for power has begun in the fields of education, social services, and the arts. The language is the language of devout feminism, and the foot soldiers are feminist women of all races. The battlecry is "systemic racism," a concept that few whites understand. Callwood—feminist icon and media celebrity—was the perfect target. In the language of the day, she is a "woman of white privilege," a designation that denotes class and can include persons of other races.

June Callwood's real crime was that she said "fuck off" to the wrong person.

The first salvo in the war between Callwood and women of colour came, not at Nellie's, but at a congress of PEN International, an organization of writers that lobbies for the release of imprisoned authors and journalists. In September 1988, the annual congress of PEN International was held in Toronto for the first time. The greats and almost-greats of literature and journalism, among them a number of Third World authors, converged on the city for a congress hailed by PEN as a breakthrough in racial representation.

But outside Roy Thomson Hall, picketers from a variety of groups representing persons and writers of colour, under the banner of Vision 21, picketed the proceedings. They claimed that they were demonstrating on behalf of the silenced writers of Canada, that Canada was a racist society, one that used grants, publishing quotas, and the jury system to keep writers of colour outside the mainstream of publication. They were few in number, but they made up for that in zeal.

Callwood was incensed. She felt the protesters were trying to undermine an organization world-famous for its support of imprisoned and dissident writers worldwide. The Third World authors in the hall and on the panels were proof of PEN's commitment, and Canada's commitment, to those goals. As she saw it, the picketers' charges were ridiculous.

After two days of attempting to get the picketers to join the authors inside the hall, Callwood was fed up. As she and her husband, sportswriter Trent Frayne, left the hall (here, versions of what happened differ wildly), she either was approached by or independently walked up to the group and said, "Fuck off."

One of the women Callwood swore at was M. Nourbese Philip, lawyer, author, feminist, Guggenheim Fellow, and, as she describes herself, an African Canadian of Caribbean background. In a more perfect world, Callwood and Philip would be on the same side, because they have much in common. They are both intelligent women of action who go at whatever cause they select with a vengeance. Issues are sharply delineated, people are for or against, and no one takes prisoners.

But Toronto isn't a perfect world, and Nourbese Philip spends a great deal of time pointing this out. She is seldom published in the establishment pages that Callwood commands—the *Globe and Mail*, the Toronto *Star*—but she's a regular on the alternative media circuit—*NOW*, *FUSE* magazine, *Border Cultures*. As expected, Philip's recollection of events is quite different from Callwood's.

Philip set down what she had to say about PEN, Callwood, and the whole incident in an essay called "Disturbing the Peace," published in the winter edition of *FUSE* (and reprinted in Philip's collection of essays *Frontiers*). According to her, the picketers were a quiet bunch, drawn from several antiracist groups concerned about the continuing focus of writers' organizations like the Writers' Union and the League of Canadian Poets on white European-centred modes of expression. According to Philip, discussions, reactions, and confrontations had been occurring since 1983. "In writing and publishing in Canada, racism was by no means a new issue."

The aim of the leafletting campaign, said Philip, was "to advance the state of the debate concerning racism and the arts here in Canada. Our aim was not to change PEN Canada or PEN International. We merely used the ethnic and racial composition of the Canadian contingent as a startling yet predictable example of the official face of racism in the arts in Canada."

A great many of the delegates in the hall, and certainly most of the white Canadians, had no idea what Philip and her group were on about. Racism, to June Callwood and most other white people, is personal and individual. It is name calling or overt discrimination. They see it as a vicious act of a nasty lunatic fringe who seek to assert the superiority of one race over another. Ernst Zundel and Wolfgang Droege are racists. Certainly not people who found and fund institutions such as Nellie's.

For Philip, however, and for other Black intellectuals with an increasingly widened view of the world of possibilities closed to them, racism is subtle, endemic, systemic, a part of the structure of everyday life in our capitalist society, and a means of keeping that society working in an orderly fashion for advancement of the white majority. This racism—an operational ideology, no longer the immoral attitude old-fashioned liberals thought it to be—permeates the very air we breathe, is explicitly taught and implicitly communicated in the schools, nurtured by the demands for obedience and humility made on the individual by church, state, and family, and played out against Blacks, browns, Natives, and Orientals in both positive and negative ways. To cite some favourite targets of people so minded, it means insisting on everyone's learning Shakespeare but not the Ramayana, Wordsworth but not dub poetry, Ernest Hemingway but not James Baldwin. It means constructing a media culture in which all beauty, all grace, all civic virtue are vested in white role models, from Terry Fox to Peter Mansbridge to the Canadian peacekeepers in Somalia. It means communicating continually, through advertising, images of young, restless, successful, and upwardly mobile whites, and of Blacks who dress just like the whites, talk like them, make the same career moves.

But it also means allowing structures of entrenched white privilege to stand as mute witness to the power of just who's in charge. Walk into any newsroom of any great newspaper in Canada, into the head office of any great capitalist institution whose judgements affect the very texture of our culture—banks, law firms, magazines, stock brokerages, and on and on. Each is a monument to the victory of whites, whether any individual in the firm means it to be or not. Each is, in its way, a judgement on Blacks and other Canadians of colour—exclusionary in a benign way, discriminatory but with kindness, and with much talk of "keeping standards high." It is the very Canadian face of our own brand of racism.

The earlier dreams of the activists—to break open the decision-making apparatus in society, to precipitate a swing towards active, affirmative action—has all but died, dashed on the rocks of indifference and the hostility of a white majority that, indeed, has much to lose from competition with bright, able people belonging to groups traditionally marginalized. Thus the gradual shift of energies into the arenas of culture, which are traditionally more liberal than society as a whole, and therefore (it would seem) more likely to accept the arguments of those seeking to expose systemic racism and make that exposure public.

And thus the picketing of PEN and the assertion that in this organization could be found just one more instance of the Canadian white hegemony in action, protecting the privileges and positions of the white race by the familiar tactic of sympathize and conquer.

By focusing on PEN, the picketers hoped to call into question the whole contemporary network of the distribution of honours, favours, opportunities, money. Writers of colour who want to be published by mainstream publishers, who want to receive major arts grants, to be recognized, and to be taken seriously by major critics— so the argument goes—must either sell out their cultures to the majority white Europeans (like the Black fashion models who have adopted the looks and postures of whites, or turned themselves into objects of white male lust), or be cut out of the pie.

In the world of systemic racism, small slights are merely echoes of the larger, more destructive, and infinitely more subtle ones inform-ing the daily, impersonal workings of capitalist culture's institutions. It is not enough to rail against race hatred, vengeance, active segre-gation. In any case, such attitudes and actions are actively opposed by leaders of opinions in all walks of life nowadays.

But if the publicly articulated race hate promoted by the older generation of Canadian racists, whom June Callwood and other lib-erals have spent their lives fighting, has largely been proscribed and rendered deeply unfashionable, it has survived intact in the social and cultural structures bequeathed by the past to the present. In Philip's view, to eradicate racism you have to fight for the disman-tling of the very bones and glue of our inherited social structures— especially the liberal ones, such as PEN—not merely wait for some-one to make a discriminatory remark.

If one is white, and particularly if one is both white and male, he will find it easy to dismiss Philip and the whole idea of systemic racism as a kind of behavioural extremism, without evidence in the real world in which the cream so often does indeed rise to the top. But if all writers and artists have difficulty finding publishers, galleries, and critical acceptance, the fact remains that those of colour and from new immigrant communities have more trouble than others. Nevertheless, the dictum is insistently pronounced: "If you're good, you'll be suc-cessful. If you're not successful, it's because you haven't got the right stuff." This seemingly plausible argument may well strike many a

Canadian woman as all too familiar. It was used to downplay the works of women in the arts as recently as a decade ago.

To Philip, this means the effective "silencing of African, Asian, and First Nations writers." She and her group wanted PEN to recognize that "such silencing of writers, while in no way equivalent to the imprisonment of a writer, was serious enough to warrant the attention of an organization such as PEN and the delegates to the congress."

In her essay, Philip acknowledges that Callwood was a good target because she was "an icon of Canadian white liberalism." It was convenient that Callwood chose to come out and strike the first blow. But it was hardly the first time Philip had taken on the Canadian literary establishment.

A year before, in the fall of 1987, she had penned an essay, "The Multicultural Whitewash," in *FUSE*. There, she took on the various arts councils and funding bodies that dispense grants to artists, writers, and composers. These agencies, funded by ever stingier governments, are presided over by bureaucrats who, according to Philip, are stunningly out of date in the multicoloured and multiracial world of today's Canadian art. Philip's point, that there are too many white representatives of "mainstream arts culture" on the juries and committees that decide who gets how much of a shrinking financial pie, is well taken. Less than a decade ago, these committees were also preponderantly male, as well as white, middle-class, and mainstream. There are now equal numbers of women, something Philip calls "a small mercy."

Philip's target here was the Toronto Arts Council, an organization under the heading of Metro Cultural Affairs and, according to their literature, committed to "express and enhance our unique ethnic diversity." Grants were to be awarded by committees, and "each committee is chaired by a member of the Toronto Arts Council Board: together they have representation from a wide range of the arts community. All committee members are volunteers with extensive professional experience in their fields."

Philip, with some cause, felt that she fit the category for a volunteer committee member, and so she inquired of the executive director how she could get onto the literary committee. She was told that the members of the committee chose other committee members; thus, unless she knew a committee member, she had no access. The list of literary committee members Philip gives in her essay are June Callwood, Kass Banning, Carol Bolt, Susan Crean, etc. It is a list, according to Philip, that "confirms my expectations." Crean, Callwood, Banning, and Bolt might be perceived somewhere as left-leaning feminists, but in the world of Philip, they are just a gaggle of "women of white privilege" holding the door closed against the rabble.

Philip made the literary committee of the Toronto Arts Council one of her pet projects and so, though she and June Callwood had never been formally introduced on the night of the PEN congress, Philip already had June's name, her place in the racist order, and her list of sins prepared. Whatever else she might be or become, Callwood was a woman of white privilege according to Philip, hence part of the problem.

In a letter to the *Globe and Mail* published in September 1990 (and republished in *Frontiers*), Philip recounts how, the day after the PEN incident, she received an early-morning telephone call from a man who called her a nigger. He was responding, she was convinced, to the version of the PEN demonstration that appeared in the *Globe*. "While I cannot and do not hold Ms. Callwood responsible for this phone call, I wish to point out that when someone of the stature of Ms. Callwood contemptuously dismisses allegations of racism in the manner she did, as well as being verbally abusive to a Black woman, such behaviour gives licence for individuals such as that early-morning telephone caller to do what he did."

In the same way that Nourbese Philip cannot hold Callwood personally responsible for the telephone call, it's not fair to say that Philip orchestrated the downfall of June Callwood at Nellie's. But there is no question that she lit the fuse that started the fire. From the day Callwood lost her cool, she was a goose waiting to be cooked.

June Callwood has established many organizations in her long career, but it's safe to say that Nellie's was the shining jewel in her liberal crown. It has always been at the cutting edge of the needs of poor women. It has always met the needs of those who have found its doors. From the day it opened, it has been a centre of struggle, as women, drawn to the issues of a feminist response to violence and poverty, fight to find a new method and a new language for social action. All these factors make it a particularly useful place to study the gradual transformation of the notion of racism as a personal, voluntary, and self-stoppable fault into a structural dynamic, afflicting all within its reach.

Twenty years after its foundation, one finds it hard to recall just how desperate the need for such an institution really was. In 1973, I was a community organizer working in the Regent Park public housing complex in East End Toronto, just a stone's throw away from the old Riverdale house that eventually became Nellie's. In 1972, the year I went to work in Regent Park, there were twelve hostel beds for women in all of Toronto and they were occupied, as a rule, by ageing street women who could no longer trade sex for a place to sleep. The addresses of these hostels were well known. Any abused woman who went there, should there be a bed, could not expect to be protected from an angry husband. There were no facilities for women with children.

Those of us who recall the bad old days before Nellie's have lots of stories about women who'd be dead or disabled, kids who were raped or worse, if there hadn't been a safe place to go. No matter what Nellie's became later, it remains a haven for women and children in trouble. You just showed up at the door and someone took you in.

Today, Nellie's is at the centre of a web of interconnected social services organizations devoted to the needs of women and kids. Street women with no place to sleep on a freezing night can get a bed and a warm meal. A battered woman can get a protected haven in which to pull her life together, legal help and eventually a safe home. There is counselling for physical and sexual abuse, incest, child molesting, sexual confusion, and drug and alcohol addiction. The organization includes two housing complexes for single women, two hostels, a special drop-in centre for teenaged mothers, and a referral and counselling network across Canada. The budget, most of it received from the Ontario government, is in excess of $6 million a year and, unlike most private social services agencies, which are chronically short of funds, Nellie's in 1991 had more than $600,000 in its reserve fund.

While others can take credit for fiscal prudence and careful shepherding of funds, it's safe to say that most of this success is due to June Callwood's high profile and her campaigning among wealthy and influential friends. When Brian and Mila Mulroney came to Toronto, June got them to drop in and meet the gang at Nellie's. When June heard there was money available from the federal government for a resource centre, she homed in on it for Nellie's. Race, creed, or colour never came up—a sure sign of health to the old-fashioned liberal, a sure sign of rot to the gender-conscious, gesture-sensitive proponents of the systemic-racism theory.

As Nellie's grew, the population it served changed. There were ex-psychiatric patients, plopped on the streets with a dime bag of haloperidol and an address. There were the lesbians and the lost kids from the North and the occasional aboriginal woman in the years before aboriginal women opened their own shelter.

As the neighbourhood and the city changed, so did Nellie's. There were more immigrants, more women of colour. The staff obtained permission from the province to be a women-only closed shop. Later, two women of colour were hired to reflect the changing face of the community and the clients served. One of them, Joan Johnson, had been an illegal immigrant. For a year, Nellie's staff hid her in the building while they worked to get her status cleared with Immigration Canada. After she became a landed immigrant, she went to work at Nellie's. She liked to be known as J.J. It was J.J. who dealt the *coup de grâce* to June Callwood, but the real destroyer—at least so the local folks believe—is a woman called Carolann Wright.

"Let me just tell you about Carolann Wright," snarls a friend of mine, a longtime resident of the Regent Park–Cabbagetown community and dedicated community volunteer, a woman who has given tirelessly of her time to every community need from soup kitchens to organizing, in just seventy-two hours, a safe, clean flophouse for men on the streets. "Carolann Wright thinks she's entitled to public office because she's Black. She ran for MPP and lost. She screams it was racism. Every time she doesn't get her way, it's racism. I'm sick and tired of these people claiming I'm racist every time they lose fairly. God help us if she ever really gets elected. What'll she do then? Scream racism every time she loses a vote in the legislature?"

It's regrettable that the confrontation, all dirty linen waving, was presented in the Toronto media as St. June versus Carolann the demon. Carolann Wright, who is a Canadian of African heritage, was born in Halifax. Like my friend who regards her as anathema walking, Wright is a longtime community activist and a member of the Coalition of Women of Colour Working in Women's and Community Services. According to a statement issued by the coalition and written by Wright and Donna Barker, the organization is a city-wide movement pledged to racial equality in the workplace. There are no "leaders" in the coalition because, like Nellie's, it is a feminist organization run as a collective. The mood is militant, but the issues are bread and butter. The poor are largely female and the poorest of the poor are women of colour, who often face cultural as well as financial barriers when they attempt to gain access to the Canadian social services network.

Cleta Baines, a gregarious Indo-Afro Canadian, born in Guyana, is one of the women Wright is sworn to help. Baines calls her five years as a single mother on Family Benefits "the most soul-destroying of my life. Every day, I felt another little humiliation, another embarrassment. I would go to the bank to cash a cheque and the teller would ask for my ID. Nobody else had to show ID to write a cheque, but I did. When I bought my son some good clothes as a graduation gift, my caseworker happened to see him. She assumed I was working on the side and gave me a little lecture on honesty and not stealing from the good taxpayers of Ontario who were supporting me and my family. I was made to feel like a cheat and all I'd done was get Clifford some shirts and pants on sale."

Baines speaks for dozens of other women of colour who have

encountered the casual assumptions and negative stereotyping that accompany colour and poverty. "The social workers came to tell me how to manage my money, and they would come in wearing expensive coats and dresses, and then ask me how much I was spending on groceries for myself and three teenaged children. My monthly income wouldn't pay for the clothes on their backs and they were making judgements about my lifestyle. I was so humiliated that I used to cry whenever they left."

These are the women Carolann Wright speaks for. They are the new Canadian female poor and, sometimes, they have recourse to Nellie's. When they get there, the coalition believes their problems will best be understood by and solved by women who share their cultural background—in other words, women of their own race. There is also an unmentioned but not unimportant subtext: if salaries are to be made in the social and women's services, those salaries should be shared equally with women of all races and social classes. The day of the white middle-class female social worker, with her M.S.W. and her briefcase, is at an end. White women, who have defined the face and race of the feminist movement for twenty years, have got to move over and share the power and what little wealth there is. Faced with this fact, the staff and board of Nellie's hired two women of colour as staff members. One of them was J.J.

The timing wasn't the best. According to all sources within Nellie's, there were severe stresses and tensions on the staff. "People thought the psychiatric patients were hard to handle," one former staff person told me. "But the incest survivors were worse."

According to experts in child abuse, children who have been victims of incest grow up feeling worthless. Because they have been betrayed by adults, they have difficulty trusting others. And when buried memories of incest erupt, they are often accompanied by depression, periods of self-loathing, and self-destructive acts. Suicide attempts and self-mutilation are common. I once saw a woman who had driven a knife through her tongue to keep from "telling."

Given the complexity of the psychological damage and the violence, it isn't surprising that some staff members felt overwhelmed.

They broached the subject at staff meetings. Was it possible that the time devoted to counselling incest survivors was stripping so much time and energy out of staff that the services of the hostel as a whole were being diminished? Three staff members, including two women of colour, said they lacked the training to handle women with dangerous mental and emotional problems. They also advanced the idea that untrained staff members, regardless of commitment, could be doing more harm than good.

Yet the policy of Nellie's was that no woman, no matter how difficult the case, was turned away, and it was a policy developed by and supported by the staff members themselves, not one imposed by an outside board of directors. If individual members of the staff couldn't handle the load, maybe they should look for another line of work. There were other contentious problems at Nellie's, but this one became divisive.

The board of Nellie's, and, of course, June Callwood, knew all about the staff's concerns. They set to work to fix the problem, had a facilitator come in to get the staff talking. What emerged were the first open accusations of racism. Board member Carey Ellis told Adele Freedman about the decline of faith between old (white) and new (of colour) staff:

"The women there the longest indeed have the power, even if there's no formal power structure....The structure is based on longevity. It's also based on knowledge, work. Lots of the service providers sit on other organizations, and go to city council meetings. I'm not saying the two women of colour didn't do that—I don't know—but they accused the white staff of being workaholics, 'obsessive and sick.' The attacks implied something purposeful, as if the whites were a corporate elite of multinationals reaping great profits. Women dealing with incest aren't in it for fame and fortune! It's turned out that we haven't spoken for years about incest, only about the horrible things white women did."

In the world of false perceptions, everyone is blind to everyone else. Nellie's consensus collapsed in a welter of accusations. Power, race, sexual preference, personalities, everything became grist for charges. The women of colour at Nellie's formed the Women of

Colour Caucus and joined Carolann Wright's larger group. They believed that the disease of systemic racism was flourishing at Nellie's in the workings of the board and the longtime white staff. The power was vested in the whites, and the non-whites were cut out, silenced, in effect told to fuck off. In fact, according to the coalition's statement, it came to a tirade from Callwood, who told them to "put aside your fucking differences. I don't want to hear that crap." Callwood denies this and other alleged incidents recounted in Wright's statement, a statement that, when she read it in the Toronto *Star*, sent her into a screaming rage.

Eventually it came to a grim impasse. The Women of Colour Caucus wanted to bring the issue of racism before the board. The other staff members told them that they would tell the board that the Women of Colour Caucus was homophobic. The battle lines were drawn between the lesbians and the women of colour: two marginal groups ready to tear each other, and Nellie's, to bits.

The only gossip network more efficient than the journalists' is that of the social services, and bad news from Nellie's was already making the rounds when the board of directors met on December 3, 1991. There are varying reports of precisely who said what at that meeting, but all reports agree that Joan Johnson, weeping with emotion, read a long, rambling, and highly personal letter that she and Karen Hinds, another woman of colour on the Nellie's staff, had written. Johnson and Hinds and the Women of Colour Caucus were claiming racist practices at Nellie's and they wanted action to eradicate those practices. There were many claims in Johnson's letter, but one cry stands out: she and Hinds felt they were being ignored by the white staff and the board. They were being "silenced." It was time for her to be heard.

Everyone who was at the meeting agrees that J.J.'s letter blew the board away. There were the usual comments: "Thank you for sharing your pain. What can we do?" Callwood, ever the woman of action, charged in. How was it possible that this woman, who had been a recipient of the service, whom the staff had harboured, nurtured, given a job, could stand up and accuse that same staff of racism? There are several deeply conflicting and emotionally charged recollections of what she said, but everyone agrees that she asked J.J., "Are you the same woman we helped for over a year?"

Johnson responded with, "Do I have to be grateful all my life?"

There was more—a lot more — but everyone was too wrought up to follow it. Words were exchanged. Emotions taxed. The Women of Colour Caucus withdrew from the room. Callwood was, by her own admission, demoralized. She ended the evening sobbing.

The news of confrontation at Nellie's travelled like wildfire. There were ugly rumours that the Women of Colour Caucus and the coalition were attempting a takeover, that the sorry saga was just a smokescreen by a small group of power-hungry women who wanted to get their hands on the hostel and its jobs and bank accounts.

There were rumours that the affair was a personal attack on Callwood, a "payback" for telling Nourbese Philip to fuck off.

There were rumours that, if the Women of Colour Caucus didn't desist in their attacks, influential friends of Callwood would shut Nellie's down. There were rumours that Nellie's was already in a state of collapse and nothing could save it. There were calls for Callwood's resignation. There were calls for J.J. and Hinds to be fired. The board instituted damage control. June was asked to apologize. She did. It wasn't accepted.

It was at this point that Carolann Wright came in to assist the Women of Colour Caucus to state their position. The March 1992 board meeting was presented with a tightly worded list of demands. Nine of the demands dealt with the structure of Nellie's. There needed to be more clarity, accountability, training, and recognition of the role and representation of racial minorities. The tenth demand was that Callwood resign for being "emotionally and verbally abusive to women of colour on staff and for violating confidentiality as to the history of a former resident."

Callwood spent a month organizing a high-profile fundraiser for Nellie's, and then submitted her resignation. When she walked, she took with her Nellie's credibility, its special place in the hierarchy of women's social services, and, most important, its access to well-heeled donors who raised hundreds of thousands of dollars to keep it financially secure. Within weeks of Callwood's resignation, an estimated $150,000 in donations were cancelled or put on hold. A large-scale women's resource centre, one of Callwood's dream projects for Nellie's, died on the planning board. Regardless of how she might be seen by the women of colour, the women of money believed Callwood had been had.

"It's not that simple," says Cleta Baines. "I wasn't there. I don't know any of these women. I've worked as a volunteer in a women's shelter and I know how it is and it's bad. It's hard work, all the time. I couldn't work in a place like that all the time. I'd just get mad and stay mad. People get frayed. But I can tell you what those women, those Women of Colour Caucus, were saying. They were saying that they were tired of being the dirt on the white women's floors. That's what systemic racism is. I don't know how to explain it but I can describe it. It's when I like someone, I sometimes call them girl. I might say to you, 'Hey, girl, let's go to the movies.' It's just an expression. But if you called me girl, it's an insult. It's racist. You might not mean it to be, but it is because when a white woman calls me girl, it makes me the maid. That's what a girl is in a white family, the maid. It's just like calling a black man boy. I can do that and it's okay. But if you do, it's racist."

This may seem like linguistic hair-splitting to some, but to others, particularly others of colour, it's the fabric of racism in our society. It's how whites are seen and heard by persons who are not white. Racism, which is always about power, is now invisible, silent. It is now part of what we call context. It's not just what the words are but what they mean in history, and the history of racism is the history of conquest, subjugation, slavery, degradation, and death. When I call a woman of colour girl, I raise all those spectres, speak with all those voices.

The brouhaha at Nellie's opened up a lot of festering racist sores in the cosy little worlds of Canadian social services and Canadian feminism. It pointed out what a lot of women had been saying for a long time—that it wasn't enough to provide services and a few jobs to the new immigrants, they wanted a place at the table with the white power brokers. That the whites were women was incidental. The time had come, the message went, for the power to shift to the aboriginal people, the people of colour, the have-nots. The women beating on the door were angry and ready to seize the day. The women holding the reins weren't ready to let go. Racist stereotypes abounded on both sides. The women of colour were portrayed as aggressive and grasping. The white women became "persons with white privilege," the all-purpose description for anyone who says no.

When the story hit the papers, women journalists, friends of Callwood or not, found themselves forced to take sides. Michele Landsberg, the influential columnist for the Toronto *Star*, took the side of the Women of Colour Caucus. Her position wasn't popular. "How dare they call June Callwood a racist?" was the responding battlecry.

The *Globe and Mail* devoted an editorial to the question and called it "The Revolution Eats Its Grandchildren." The *Globe* was displeased with the attack on Callwood and said so. The Women of Colour Caucus was confused. "Ms. Callwood's mistake is to think that racism means belief in the superiority of a particular race, or that racial attributes explain social phenomena. Her mistake, indeed, is to think that racism 'means' anything at all, in the sense of a word having a commonly understood meaning. For if June Callwood is a racist, then the word has no meaning we can share. It is no longer a word, really, but rather a weapon, to be flung at whomever one wished to silence."

In December 1993, Nourbese Philip finally won her war against Callwood. After a rancorous series of letters condemning her "racist attitudes" was exchanged in its house organ, Callwood resigned as president and member of the Writers' Union. The union extended to her a life membership, but the damage was done. The silencing of Callwood should not be seen as a victory for anyone.

Silenced. Shut up. Those words keep coming back. The Vision 21 demonstrators at the PEN conference, with their claims that Canadian publishing policy and Canadian critics were silencing writers of colour. Nourbese Philip's impassioned attack on the arts grants system that keeps the Other shut out. What Joan Johnson and Karen Hinds saw were "women of white privilege" telling them to fuck off, shut up, and go away.

A long time ago, when I was a revolutionary, I had a poster in my bedroom. It was a picture of Dolores Ibarrubi, a Communist leader in the Spanish Civil War. The text, which supposedly came from a speech she made at the barricades in front of Madrid, read: "It is better to die on your feet than to live on your knees."

Telling people to fuck off when they made me mad was part of my transition from knees to feet, a transition that took years and a lot of help. In some ways, it isn't finished even for someone like me—a woman of white privilege, a woman with education, resources, friends, family, and money in the bank. I am a lot like June Callwood in that sense. I'm also like her in another. Given the same set of circumstances, I probably would have told Nourbese Philip to fuck off. I would have told J.J. to shut up and moved on with business. I would have taken a side off anyone who dared to call me—who marched in Selma with Martin Luther King—a racist. Wolfgang Droege and Carney Nerland are racists.

But after the Nellie's incident I have to think again. The *Globe and Mail* wrote: "If racist can be attached to Ms. Callwood, what are we to call those who do believe and act on those principles with which the word has traditionally been associated?"

Maybe we have to call them us.

6

THE REAL WORLD

A LOT OF TORONTONIANS might not know Dwight Drummond in the flesh, but we know him on our television screens. Twice an evening, at six and ten, Drummond appears as one of the genial multiracial group that hosts various segments of the popular CITY news. You want to know whether to bed down the roses? Harold Hosein gives you the real dirt. What's happening at City Hall? Colin Vaughan is the CITY man on the inside.

Dwight Drummond is the chief assignment editor. He sends the reporters to get the stories. On camera, he's the man on roads, taking to the Eye on Toronto camera that points out the jams and streets to avoid and the seemingly never-ending repairs that make the rush hour a torment. A lot of people, including me, rely on Dwight. He's familiar and pleasant and we "know" him, in the sense that we "know" all good television characters.

So it came as a special shock when Drummond became the news instead of reading it. On a warm night in October 1993, he was on his way home after his evening shift, which had ended shortly after eleven. Like most people, his social life begins after work. That night, he met with some colleagues and about 2 a.m. he and a friend grabbed some take-out food and headed home through downtown Toronto past City Hall, five minutes from his CITY studio, just around the corner from the RCMP Toronto headquarters. It was an area where any law-abiding person should be safe.

Drummond noticed a police car. When it signalled, he pulled over, thinking it wanted to pass him. When the car pulled up behind, he wondered, as any driver might, what was up. He wasn't worried because this had happened to Drummond before. The police stop him regularly to check his ID, his ownership, his insurance. This time, however, was different.

Drummond heard a loudhailer demanding that he and his companion get out of the car and put their hands on top of the car. Drummond complied and, when he looked back, saw what appeared to be two armed officers positioned behind the open doors of the patrol cars, with guns drawn and pointed at him.

When Drummond and his companion were out of the car, they were thrown face-down on the street and handcuffed. The police proceeded to search the car. Nothing, of course, was found. When Drummond was released, he was told that "a lady of the night" had reported that she thought she heard gunfire. There was no confirmation of the story, no report of what the man looked like or what kind of car he might be driving. There was, in fact, no gunfire, no criminal activity at all. When Drummond asked why he had been stopped and treated like a criminal he was told, "You looked at us as you drove by."

Drummond's real "crime" is that he happens to be Black.

Because Dwight Drummond is a well-known and respected member of the Toronto media, this saga made the evening news the very next day. Reporters and editors were outraged. One of our own had been subjected to a racist rousting by the Toronto cops. We were duly disgusted that this could happen in our city. Furthermore, we were infuriated when Drummond reported that he'd been stopped five times before and handcuffed once. A Black editor, driving a nice car, treated like a felon. Colin Vaughan spoke for everyone when he wrote in his weekly *Globe and Mail* column: "As for you out there who scoff, ask yourselves: When did this ever happen to you? Never. It's called racism."

In all the expostulations, one important point was lost. It wasn't the first or even the hundredth time this had happened in Toronto. Blacks, Natives, and Orientals report that they are regularly stopped by the police and have to prove that they are law-abiding citizens just to continue walking along the street or driving to work. All that set Drummond apart was that he could rally some media outrage. When he said he was scared to death that an overeager SWAT marksman might shoot him down in the street, people listened.

Harry Lee, a Chinese Canadian student who drives a Nissan sports car, gets stopped "at least twice a month." He has, to date, not a single infraction except for "a couple of paid parking tickets." Yet he has been questioned about everything from break-and-enters in Scarborough where he lives to a ruthless gang-related murder in Chinatown where he happened to be passing by on the street. "It's not just me," he says. "My friends get stopped too. If the police are looking for a crook and a Black or Chinese happens to be around, we're it. I really believe that white people think that all Blacks and Asians are criminals. And, of course, there's the fact that cops really do think we all look alike. You get used to it after a while."

Though I am still partial to the idea of racism as a pattern of voluntary actions that an individual can and must deal with in the depths of the soul, the argument for systemic racism—a drift, an ideological and impersonal set of images extruded by the institutions of mass culture—is a powerful one. A case in point is the remarkably stubborn notion, slowly dripped into our veins by the mass media and the less formal educational structures of the modern middle-class home, that race and crime are linked. It's never stated as a theory and always stated as a fact—hence it attains a kind of facticity. We act upon it. We set the police on the trail. We convince ourselves that our streets aren't safe because the Other is there. In the shadowy realms of the invisible empire, the police are the majority's weapon.

In Vancouver, Asians are feared by whites, the justification being scary stories about tongs and Asian gangs. But in Toronto, Asian gangs are shooting, not whites, but each other on the streets of Chinatown. My neighbours, mostly Portuguese and South Asian, are convinced that Blacks are committing crimes at a record rate. They believe this even though the drug dealers on the corner have South American names and white (or brown) skins. The major gang fights in our neighbourhood are between warring factions of Tamils from Sri Lanka. But the neighbours are convinced about the Blacks.

It's impossible to isolate where this slippage from reality into generalized mythologies comes from. From earliest childhood, Blacks meant safety to me—the cook who made my special birthday cake, the nurse who cared for my dying grandmother. At the same time we were also taught that there was an indefinite evil about the Blacks, a penchant for crime from which we could never be completely safe. What Southerners call "uppitiness" was the first sign of this emerging evil, the first sign of transformation of the faithful servant into the bogeyman who would come climbing into your room at night and do unspeakable things. We were taught to trust and to fear simultaneously. Black women, children, and old men were safe. Other Black men, particularly young Black men, were dangerous. Even if all they did was wash the car or serve the meal, they could become fearsome.

Or so the stories went. The fact that I never saw any evidence to support any of these views is irrelevant. As I have argued throughout this book, racism defies statistics, fact, and reality with an implacable force. It more than defies them, it warps them to suit its own malign purposes. In my small home town—and in those days, statistics were kept according to race—Blacks did not commit a disproportionate amount of crimes. They did, however, get caught more often, receive longer sentences, and have less legal representation than whites. Where did the bogeyman come from?

One place it begins is in the fears and gossip of childhood. Last winter, my daughter was invited to a birthday party. It was an upscale affair, featuring a gang of ten-year-old girls, and it was to be held in a roller rink. The girls were excited. Most had never been to a roller rink and they were looking forward to flashing around on their Roller Blades. Then one child came with a story. Her friend, she reported, had been to a party at a roller rink, when a gang of big Black guys had jumped over the side, taken over the rink, and run the smaller children away. They had been loud and threatening. Her friend never went back. This girl wasn't going to the party because she was afraid of being hurt.

Most of the kids ignored this cautionary tale and went to the party, where, true to form, they had a good time. But the idea was born. Big Black kids are threatening. Places where big Black kids hang out are dangerous. These people are thugs. They hurt little kids. Black people are dangerous. They do bad things.

Living in a city with a moderately large Black population where this stereotype is thriving can be dangerous to the mind and soul. Scared little kids grow up to be scared adults, adults who see a Black man coming and shoot first, then ask questions.

Howard States is a charming, intelligent schoolteacher who likes to be with people. Well-read and socially committed, States enjoys the old-fashioned art of conversation, where folks get together to listen as well as talk. I don't see Howard as often as I'd like, largely because we're both busy people and because our paths cross too rarely, but I'm always impressed by him when we do meet. I like and respect him and I like to think that it's mutual. So I was a bit surprised when I invited him to a party and he almost didn't come. "I was concerned about the neighbourhood," he confessed, looking away. "And the police."

Howard was telling me, in his delicately polite fashion, that my streets are not safe for him. Howard is Black. Two weeks before, the police shot and killed a young Black man four blocks from my house. His name was Raymond Lawrence. He was an illegal immigrant, a suspected drug dealer, and, according to the police, he had a large knife. All of that pales beside the fact that Lawrence was shot in the back. Then there was the Scarborough teenager driving a stolen car, also shot in the back. There was the young man shot in the head by an officer who claimed that he tripped and the gun went off accidentally. Sophia Cook, a young Black woman, was hitching a ride with a total stranger when the police stopped the car. Cook, shot in the spine, is partially paralysed.

There is an ominous similarity in these accounts that can be traced through police killings of Blacks in Montreal, and across the country to Winnipeg, where, once again, a Native Canadian was shot dead, unaccountably, irrationally, by a police officer obviously afraid of what the dark force inside this person might do to him. In Vancouver, a SWAT team acting on an anonymous tip invaded the apartment of two Chinese students. One student was beaten over the head for refusing to obey an order to put his hands on his head. The student, recently arrived from China, did not speak English.

All of these confrontations between police and suspects were reported, some heavily, in newspapers and on broadcasts across Canada. Minority groups have claimed that racism in the police forces is encouraging attacks on Blacks, Orientals, and Native people. Whites, on the other hand, assert that lax immigration regulations are permitting criminals into Canada, destroying the peace and contentment we have previously enjoyed. "There was no crime to speak of before they came" is a familiar lament in Montreal, Toronto, and Vancouver.

"I could tell you things but I won't."

The speaker is a cop in a major Canadian city. He is talking to me on the telephone, after requiring and getting assurances that I will not reveal any identifying information about him other than that he's white. Racism, according to this veteran officer, is present but "not rampant, like the media want to believe.

"Cops aren't saints," he says. "They're just as bigoted and stupid as anyone else. Look around you and you'll see that cops are the same as everyone else. If, say, 10 per cent of the population are bigots, then 10 per cent of the cops are bigots, too."

But bigots with the right to bear arms and shoot people.

"If this was an ideal world, cops wouldn't kill people. Nobody would kill people. But it's not ideal. The facts are that crimes get committed and people want the perpetrators caught. If someone robs your house, steals your car, rapes your daughter, you want the criminal caught, locked up, throw away the key. Then, you want the cops to get out there and do anything it takes. But when it's not your house, your car, your kid, you're all for tying the hands of the police. They're the bad guys unless someone needs them."

There is more truth in this statement than I want to admit. It is easy for me to write and talk about police brutality. I also am quick to insist that the streets of my neighbourhood be kept safe from drug dealers and prostitutes and that my property be protected. When I visit relatives in the States, I like to tell them how in Toronto I can take the subway late at night in perfect safety, walk down the streets in the evenings, and let my daughter roller-skate on the sidewalk without worry. Like most Torontonians, and most Canadians, I'm proud of the safety, cleanliness, and order in our cities and I don't want to lose it.

"It doesn't matter about whether you do or don't keep statistics on crime," the officer says. "In Toronto, you have a Chinese cop"— Ben Eng —"saying that the highest proportion of crime in the Asian community is committed by Vietnamese. The Vietnamese get up in arms, claim this is discrimination, all that. They can shut up the officer, but that's just shooting the messenger. Any police officer in a big city can tell you that certain groups of people are responsible for certain kinds of crimes. If you have a large Asian population, like in Vancouver, you're going to have Asian gangs. Most of the members are Vietnamese and they extort money from Chinese people. They rob, they run vice and fraud, illegal gambling, prostitution, stolen credit card rings, drugs. When there's a killing in a Chinese restaurant in Toronto, it's Vietnamese gangs.

"In Toronto, you have your Asian gangs but you also have posses [West Indian gangs]. They're armed and they commit armed robberies: corner stores, banks. The younger ones go for B&E, car thefts, stereos, computers. Stop a kid in a mall and steal his jacket or his running shoes. Doesn't matter about the race of the victim. Black or whatever. If they want it, they take it. They're also into prostitution and drugs. These are facts. The Black community or the Asian community says that we shouldn't keep statistics of race and crime.

We don't have to have statistics, we have our eyes. We know who's doing what out there.

"Winnipeg, you have a big Native population. Lots of drinking, prostitution, street people. You get crimes of violence, rape, beatings, manslaughter, sometimes murder. Folks want to feel safe and so they yell for the cops to clean things up but they don't want it to be messy. Well, things get messy."

The issue of keeping crime statistics by race is a contentious one. On the one hand, keeping clear statistics of arrests and case dispositions would mean that minority group leaders, who have long argued that the justice system discriminates against their members, particularly Native people and Blacks, would have a powerful weapon against unfair justice. Human rights groups would have not just proof of systemic racism but a chart showing at what point—arrest, bail, legal assistance, sentencing—discrimination occurs.

On the other hand, those same statistics, if they show that a disproportionate amount of crimes are committed by visible minorities—Asians, Blacks, Natives, new immigrants—will be a powerful weapon in the hands of people who already suspect or believe there is a link between race and crime. That the government has chosen not to keep statistics by race simply confirms, in some minds, that visible minority groups, who constitute less than a third of the Canadian population, commit far more than a third of the crime, particularly violent crimes—murder, rape, robbery, assault.

Because racial statistics aren't kept, or, if they are, aren't made public, fears grow on both sides. In the middle are the police, and they have their own fears to contend with. Sgt. Ben Eng, of the Toronto force, revealed in a public speech that most of the violent crimes in Toronto's Chinatown were committed by Vietnamese gangs. He was censured by the force, roundly reviled as a racist lackey by the Vietnamese community who denied everything he said, and condemned to a job on the force where he could be kept silent and invisible. Seeing his law enforcement career at an untimely end, Eng resigned.

What is tragic about the Ben Eng affair is that the Toronto force lost a good officer, one from a minority group not ordinarily drawn to police work—for telling the truth. There have been at least three highly publicized gang-related murders in Chinatown since 1991. In 1989, when I was researching a book on Hong Kong immigrants, I was told by Asian crime experts on both the Toronto and Vancouver police forces that the majority of Asian gang members were young Vietnamese men who had, for many reasons, failed to assimilate into Canadian society. These same officers told me that law-abiding Vietnamese, who are by far the majority, seldom cooperated with the police in investigations, were in fact deeply suspicious of police. In such an atmosphere, they said, gang violence from petty extortion to gambling goes unreported and murders go unsolved.

The code of fear and silence that protects these gang members works against the police, and it's not difficult to understand why they often feel thwarted in their work. When Ben Eng went public, the reaction was the expected. The Toronto Police Commission, the Vietnamese community, the immigrant groups all banded together to demand action, not against crime, but against Eng. In the absence of hard facts, they shot the messenger.

"Happens all the time," says my cop.

One area where there's no shortage of statistics is the relationship between poverty and crime. There is no question that poverty breeds crime. Poor people steal, and they have a higher incidence of assault and break-and-enters. They are seldom seen in the worlds of large-scale fraud, computerized crime, or murder-for-hire. Those categories tend to have more affluent whites. But Legal Aid statistics show that poor people—and many of these are new immigrants and visible minorities—get caught more quickly, and, because they can seldom afford expensive lawyers, they get longer sentences. They often end up as repeat offenders.

The police officer: "I don't know about all that. I know that every time I bring in some kid who's broken into a house and stolen or vandalized it, there's a social worker or a psychiatrist saying that the kid is the victim of poverty. That he—or she, because a lot of the girls are worse than the boys, if you want the truth—was abused as a child, or poor, or thrown out. Well, I know plenty of people who were poor or abused or whatever and they don't go out and kill people or rape them or break into houses.

"I won't deny that I've heard racial slurs against certain racial groups, especially Blacks. But it's not all because police are racists. There was all that to-do about the kid in Mississauga who was shot in the back. Well, that kid was driving a stolen car. He was not a good little boy parked in his mama's driveway, like the Black community in Toronto tried to paint him. He was a car thief. I don't say he should have been shot. I think that was really an accident, the officer was aiming for the tires or whatever, and it was accidental. But trying to paint him as a good little boy won't wash."

Minority complaints should get short shrift from police, most judges, and Crown attorneys, the policeman claims. I point out that Sophia Cook was unarmed, simply sitting in a car with a man who had offered her a ride. She didn't even know the man.

"It's all out of proportion, as I say," says the police officer. "That was one incident. One special case. You get your bigots, but by far the majority of the officers are racially tolerant. I've had occasion to speak to my men about language and behaviour. We have to be careful nowadays about how we're seen by minority groups. We're aware of that.

"This situation is a bit like the situation with women some years ago. When I started in law enforcement, you got a call to a domestic violence situation, there wasn't anything you could do, really. I went on calls where the neighbours said the man was beating his wife. I'd go to the door and you could hear her screaming. When they opened the door, she'd be off in the kitchen and he'd say it was the TV or a fight that got out of hand, whatever. I could go inside but even if I found her and she was black and blue, there wasn't much I could do. If she swore out a warrant, and I have to say that in those days no one ever did, the judge usually gave a suspended sentence or nothing at all. Now, with education, people are becoming more aware. We have more education for officers. They learn about domestic violence. We have teams to deal with it, real specialists. This is a good thing. I think that racial altercations could be the same."

What about hiring more minorities in the police forces? This is a recommendation that comes up repeatedly in all the studies, inquiries, and reports. Some kind of affirmative action. Wasn't that what happened with women? They got some female officers and that helped further the education of the men?

"Not really. We've always had women on our force, always since I've been here. The women officers, they had the same problems as the men when it came to domestic violence or rape or whatever. I don't believe a man or a woman makes any difference in the situation. It doesn't make any difference what race. We have merit tests and that's all anyone needs. I don't believe in giving quotas to Asians or Natives or whatever. All that does is create problems. Some person who's not really qualified gets the job over others who are more qualified. Law enforcement officers should be the best for the job."

But what if the merits are equal, the minority person is qualified? Is it then permissible and even desirable to lean towards women and minorities, as the Toronto Fire Department attempted to do?

"I don't know about the fire department thing. I heard a little about it. As I understand it, the affirmative action people tried to change the rules after the tests were done. The candidates were told they would be placed in order of performance on tests and whatever and then the city came in and said they were bumping the white candidates in favour of women and minorities. First of all, if all things were equal, why were the minority candidates further down on the list? Why did they have to be given special treatment? The women and minority officers who serve with me didn't need any special treatment. They got the job fair and square. No one had to be bumped for them.

"If you want to know what I think, I think these affirmative action policies create racism. If I knew I was the best person for the job and I'd been bumped to make room for someone less qualified, I'd be pretty angry. I wouldn't see that person as my coworker.

"That kind of thinking is very divisive in any kind of work, but it's more so in law enforcement. We have to work together. We have to believe in what we do and in each other. We carry out the laws. We don't have a lot of leeway for action. I mean, you're not supposed to let your personal feelings get in the way of law enforcement. That's our job. To enforce the laws.

"Remember that case in Ontario, that officer who wouldn't work at the abortion clinic because he was a Catholic and he didn't believe in abortion? Well, I don't believe in abortion, either. I would never allow my daughter to get an abortion. But I would have gone to that clinic and done my job. If policemen let their personal feelings dictate what they did, we wouldn't have law, we'd have anarchy."

The personal is political. That's an old feminist shibboleth that's still in force today. Perhaps more in force than in the sixties when it was coined. When it comes to race, my personal experience is translatable to the political arena. Dwight Drummond's rousting by the Toronto police is a personal assault that has a political edge. The shooting in the back of a Black teenager, even if he is a car thief, is political. What would have happened if that teenager had been white?

The officer: "You want to know? I'll tell you the truth. Nothing. I wasn't there, but I'd stake my life on it. There'd be a coroner's inquest and a hearing within the department. They'd probably find the officer did what he was supposed to do and that it was a really unfortunate accident. We're supposed to catch thieves. That's what the public wants us to do. If that kid was driving your car, you'd want the police to catch him and catch him before he damaged your car. I'm not saying that what happened was right. It wasn't. It was a mistake. But in the real world, people get injured protecting other people. And, yeah, in the real world, you get people who are in law enforcement for the wrong reasons."

The real world. That phrase keeps coming up when I get into discussions of race.

White Canadians tell me that minority groups, pampered by multiculturalism, don't want to join the Canadian mainstream. Insistence on hanging on to dress and religion and lifestyles that belong to the old country is seen as a rejection of Canadian culture, ways, lifestyles. The justice system, in my thinking, is the place where the real world should operate. There should be justice and fairness and equality for all before the law. I have a lot of respect for laws and the people who enforce them and administer them. I want the system to be just and I have the dreadful feeling that it isn't. The names of Donald Marshall and Betty June Osborne and J. J. Harper keep floating in my mind.

Donald Marshall spent twelve years in prison for a crime he didn't commit because he was a Micmac, and because the white police force in Nova Scotia didn't bother to investigate rigorously a case involving Native people. Betty June Osborne was raped and murdered by a gang of white toughs in The Pas, Manitoba. Everyone in town knew who'd killed the Native girl, but no one investigated the case because her death wasn't seen as important. She was, after all, just an Indian; rape and murder were her destiny. J. J. Harper, dead in Winnipeg, was a Native rights activist. When a policeman shot and killed him, the force covered up the evidence. After all, a dead Indian could make more trouble than a live one.

Increasingly, minority groups in Canada are zeroing in on the police forces of major cities (and not-so-major ones) as racist. Carney Nerland in Saskatchewan had ties with the RCMP and the local police force. Wolfgang Droege has often alluded to invisible ties with the Toronto police force—ties vehemently denied by official spokespeople. The Metro force has its own hate crimes squad, which monitors extremist groups, including the Heritage Front. It is difficult to believe that a member of the Toronto police could belong to the Heritage Front or any other extremist group and fail to be recognized by members of the hate crimes squad, and yet the rumours of police involvement in far-right activities continue.

But far beyond the suspicion that the police are right-wing extremists is the conviction in the minds of a good many leaders of minority groups that the police abuse their power and act indiscriminately with force against members of visible minorities and that the entire justice system—from investigation to jury representation to judicial sentencing—is permeated with racism.

Two investigations and a royal commission show clearly that racist attitudes on the part of highly placed members of the Halifax Police Department were responsible for the arrest and conviction of Donald Marshall for a murder he didn't commit. Marshall served twelve years of a life sentence and, but for the jailhouse confession by the real murderer, would be in prison still.

Tony Hall, an associate professor of Native American studies at the University of Lethbridge in Alberta, has likened Canada's treatment of Native people to the treatment of Blacks in South Africa. In a 1993 interview with the Toronto *Star*, he points out that, in courtrooms in more than a hundred Canadian cities with large Native populations, one can find that most of the people on trial are Natives. The judges, police, Crown attorneys, and jurors are non-Natives, "mostly white," says Hall. "And it does look like a South African–type situation." In 1990, Manitoba's Aboriginal Justice Inquiry pointed out the underrepresentation of Native people on juries. A year later, an Alberta task force on the criminal justice system spelled out the problems and urged Alberta to make an intense effort to get Native persons on juries.

But Hall's analogies and all the inquiries pale beside the awful drama played out in Winnipeg over the death of J. J. Harper, killed by a Winnipeg policeman on a chilly night in March 1988.

The facts of the case have always been clear. Const. Robert Cross was on the trail of a suspected car thief when he happened upon Mr. Harper, a local Native leader, walking along the street. Constable Cross believed Mr. Harper to be the wanted man and he stopped him. Mr. Harper, innocent and angry, refused to halt. Constable Cross drew his gun, a scuffle ensued, and the gun went off. Harper died. Cross was investigated by the Winnipeg Police Department and found to have acted appropriately.

But the story didn't end there. J. J. Harper had friends among the leaders of Native groups in Manitoba. He also had a family who believed justice hadn't even been attempted. The aboriginal groups demanded an outside investigation of the Winnipeg force. The Harper family hired feisty lawyer Harvey Pollock to represent their, and their dead son's, interests. It took five years and repeated court challenges, hearings, and inquiries before the facts of J. J. Harper's death were known. What was clear, finally, was that the Winnipeg police force had covered up the facts of Harper's death in a misguided attempt to protect Constable Cross. What was also clear was that if J. J. Harper had been a white man, he would still be alive.

The Winnipeg investigations, covered by the media nationwide, shocked many people. Before the final report was delivered—one that was a scathing indictment of the Winnipeg force—one Winnipeg policeman was dead, a suicide, another had had a severe nervous breakdown, and the chief of the force had been forced to retire.

The Harper story was nasty enough as it stood, in a welter of wasted lives and smashed careers. Bad as it was, though, it didn't end there. That's because the tentacles of the invisible empire stretch beyond events, to poison and taint the lives of people on the periphery of the original incident.

Harvey Pollock was charged in 1990 with sexual assault. Pollock, claiming police harassment because of his actions in the high-profile case, demanded a judicial investigation of his arrest, trial, and stay of conviction. The conclusion of that inquiry, conducted by Mr. Justice Ted Hughes, found that "the police investigation was conducted with indecent haste and with no apparent need for that haste that is rooted in either effective law enforcement or the administration of justice."

Hughes goes on to state, "I have concluded that there is no rational explanation for the conduct of the police officers involved.... Having discarded all other reasons advanced by the officers for their conduct, I must come to a consideration of Pollock's suggestion that the charge of sexual assault against him was an attempt at payback by the Winnipeg Police Department because of his role in the Aboriginal Justice Inquiry into the death of J. J. Harper."

What happened to Harvey Pollock was a nasty attempt to get even with a lawyer whom the police saw as an enemy. What if their attempt to silence him had been successful? How easy would it be for another family with a dead son and brother to get a lawyer to represent their interests against those of the police?

"I don't think the Winnipeg force got a fair deal in the Harper case," says my source the cop. "Accidents happen, but they don't happen often. Winnipeg was blown way out of proportion. The cop there was young, inexperienced. He was frightened. He was attacked. He reacted, but everyone else overreacted. I think they would have lynched that guy if they could have got away with it. It was vicious."

It is difficult to be objective about the Harper case. A lot of people I talked with agree with my officer: they believe that the Winnipeg police got a bum deal. They say that the Winnipeg cops were made the scapegoats for other incidents involving Native people, most particularly the abuse of justice in the Betty June Osborne case in The Pas. The Winnipeg cops, viewed only on the nightly news and in the odd newspaper article, came across as a gang of licensed hooligans, corrupt, racist, cold-bloodedly self-serving.

It was an image made for the current climate of confrontation between white and Native Canadians. After armed Natives resisted at Oka, Quebec, a whole new structure of rhetoric was hatched, which in turn seems ready to provide new nourishment for the enduring culture of racism in Canadian society. This overheard from a journalist: "Who'd have thought Tonto would go to war over bingo and untaxed cigarettes? Just goes to show what's important to the Mohawks."

Oka, with its nightly newsbites and superficial media coverage of deep issues, helped to enhance an existing climate of distrust. Manitoba MP Elijah Harper (no relation to J. J. Harper) was holding the country to ransom over the Meech Lake accord. Across Canada, Native groups were demanding land and compensation, redress for four centuries of wrong. Natives like Rodney Bobiwash were challenging the stereotypical view of Natives as drunken bums, unable or unwilling to take responsibility for their own lives.

"It's not as bad as it used to be," says Molly, a street worker for a Toronto agency that assists Native people in the city. "I'm from Kenora and I remember when people just died on the street and nobody cared. Nobody even bothered to stop. I went into a store to buy some milk for my baby brother and the lady called me a little squaw and said I was young to be breeding more welfare bums. I didn't know what to do, so I just took the milk and ran out of the store. But I remember that. I remember that woman's face to this day. I had never seen hate on a face before and she hated me. Just because of who I was."

Molly left Kenora fifteen years ago. She was still there when the notorious pamphlet "Bended Elbow," a savage parody of Native life, appeared in town. "You can't imagine what it's like, having people reading this piece of filth and laughing. I know more about sniffing glue and drinking than those people and there they were, mocking my people's problems. They weren't interested in helping any of us, even the kids. They just laughed and bitched about having to pay taxes to support us."

Just what are the improvements Molly sees? "Name calling—Chief and Squaw and Tonto—that doesn't happen hardly at all now. Oh, the old guys on Skid Row still do it, but they're too old to change and they don't really mean it in an offensive way. Young people are more sensitive. And there have been some positive things about Native people. I think the Klanbusters is positive. Getting out and doing something, showing we're not just standing back, waiting for help. There are medicine men in Alberta who are working with people, especially kids, who sniff. These are good things. Oka was a good thing. It was good to stand up and say we weren't going to take it any more. We have our pride too."

Molly's positive view doesn't extend to the Canadian criminal justice system. Here, the reality of Native life in Canada today is appalling. Depending upon which province you select, Natives constitute 30 to 40 per cent of the prison population. Two inquiries on aboriginal justice have called for immediate and radical change, but change isn't happening. There are recommendations but no money and, as Native leaders see it, no will on the part of the white majority to carry out the changes.

The prevailing opinion of the police I spoke with in six major Canadian cities was that they were getting a bum rap. "You people are making it up as you go along" was a constant complaint. It was also the reason why, aside from press officers and my unnamed cop, no police would speak to me on or off the record. "The media are biased against the police. They see racism everywhere. They don't know the real story."

The real story, like *the real world*, came up again and again in discussions about crime. The real world, so I was told, was one where crimes happen and where journalists don't go. I don't believe that, so I decided to go and spend some time in four so-called high-crime areas of Toronto.

I say "so-called" because, by my own standards of crime, those born in places like New York City and Detroit, there are no high-crime areas in Toronto. But when crime is mentioned, when the police talk darkly about drugs and guns and bad people, these are the areas they mention. When the newspapers print stories about places nice people don't want to live, these are the neighbourhoods they list. These also happen to be communities where there is a large concentration of poor people and concentrations of new immigrants and racial minorities. There's no shading of facts there, just simple truth. If there is a "real world" of race and crime, these are the places where it's bound to happen. They are also the places that people who don't live in them associate with crime and, by implication, the racial relationship to crime.

The first community is my own, the Lansdowne and Bloor area of West Toronto. There are crack houses in this neighbourhood, at least so I've been told by the police and by neighbourhood activists, but I don't know where they are. I do know that you can buy anything from angel dust to crack on the corner by the subway and that, after ten o'clock at night, most of the single women on the street are not waiting for cabs.

In the daylight, it's easy to spot the signs. There are used needles tossed on the sidewalks, pop cans used to puff crack left on the lawns. I don't have to go far to see too-thin girls wandering around in a haze of whatever they ingested most recently. I came of age in the 1960s. I know the pasty-faced, stringy-haired look of a kid on a drug. As a social worker, I learned to spot the incoherent staggering youth who'd been sniffing gasoline or glue. No one has to tell me what drugs do or what the people who take them or sell them look like.

On Saturday nights, the police sweep the area regularly. They cruise the corners and they keep a sharp eye on the little groups of people gathered in restaurants. Once, they came up to question me at my own front door. I was chatting with two of my neighbours, just three white women on the porch. Where three are gathered together, there's suspicion.

So I went down to the local corner where the dope is sold and the hookers work. I went for several nights and I hung around and gathered my own little statistics. I found that a majority of the dealers were Black or South American. A majority of the hookers were white. Most of the customers for both were white. There were very few Orientals and no South Asians, although there have been at least two major incidents of violence between Tamil groups and, several months after my own evenings, there was a gang-style shooting at the local Vietnamese restaurant.

After this little experiment, I polled my neighbours, including the Sikhs and the one Black family. Everyone, to a person, agreed that the dope trade was run by Blacks, that they were Jamaican immigrants, that they also controlled the hookers, and that the whole community was in a state of chaos. All loudly insisted that the police weren't doing enough and that uncontrolled immigration was the problem.

Since all of these people, except for the Blacks, were immigrants, their reaction was a surprise to me. When pressed, each ethnic group blamed the others for crime. When I asked for incidences of crime— have you been robbed? molested? mugged? accosted?—no one said yes but everyone knew someone who had been. In short, what we have is a stereotype that cannot be confirmed.

Next I went to a community that has been synonymous with crime in Toronto for nearly twenty years. The notorious Jane-Finch corridor, built up on farmland only a generation ago, is one of the ugliest neighbourhoods in a town full of ugly neighbourhoods. At the junction of the two main streets squat three large and undistinguished shopping malls. There are the usual grocery stores and fast-food restaurants. Along Finch, the east–west axis, run more strip malls, highrise residential blocks, some homes set back on nice lots. Along Finch at Keele, one enters York University, where forty thousand students come daily to learn. Most of them are not from the neighbourhood.

Behind York, tucked into a nest between highrise housing and campus parking, is Black Creek Pioneer Village, a reconstructed nineteenth-century town where my daughter and her friends go for educational outings to learn how their pioneer ancestors lived. It is pretty and full of attractive people in pioneer dress making horseshoes, candles, and candy. This is not about everyone's ancestors.

Hard by Pioneer Village, in fact close enough to smell the candlewax, is Edgely village, an ugly rabbit warren of condominium apartments and townhouses. On the route into Pioneer Village and York University sits Shoreham Drive Public School, on the edges of a public housing development. Along down Jane, towards Finch, is a community centre, and blocks of rental townhouses. I used to live in one of those townhouses, more than twenty years ago. Edgely and Shoreham were new then, full of optimistic people recently arrived in a new land, and living at what was then the far northern edge of Toronto's urban sprawl. The countryside, and beyond that farms, lay only a few minutes' walk away.

But the first winter I was there, there was a race riot in the mall across the street from Edgely. A group of white youths attacked some East Indians who attempted to play shinny on the minute slab of outdoor ice behind the local supermarket. Police were called. No charges were laid. The East Indians didn't play shinny there again.

Shoreham's public housing has been kept in good repair (Americans are always amazed at the condition of Canadian public housing), though keeping the graffiti at bay is obviously a full-time job. I went to the local sweet-shop and hung around, hoping to find some teenagers who'd talk to me about life, crime, and the like. The owner came out and asked what I was doing there. I said it was nice to know someone was looking out for perverts. He told me that if I was looking to talk to people about real racial and crime problems, I should go to Grand Ravine, about six blocks south. I told him that I was familiar with Grand Ravine and I had no intention of going there. People were dying in Grand Ravine. It's as close as Toronto gets to Detroit.

The teens I eventually lined up were an attractive mixed bag. Soca and Dana are girls, fifteen and sixteen, students at the local high school. Both have lived at Jane and Finch "ever since we can remember." I asked if they had ever been to the events at Pioneer Village. They had gone a couple of times in grade school but neither found it a memorable experience. Soca remembers going on a hayride. It was her first and last hayride.

Dana is six months pregnant, planning to move in with her boyfriend as soon as he finishes school. Until then, she'll stay at home with her mother, continue her education, "get help with the baby," and get on with her life. "I have plans. I have ambition. I'm not dropping out."

Soca and Dana were both born in Canada. Their parents were from Guyana and both are mixed race. "I'm not Black, I'm not white, I'm not brown, I'm a bit red," says Soca. "I tell people if they ask that I'm everything in one package."

Drugs, according to Soca and Dana, are "everywhere. You can buy anything on the playground. The dealers use little kids to carry stuff. The kids know that if they get arrested, it's no big deal. They get a couple of weeks in Juvenile and that's it."

Soca and Dana don't see the police as their protectors or defenders, but they don't see them as racist hounds, either. "They've been around, having community meetings, coming to the schools. They tell us to let them know if we see people selling drugs, people getting hurt. I wouldn't do that. The police's job is to catch criminals. It's not my job. There are times when I would. I don't believe in selling to kids. If I saw someone around the grade school, I would probably call the police."

As for racism, "I think there's too much talk about it. It exists. Let's be real. I think the police are quick to judge people as criminals if they are members of a visible minority. I think there is too much using guns. But there's a lot of crime up here. Down on Grand Ravine, they are selling crack in the halls of the buildings. Those people selling have no morals. They sell to kids or anyone. If the police shoot one of them, I don't think it's much of a loss."

"I've never had any racial problems with the police," says Dana.

"I know people who have. My girlfriend and her boyfriend were out riding and they got stopped and he had to answer a lot of questions and they checked to see if the car he was driving was really his. That kind of thing happens a lot more than people realize. Especially if the person they stop is a Black person driving a really nice car. They just assume that he's a drug dealer or a thief. Still, it's not like in New York where they call you names and push you around. It's not perfect here, but it's better than there."

After listening to Soca and Dana, I decided to take my chances in Grand Ravine, a nest of highrises surrounded by attractive ranch-style homes. Oddly enough, Grand Ravine doesn't look tough. From a distance it can almost pass as an ordinary suburban strip with its highrise apartments, townhouses, mall, and community centre.

The police are very visible in Grand Ravine, which is considered one of the most dangerous areas in Toronto. There are dealers in Grand Ravine but, unlike the cheery entrepreneurs who sell stuff on my corner, the dealers at Grand Ravine, and the gangs who control parts of it, are armed.

The police patrol regularly, sweeping the area in search of drug users and dealers. It is a cool evening when I go there, and in some Toronto neighbourhoods people might be out for an evening stroll. Not in Grand Ravine. Cars cruise the short streets or wait by the parking lot. Whether these men and women are dealers and sellers, I don't know. I do know that they are almost all people of colour, as are many of the residents of the buildings. Inside, children are hustled into the apartments. Nobody plays outside on the playground. A handful of large Black teenaged boys lounge around sporting their Chicago Bulls caps, shirts, and jackets. The police drive by, observe the group, get out and check, then go back to their car. The boys wait until the car is down the road and then shoot the finger.

When I attempted to approach the little gang, I was summarily dusted off. There was a great deal of expressed attitude and considerable profanity, but there was no danger. These teenagers were bored and sullen and possibly in search of some chemical excitement, but they weren't hostile. They told me they didn't want to talk to me and then resumed their own conversation. When I wandered down the wrong street, a pair of them cheerfully showed me back to my car. I asked if they liked living in Grand Ravine and they said it was okay.

Later, I spoke with a trio of Black parents who live in the community. They assured me that drug dealers "of all races" were a problem and that illegal guns were in the hands of "punks of every race." They said the police tended to assume the worst about the Black youths and to let the white kids have the benefit of the doubt. These parents, all from Guyana, assured me that the Black troublemakers were all Jamaican.

A few days later, I went to another Toronto neighbourhood known for crime. Parkdale was once one of Toronto's finer addresses. There are still beautiful mansions on large treed lots, but most of them are now rooming houses. Interspersed among the old elegant houses are ugly functional highrises and a handful of older more attractive lowrise apartment blocks. You can see Lake Ontario from the lower edges of Parkdale. You can get good West Indian patties or hear Tagalog spoken at the Filipino store. Parkdale is the address of necessity for a good many former mental patients and has On Our Own, a self-help project for them. It is also the scene of one of the most brutal crimes in Toronto's memory—the kidnapping and murder of a three-year-old girl from the playground at her own apartment block.

Janice Murray is white, describes herself as "over forty and overweight," and she's lived in Parkdale for most of her life. "This has always been a place for working people," she says. "But it wasn't dangerous like it is now. I don't go to the McDonald's after dark. It's full of mental patients and Blacks. The police don't do anything. They don't dare. They're afraid some group or other is going to scream racism. Blacks can do anything down here."

After walking around with Janice, I'm hard pressed to see her point. There aren't that many Black people around. There are several white prostitutes plying their trade and a couple of dealers in cars, but it's tame here compared to Jane-Finch. Still, the reputation has gotten around. "Cabs won't come here at night," says Janice. "I don't call. I just plan to get home before dark or I take the streetcar."

The American in me that won't die is perplexed. How dangerous can a street be if you can take a streetcar home?

"I take my life in my hands. Sometimes I have to be out after dark. I could be robbed, killed, tossed on the sidewalk. If it was Blacks, the police wouldn't lift a finger."

As in Jane-Finch, and Bloor-Lansdowne, the police sweep Parkdale, rounding up dealers, pimps, prostitutes. They pass by a mental patient hallucinating on a corner. He calls for hellfire to purge the streets. They stop by a man apparently passed out in the doorway of an empty building. Check his breathing. He's still alive. They leave him in the doorway and drive on. The police are in teams. One team has a Black patrolman. As he drives by, he waves to Janice. She grins and whispers "Black bastard" under her breath.

As we walk along Queen Street, Janice keeps up a running commentary on the decline of the neighbourhood since the non-whites arrived. They are dirty and don't look after their children. They don't keep their property neat, have no regard for others, are selfish and short-sighted. They don't support neighbourhood events, aren't interested in the schools. She hardly stops for breath. Yet nothing that I see bears out what she's saying. A group of Black children playing on the sidewalk breaks up to let us pass. The kids are cute, clean, well dressed. Better dressed, if truth be told, than we are.

The truth is that, in my own city, which I know well, there is no empirical observation to back up the claim that Blacks are responsible for a crime wave. If Blacks aren't murdering, pillaging, mugging, and selling dope in these areas, they're not doing these things en masse anywhere. Aside from Lansdowne, in no area did I see a majority of Blacks engaged in the drug or prostitution trade. In Parkdale, despite Janice's best efforts, I saw no suspicious Blacks at all. I went back several times, at various times of day, and I spent a lot of hours in the local McDonald's, which does have more than its share of lonely poor people who talk to themselves and chain-smoke. There were simply the usual people who hang out at places late at night and a large number of people who appeared to be former mental patients. I say "appeared to be" because, aside from the tics and starts caused by continual use of drugs used to control major mental illness, they looked just like poor people anywhere.

I had occasion to recall my evenings in Parkdale in the summer of 1993 when Audrey Smith, a Jamaican tourist, was approached by the police as she waited for a bus. Mrs. Smith, a civil servant in the Jamaican government, was accused of having drugs. She denied it and consented to be searched. What she didn't count on was that the search was to be thorough, and immediate. On the streetcorner, in the bus shelter, she was stripped and body searched by a female police constable. When the search produced no evidence of any kind, she was left, shivering, on the street.

When the story hit the headlines, the Toronto police denied the events. There was a policy for strip searches, and the person was "always" taken to a nearby washroom. The woman must have been suspicious or the officers wouldn't have stopped her in the first place. What evidence of suspicion? Why was she not taken to a washroom? Faced with a very persistent woman, the police commission began an investigation of the events. Long after she had returned to Jamaica, where the story made banner headlines for days, the police admitted that their treatment of her had been wrong. Her account of events, which contradicts every aspect of police procedure, to say nothing of human decency, was corroborated.

The police tell me that these four communities are "the real world" of law enforcement, and I believe them. But I also know that I, a white middle-aged woman, move freely about these communities without fear and my Black neighbours stay indoors, convinced that they can be shot, rousted, or strip searched in the streets.

Different city, same story: Tran is a gang member in training. Part of his training is not telling anything about himself or his life to strangers, particularly strangers who are white and from the press. All I know about him is his age—nineteen—and his first name. I know he is Vietnamese and that he came to Canada when he was nine as a refugee. He must have had English lessons and gone to school, but it's hard to tell. His English is hardly understandable. He lives in Vancouver, in an apartment he shares with four young men. He describes himself as a student. As far as I can determine, he is not attending any certified B.C. educational institution. "I am a student of life," he tells me.

Tran is in the process of becoming a foot soldier for one of several well-organized Asian gangs operating in Canada. Recruits are usually young Vietnamese, children of the boat people. Their lives in Canada have not been easy. Their assimilation, if Tran is an example, is, at best, fair.

Tran tells me that his father was a high official in the Saigon government. This is probably not true, because Tran has taken great pains to hide everything, from his name to his date of birth, from me. In any event, whatever influenced his parents' lives happened before Tran was born. Tran doesn't remember his family's reputed wealth and reputation. He was just over a year old when they left Saigon forever, sailing off in a freighter with several hundred Vietnamese eager to escape the new people's republic.

Tran's parents, along with Tran and his four brothers and sisters, his grandparents, and assorted other relatives, ended up in a refugee camp in Hong Kong. That is where Tran spent his early childhood. That is where he made friends who are still with him today. "We were children together. We went to school in the camp. We worked, fought, everything together."

Tran's family was always "very lucky." After seven years in a Hong Kong refugee camp, during which time they never set foot on the Hong Kong mainland, they were picked by a Canadian church group for sponsorship. "Very good people," says Tran. Tran is unsure which denomination it was, although he thinks it may be Mennonites. Again, it's hard to say if he's genuinely ignorant of his past or if he's deliberately covering up any traces that might identify him. The church group provided a home, furniture, and jobs for Tran's parents and arranged for the children to enter school. Tran spent three years in an English as a second language program and never mastered enough English to enter a regular school program. "I am not very intelligent," he says, with a smile. "I can't learn English."

One of Tran's brothers and both of his sisters managed to get through high school. Tran stayed on the rolls until he was sixteen, but he rarely attended classes after the seventh grade. "I was in shop.

It was okay, but I learned all about cars and welding in a few months. After that, I didn't need to go."

Tran found one of his old friends from the camps in Hong Kong and the two spent their days hanging out in Chinatown. Here, Tran was at home. English wasn't necessary.

Tran's family, ambitious and hard-working, didn't approve of his peripatetic lifestyle. "My father beat me. My mother cried. They wanted me to be a good student, to learn, to graduate. They didn't like my friends. Finally, I left."

Tran left for a life of petty crime. At sixteen, on his own, he could steal food from stores. He slept in his friends' homes or cars. He drifted up and down the Vancouver mainland, always staying in the orbit of the Chinese community.

"Chinese people in Vancouver are very rich," he says. "They don't like Vietnamese. They don't like anyone but other Chinese." That, in a nutshell, is as close as Tran gets to saying why he feels no shame for victimizing Chinese shopowners, burgling Chinese homes, stealing Chinese cars. As a youthful offender, he managed a long list of small-time crimes. He terrorized kids for their lunch money, joined with his friends in extorting money and food from local shop-keepers, acted as a legman for older Chinese criminals.

I ask him if Sgt. Ben Eng, the Chinese policeman who was disciplined for saying in public that the Vietnamese are two-thirds of the Asian gang population, was correct. He grins. "Maybe a little more than two-thirds. Sergeant Eng is in Toronto. Here in Vancouver, it's a little different."

Not too different. There and in Toronto, the operations are run by Chinese, many of them veterans of the People's Liberation Army, who are in Canada illegally or who claim to be refugees. Some, who have no criminal records, have emigrated legitimately as business-people or entrepreneurs. These Chinese criminal organizations have centres in New York, Los Angeles, Vancouver, Toronto, Amsterdam, Taiwan, and Hong Kong. They have taken over the heroin trade from the Mafia, shipping heroin from the fabled Golden Triangle of Southeast Asia. They deal in so-called designer drugs, leaving the cocaine trade to the South Americans.

Closer to home, the Chinese criminal organizations run elaborate and profitable financial frauds, particularly frauds involving fake credit cards and extremely sophisticated computer frauds. They have also been known to hijack a load of cigarettes, a container of furs, the odd batch of Swiss watches. They make large amounts of money.

While the Chinese run the operations, the Vietnamese are the local foot soldiers. The Vietnamese work their way into the crime rings through youth gangs. In Toronto, the Asian gangs settle scores by shooting enemies in crowded Chinatown restaurants. There's an Al Capone–style déjà vu about it all. Although the big money is reserved for the leaders, there's no shortage of jobs for a smart young man. Petty theft, extortion from Chinese merchants, and, always, gambling.

"I play *pai gau*," says Tran. *Pai gau*, a fast and furious game vaguely resembling dominoes, is the Asian high-rollers' game. In Toronto, you can lose thousands in minutes. In Vancouver, both legal and illegal *pai gau* parlours are tucked behind houses and atop buildings. They are small, bare, and ready for action. Tran claims to play almost every night. "I stay even," he brags.

Tran may be gilding the lily about his gambling losses but he's not hiding his profits from crime. His car is a snazzy black Nissan sports job with black leather seats and a top-of-the-line stereo. He's dressed in expensive black jeans, a black T-shirt, black leather jacket, and his glasses have Armani frames. A discreet glance at his wrist shows off a steel-cased Rolex oyster watch. It isn't gold with a diamond bezel, but then he's only nineteen.

Lack of education and skills doesn't concern Tran. He's on the route to success of a sort. It's hard to imagine what he'd do if he wasn't a criminal. Work in a restaurant? Sell Korean toys from a street stall? What options are available to a young man without skills or training? Could he get help? That implies he wants or needs it. He doesn't think he's doing badly.

It's unlikely that Tran would qualify for most programs. He's a surly kid with a definite attitude. In addition to his lack of skills for a traditional job market and his poor English, he shows the physical signs of a childhood with poor nutrition and deprivation. His teeth are crooked and unhealthy, he's skinny and stooped. In a community that values good looks, perfectly shaped almond eyes, sensational smiles, and the slick preppy good looks of Hong Kong rock stars, Tran is at a distinct disadvantage. Even if his English was better and he wanted to get a job hauling vegetables or waiting tables, employers would pass him by for better-looking and more personable kids.

The anti-Asian chorus in Vancouver declares, of course, that Tran and his ilk are the result of Canada's too-generous immigration policy. They believe that ease of immigration leads to Asian criminal gangs, which in turn destroy good Canadian neighbourhoods and good Canadian lives. The solution, they say, is to keep these people out. It's a solution favoured by, among others, the Reform Party.

At a Reform Party rally in Toronto in 1992, just as the movement peaked in southern Ontario, I met Bill and Maggy of Mississauga. They were keen on Reform, intent on finding a way to "save" Canada. They were concerned about the deficit and NAFTA, but mostly they were worried about immigration.

"We're becoming a dumping ground," said Bill. "We're getting criminals, uneducated thugs, people who are going to spend their lives on welfare or in prison, and either way, they're going to be on my tax bill. I want it stopped and I want to hear Manning's views. The Liberals are hopeless. They started all this in the first place and the Conservatives have just continued it."

Bill and Maggy have a long list of complaints about immigrants, but the one at the top of the list is that it has opened Canada to crime. They are concerned about a couple of gangland slayings in Toronto's Chinatown and they've heard about drug lords and Chinese gangs in Vancouver. Maggy's sister lives in Richmond, B.C., and, she says, "we've seen firsthand what Chinese immigration is all about. They just move in and take over. That goes for shopping, housing, and crime too. I don't think our police are equipped to handle tongs and Chinese gangs."

Bill and Maggy's Mississauga neighbourhood has problems of a different sort. "We have a number of Black families—nice people, no complaints—but they have a lot of problems with their kids, particularly the boys, and they don't seem to know how to handle them. These big fellows are just hanging around the neighbourhood, not working or going to school, and they are bound to get into trouble. There have been incidents at the mall and joy riding in cars. That sort of thing.

"When you raise these issues, the Black parents say we're butting in or we're racists. I think everyone would be better off if they admitted that there are problems. Some of these fellows are bad hats, and their parents ought to be able to admit it."

Limiting immigration is an attractive option for the government. It seems to answer the issues of race and crime without ever admitting that there are any relationships. At the private level, things are different. Mention crime or race at any dinner party and you get a capsule version of the Bill and Maggy's concerns. In Toronto, there is a widespread feeling that Blacks commit a disproportionate amount of crime based on their percentage of the population. Mayor June Rowlands, when a candidate, said so at an all-candidates meeting in my West Toronto riding—a riding with a large Black and South Asian population. While the Black residents were appalled, several South Asians quietly agreed with Ms. Rowlands. The reason they gave? They lived on Lansdowne Avenue and, from their windows, could see drug dealers or persons they suspected of being drug dealers walking along the streets. Also on television, they claimed, whenever there was a report on a robbery, the suspects were "usually" Black men.

Would crime stats by race prove any of this? Would anyone believe them if they didn't prove it? The answer if probably no on both counts. Real figures aren't what anyone wants. The racists and those who are scared of change, fearful of new faces, new cultures, aren't going to be persuaded by numbers that their notions of crime and justice are unfounded. Just as those statistics would probably prove that most major crimes—murder and rape—have no racial connotations, they would also show that poverty, race, and crime do have a correlation.

Based on what I've seen, what I've been told, and the bits of information I can glean, if statistics were kept of crime by race they would probably show that the Vietnamese do make up a high proportion of the members of Asian gangs. On that score, Ben Eng was correct. Privately and not for attribution, a member of the Asian crime squad in Vancouver says the same. The Vietnamese are the low group on the Oriental ladder, poor, badly educated, without many prospects. Joining a gang is a route to respect and a form of success.

But those same statistics would also show that gang membership is an almost minuscule percentage of a community that is, on the whole, the most law-abiding in Canada. If the gang members were the children of Chinese Canadians, graduates of excellent high schools, they'd probably be in university, racking up scholarships. Instead, they are the children of poverty, war, and hopelessness. Many of them, like Tran, learned far too early that survival on the streets is a con game.

Crime statistics by race would probably show that Black youths commit more petty crimes than their represented percentage of the overall population. They too are often poor, ill educated, without prospects. But petty crimes—pimping, purse-snatching, burglary—while bad, aren't in the same league with mass murder or multiple rapes. Like the Chinese, statistics would also show that the vast majority of the Black community is law-abiding and safe. What we see when we see crimes are the aberrations, the exceptions, not the rule. We also see the results of ignorance, poverty, and social stigmatism.

Twenty-five years ago, I briefly taught European history in Little Rock's notorious Central High School. My students, nine out of ten of them Black, were the bottom level of the high-school stream. They were the last products of the "separate but equal" days of segregated grade schools and most could barely read and write. The girls planned hard lives—dead-end jobs, kids, work. The boys knew that their last day of school was their first day in the army. There were no draft deferments for poor Black men in 1968. Vietnam was just over the high-school horizon.

Many of my students had criminal records, not serious ones, but long rap sheets of petty thefts, shoplifting, the odd break-and-enter.

For all that, they were typical teenagers, full of beans and hormones, wedded to wearing the latest fashion and hearing the latest music. Since they couldn't read the textbooks, we engaged in a lot of creative learning about history. One of the assignments was to find out all they could about what a grandparent (or any other relative who remembered) was doing on December 7, 1941. That assignment netted several grandfathers who had fought honourably (and unrecognized later) in the Second World War.

Another day, I asked them to fantasize about the future. What did they want to be after the war? They could go to college on the GI Bill or get technical training. Some opted for pure fantasy—law school, medical school—but the smartest kid in the class knew exactly what he was going to do. He was going to become a pimp like his brother.

Half a lifetime later, I read Marlene Nourbese Philip's collection of polemical essays, *Frontiers*. The book made me angry—one of her intentions. Yet it also made me seriously rethink my cherished hopes for multiculturalism in a society given to shooting people in the back for no other apparent reason than the colour of their skin. She wielded her sledgehammer and thwacked that old smug, self-deluding fantasy of the Canadian mosaic pretty hard. According to Philip, multiculturalism in Canada is largely an attempt to rationalize relationships between the two founding races—the French and English—both of whom are European, and keep at bay the Other, whether aboriginal, Black, Islamic, Oriental.

One of the ways to do that is to continue to demonize and mythologize the Other, to see him or her as diseased or dangerous. In the hue and cry about immigrants and crime, it's easy to see the demonology at work. In fact—and facts appeal to no one in this intractable dispute—1991 census data confirms that, while foreign-born people make up 16 per cent of Canada's population, they constitute only 12 per cent of the prison population. Non-whites make up 9 per cent of the population but are only 6 per cent of penitentiary inmates. That's the real world everyone is referring to and it's the world no one wants to embrace.

It should not surprise us that the dream of multiculturalism is a dying ideal in Canadian culture. Language and the images in the mind to which language gives power are the problems, deep as the soul, that well-intentioned multiculturalism, with its fearful silence in the face of blatant gaps between races, cannot touch. Each time another person of colour is shot in the back, and a police officer exonerated, and white society is given another chance to congratulate itself on the solidity of its justice system, the silence at the heart of the multiculturalist dream is heard—in the moans of the dying, in the mindless prattle about the inclination of "those people" to bring such terrible fates upon themselves, in the sighs of liberals once again disappointed by the failure of humankind to live up to their ideals.

One final note from 1992. After the Donald Marshall inquiries, after the Harper inquiries in Winnipeg, after the reports and royal commissions on aboriginal justice from Alberta and Manitoba, after all the publicity and the talk and the testimony and the cant, Judge Charles Huband of the Manitoba Court of Appeal, in a public speech, said there was no racism in the courts. The Manitoba Aboriginal Justice Inquiry wasn't just bad, it was "egregiously awful." The judges who wrote the report were wrong and utterly impractical. They had missed the point. There were more Native people in Canadian prisons, Judge Huband said, because of "a higher incidence of criminal activity by aboriginal people."

Of course, there weren't any statistics to prove it.

7

How Many Is Too Many?

Liz and Phil are rich. They have a large home in an upscale Toronto neighbourhood, a winterized country house for skiing and summer swims, and a Florida condominium where they escape the worst of winter. Their children attend elite private schools and American universities. Liz has the luxury to stay at home full time, employ a live-in Filipina housekeeper, and have plenty of free time for charitable committees and to supervise the kids. Phil, after some years of struggle, owns his own business. Their income, "in the mid-six figures," according to Phil, puts them in the rarified upper 2 per cent of Canadian families. Liz and Phil are, for now, members of the Conservative Party. They voted twice for Brian Mulroney, although they never really liked or trusted him: "too oriented towards French and Quebec," says Liz. The alternatives to Mulroney—the Liberals and the NDP—get short shrift. "Don't make me laugh," says Liz. In the upcoming federal election, Liz and Phil were planning to vote Reform "strictly as a spoiler and a protest," says Liz. "I like a lot of what Manning has to say but I don't think he has a prayer of getting elected or of having the power in a minority government."

Unlike many of their neighbours, Liz and Phil haven't suffered substantially in the recent recession. "Our house is paid for and its current value is what we paid for it, so we don't have to worry about negative equity," says Phil. The business, if not exactly booming, isn't collapsing, either. By any criteria, Liz and Phil have a substantial share of the good life in Canada. Yet, for the past two years, they've been exploring the possibility of emigrating to either Australia or the United States. "This country isn't what it was when we were kids," says Phil. "It's becoming a place that I don't recognize and that I don't think will be good for my kids."

Liz and Phil speak for a large and growing group of white Canadians who believe that Canadian immigration levels, which are now at their highest since the Hungarian uprising of 1957, are too high. They believe that the immigrants coming in are of a lower quality than those in previous decades. They believe that "phoney" refugees are taking advantage of Canada's immigration system to "jump the queue" and come into Canada ahead of immigrants who have more to offer the country.

Liz and Phil aren't opposed to immigration per se. Both, in fact, are the children of first-generation immigrants to Canada. Liz, whose family came from Hungary in the 1957 exodus, remembers a lot of bad years. "My mother cleaned houses and offices for ten years and my father worked in a factory. There were times when having a new pair of boots meant eating wieners and beans for a week," she says. "From the time I was fifteen, I paid board to my parents for my food. I bought my own clothes, paid my own gas bill if I used their car. I see these cleaning women from Jamaica bringing their teenaged kids in and expecting the government to support them forever and it just makes my blood boil. They come in, work for a couple of years, get landed, and then quit and go on welfare forever and they bring in their kids who don't work and who get pregnant and go on welfare too. We pay out more than 40 per cent of our income in taxes to support this, and I'm sick of it."

Della and Jack aren't rich, but they have a lot in common with

Phil and Liz. "We're barely middle-class and hanging on by our teeth," says Della. They live in B.C., in a modest neighbourhood — "Don't say where because I don't want hassles," says Della. Their children are all in public school. Della has worked for most of their marriage and is currently receiving UI after being laid off from her job as an office manager. "And let me tell you it's a lot less than you think," she says.

Jack, "a first-class salesman," is travelling more, keeping much longer hours, and hoping the recession is finally over. "A lot of my business is in central Canada," he explains. "And the bad times just seem to go on and on."

Like Liz and Phil, Della and Jack are disillusioned Conservatives. "I think Brian Mulroney had a chance to really do something for this country," says Jack. "And he blew it trying to get some sort of accord with Quebec. When will politicians realize that it's in Quebec's interests to stay outside, to keep threatening to leave so they can soak the rest of the country for more? I'm ready to say, 'Fine, you want to go. Go.' See how long they last on their own."

Jack also thinks that Mulroney opened Pandora's box with his "distinct society" clause. "This is already haunting us out here in B.C.," he says. "Every Indian tribe, every ethnic minority is going to want its own land, its own schools, police, services, and they expect us—the working people—to pay for it all. It was bad enough before, with the government pumping all that money into multiculturalism and French services. Now it's going to be services in everything from Vietnamese to Tlingit, and I'm going to have to carry the can because these people don't work, don't pay taxes, don't contribute.

"I know it sounds racist, but I just don't see how we're building Canada by allowing all these Asians in. I read your book about the Hong Kong Chinese and I can see the benefit there, but the East Indians? No. And even the Hong Kong Chinese are too much. We shouldn't be letting in too many of the same ethnic group and allowing them to all settle in one place. It overbalances cities like Vancouver."

"*I know it sounds racist, but...*" I heard those words ten thousand times in the years I researched and wrote this book and, increasingly, as time went on, they prefaced a concern or a comment about immigration or multiculturalism. Put it down to hard economic times or whites losing their grip on Canadian institutions, but immigration and multiculturalism are the place where the far-right views of people like Paul Fromm, the immigrant-bashing Etobicoke schoolteacher, and the more moderate concerns of ordinary Canadians converge. Immigration backlash is the dirty little orphan in the Canadian psyche. No one publicly admits it, but privately it's chewed on endlessly, right after the worries about the downbeat economy and rising crime.

The day after the 1993 federal election, I called Liz and Phil and Della and Jack and asked them how they had voted. All four admitted that, after considerable soul searching, they had voted for the Reform Party. "I knew he was a long shot," said Della, "but I really believe that Preston Manning is the only politician in Canada who had the intestinal fortitude to say no to immigration."

Immigration reduction was the unspoken issue in the election, surfacing in Manning's platform and, despite ugly incidents like the Toronto Reform candidate who was an out-and-out bigot and anti-Semite to boot, carrying a lot of votes in Ontario and giving Manning fifty seats in the west.

Not a Tory I know doubts that the next election will be fought between Reform and the Liberals. Some are already discussing what a refurbished Reform–Progressive Conservative party will look like. Reduction of immigration levels, reduction of refugee admissions, more control over sponsored migrants, a linking of immigration levels to job skills and to internal Canadian unemployment are all discussed as potential winners in an election campaign against the Liberals, who have a long history of support for immigration and have substantial followings within ethnic communities. "Even if I was a supporter of big spenders like Chrétien," says Phil, "I'd be opposed to more immigration into Canada. The Liberals have opened the gates and caused nothing but problems."

Canadians like these aren't alone in their concern for the rising tide of immigrants pushing to get into their country. Germany, which once prided itself on its liberal immigration policy—the most open in the world, the legacy of the Holocaust—slammed the doors in mid-June 1993. France, never comfortable with *étrangers*, even those who speak flawless French, has heard the sibilant hiss of the Le Pen followers and is battening down its hatches. In July 1993, the National Assembly passed a law that forbids foreigners to marry or bring their families to France. Britain, the new European economic invalid, with its millions of unemployed and seemingly perennial fiscal problems, was no longer accepting immigrants unless they came with large bankrolls and larger assists to industry, trade, or commerce. The United States has for decades adhered to a strict quota system that means that the majority of the traditional "huddled masses" will not be arriving from Jamaica, Yakutsk, or El Salvador.

According to the United Nations High Commission for Refugees, there are, in 1994, 100 million emigrants throughout the world. We are living in the midst of the largest mass migration of humanity since the Middle Ages. In Africa, drought and civil unrest, wars and repression, have whole populations on the move. The collapse of communism has left millions of Eastern Europeans eager to leave the crumbling countries of the former Soviet Bloc for the more promising economic waters of the West. There's war in former Yugoslavia, ethnic repression in Sri Lanka, religious repression in Pakistan and Iran, and five million Hong Kong Chinese who don't want to become part of the People's Republic of China in 1997.

Add to that mix the hundreds of thousands who'd like to get out of underemployed and overpopulated Mexico, escape the death squads in Guatemala or El Salvador, live without the Bolivian drug lords or either side in the endless Irish Troubles. There may no longer be an Evil Empire in the East but there's still no shortage of wars, famines, plagues, and pestilences. Today, all around the world, there are hundreds of thousands of people begging, praying, hoping to get somewhere else, someplace better, someplace safer, and Canada—safe, clean, multicultural—is high on anyone's list.

And Canada needs immigrants to remain competitive, to keep those social services rolling, to keep the population from ageing and dwindling in both strength and numbers. That message, sent out endlessly from Ottawa in a constant media-friendly dribble of studies, statistics, and analyses, is accurate, widely read, and ignored or disbelieved by most people.

"I'm concerned about immigration," says Daniel (not his real name), an Alberta educator and longtime immigration activist. Daniel, son and grandson of immigrants, knows the needs but he's worried about the current crop of new Canadians. "I don't want to shut the doors but I want our government to be more selective, to be more conscious of the needs of Canada. I think our system is being abused by unscrupulous immigration lawyers and consultants. I want real immigrants to this country, the kind who are going to build. I'm in favour of accepting any refugee whose claims can be backed up by an outside agency like the United Nations High Commission on Refugees.

"I'm completely opposed to letting in anyone just because he or she is related to someone who immigrated a couple of years ago, irregardless of age or education. And I'm opposed to economic refugees, people who want to come just to make money. If there are so many people in the world trying to get into Canada, our immigration people should be even more selective on our behalf, pick the very best, the most highly skilled, the most highly motivated, or the most endangered. Quality, not quantity, should be our goal."

It can be argued—and often is—that Canada has been doing just that for more than a decade. Folks at home might fret over those photos of reunions between ageing family members or men with mail-order brides, but out there in the immigration offices around the world, the hopeful applicants line up and wait. If you don't have relatives to sponsor you or you don't qualify as a refugee, you fall into the independent immigrant category. Here, preference still goes to those with good educations (postsecondary), better-than-working knowledge of French or English or both, needed job skills (from a list updated weekly), and money to invest or professions (lawyers and doctors need not apply) that can support them and a family as well as create jobs for Canadians.

If you want to see the policy in action, there is perhaps no better place than the Hong Kong office. It is one of the largest and busiest

Canadian immigration offices in the world. On any given day, more than a thousand people hand in documents, check on the status of their immigration procedures, meet with officials to discuss their future.

Glance around and rejoice. They are uniformly young, wealthy (the downright rich have already immigrated to Canada or the United States and are established), highly skilled and educated. The average Hong Kong immigrant to Canada is male, under forty, and has one or more university degrees, usually from a Canadian or American university. He has a track record in communications, international finance, accounting, banking, or international trade. He is married, and his wife also has one or more university degrees and a career in banking or communications. This couple has two children and a net worth of more than $500,000.

Those are the ordinary immigrants. Their applications for admission to Canada can take as long as two years to process. But there is another route. If the couple has $350,000 to put into an Investor Immigration fund approved by one of the provinces, as well as money to live on, they can receive Canadian landed status in less than a year. At least, that was the case until November 1, 1994. On that day, Immigration Minister Sergio Marchi put the Investor Immigration program in mothballs. The moratorium, while the program is studied, should last at least six months and many immigration experts believe it will never be reopened. The reason? Scandals involving Canadian-managed investor funds. Exact figures are not available, but as much as $500 million of investors' funds have been lost in failed business ventures and, in some cases, outright fraud. Multi-million-dollar fund failures—which caused hardly a ripple in Canada—were front-page news in Taiwan, Hong Kong, and Seoul. That means that the flow of investor funds were already drying up when Marchi slapped his moratorium on the funds.

Manitoba was another bargain-basement destination until unscrupulous Canadian con men discovered that they could sell the desperate in Hong Kong $150,000 of collapsed Manitoba real estate or shares in a bankrupt hotel. Faced with a polite revolt from Hong Kong and the recognition that the fault was in Canada, Manitoba withdrew from the Investor Immigration program to await a better, more honourable day.

The Hong Kong office also serves the needs of other desirable immigrants—those from Taiwan, a cheery little totalitarian state where laissez-faire capitalism is the norm and heavy industry the form. The Taiwanese, even more frightened of the Chinese Communists than Hong Kong, are getting their money and their kids out of Taipei. California is the Promised Land, but the Lower Mainland of British Columbia is an adequate alternative. You can spot the Taiwanese in the Hong Kong office by their American-style wardrobes and their melodious Mandarin accents. Everyone flips through copies of *Emigrant* magazine, a bilingual local rag whose pages are full of lifestyle tips about everything from interior decor (California styles are big in Vancouver, no-nos in Toronto) to power schools for the kids. Everyone here is young, smart, and hopeful.

There are no copies of *Emigrant* in the refugee camps that circle Hong Kong. Approximately 200,000 men, women, and children are crammed into these dingy prisons. Most are ethnic Chinese who fled Vietnam in hopes of a better life. Here they wait, unable to get the job skills, education, or fortune that would make them desirable in the eyes of immigration officers. Canada, more generous than most, accepts just under a thousand each year. They are the other side of the desirable immigrant equation in Hong Kong.

The boat people used to be a hot immigration topic. Back in 1978 when the first reports of pirates, rape, and pillage hit the Canadian media, Canadians raised thousands of dollars and sponsored thousands of refugees into their country. Liz and Phil, the images of camps and Budapest still alive, gave time, money, and support. "There was no question of not supporting them," says Liz. "They were in need, but they were also the crème de la crème of the refugees. They were checked and rechecked. No criminal past, all that. And I think most of them have done well. They've succeeded. I think there were some too-high expectations on everyone's part, but most of them settled in. It's terrible that the younger people aren't satisfied just to work their way into Canadian society the way the rest of us immigrants had to, that they're turning to crime and gangs. Is that a cultural thing? We all have to lower our expectations sometime."

Note that Liz is talking about *new* Canadian expectations. Her own ideas of comfort, honed over years of hard work and plenty of what even she admits is conspicuous consumption, are her just desserts. "My family worked hard so I could live like this," she says. "Phil and I worked hard so our kids could live better. We wanted them to have everything we didn't have and we want the same things for our grandchildren and great-grandchildren."

When Liz and Phil look around them, they see that, while their own lifestyle is lavish, the standard of living for their children is declining, and that isn't acceptable to them. They pay high taxes and feel they aren't getting their money's worth. Canada is one of the wealthiest countries in the world, yet there is a chilly feeling in the air that things are getting worse. The industrial base is shrinking. Jobs are heading south. Goods and services cost more, and taxes at all levels are too high. There is a voice, just a bat squeak, that says perhaps Canadians should lower their living standards, do a bit more with less, relearn those lessons from immigrant parents and grandparents.

But as soon as that voice gets loud enough to be heard, we drown it out. If the standard of living is to be lowered, I don't want them to be mine. I need my microwave and my VCR. My daughter deserves her private school and her skiing lessons and her summer camp. My husband works hard. He needs his CD and his stereo and his high-performance car. We work hard for these things and we feel they are our due. When our hard work buys less and we find ourselves putting more money into the tax accounts, then we look around to see who's at fault.

The Other. There are too many of Them, taking our jobs and running up our welfare rolls. Keep them out—at least the ones who don't have money—and we can keep our toys and our public services and still keep taxes down.

The major debate over immigration in Canada has to do with selecting the crème de la crème. Plenty of immigration activists claim we're already skimming the top of the refugee crop, passing over people with dreams and hopes to get those with skills and education. Refugees constitute nearly 20 per cent of the people admitted to Canada each year, the second-highest ration of resettled refugees in the world. Only tiny Sweden has a more generous policy. In 1993, approximately 46,000 refugees entered Canada, and in 1994 the numbers are higher. Of that group, 25,000, or more than half, are people who came to Canada on their own and declared themselves refugees at airports or borders or who managed to enter as visitors and then claimed refugee status. That leaves only 20,000 spaces left for the throngs of people in refugee camps, in holding centres, in danger in the rest of the world.

Canada is continuing to resettle refugees at a time when other countries are shutting the doors, and there is no shortage of people in this country who would like to see our doors slammed shut as well. "I believe that if they arrive by boat and just jump over the side, they should be sent back to wherever they came from," says Della. "I think that if people are legitimate refugees, they can prove it and come in through the legitimate routes. I think that we should, on principle, turn away anyone who comes in illegally and then tries to claim he's a refugee. I've heard there are rackets where immigration counsellors tell people to say they're Seventh-Day Adventists or Mormons or something and that they're a persecuted religion. This is contemptible. This is making fun of people's deeply held beliefs. I think those people should be sent packing on the next plane and no waiting around for hearings and appeals."

That's one point of view. On the other hand are the equally adamant views of people like Sister Brenda Duncombe, a longtime immigration activist who believes the doors should be opened without restriction. "We should take anyone who comes. We have an immense country and great wealth. We have room. Immigrants contribute to this country. They've made it rich. As well, they're the labour source in the Third World that makes us all rich. Why shouldn't they be free to go where they please?"

To people like Brenda, any attempt to control or inhibit people, particularly refugee claimants, is tantamount to state-sanctioned murder. "If you're sending someone back to a country to be tortured or killed, what is that? As well, if you send someone back to starve in Somalia or Ethiopia, how can you say that's morally correct?"

People like Brenda presume, and the Council on Refugees seems to agree, that the Canadian policy towards the well educated and well off is also inherently racist. It would appear, on paper, to favour immigrants from Europe or America over those from Africa or Asia or the Caribbean. Immigration statistics, though, don't support this. By far the largest percentage of independent immigrants into Canada are now the Hong Kong Chinese, followed by those from the Indian subcontinent. In Quebec and Nova Scotia there are substantial numbers of migrants from Arab countries, particularly Lebanon and Iraq. For the most part, these immigrants are wealthy, French-speaking, and easily assimilated into Quebec society. To people like Brenda, these people are irrelevant because their wealth makes them "as good as white." They can blend in to Canadian society, buy homes in nice neighbourhoods, send their kids to the best schools. The ordinary barriers of race do not apply to these favoured few.

And they are just a few. What confuses people like Daniel is that these immigrants—the ones he reads about—don't seem to be the ones that are turning up in his ESL classes or being served at the local Welcome House. "The immigrants who are coming here have very little language. Many of them are illiterate in their native language as well as in English, and this makes it difficult if not impossible to teach them to read and write English. And, if you can't read and write, you just aren't going to get a job in today's market. You just aren't and that's a fact. I guess these super-people are going to Vancouver and Toronto and Montreal. If so, then that's a problem too."

Daniel becomes confused when I point out that under such selection processes as he and others suggest, his own relatives might have remained in eastern Europe, to survive (or perhaps not) the rigours of Nazism and communism. They were, by his own admission, "simple people," hard-working, dedicated to making a life for themselves in a not terribly hospitable new country. People made fun of their accents, their clothes, their habits, even their food. And didn't the phrase *better life* include making more money? "I don't have anything against so-called economic refugees," says Daniel. "But I don't think that an illiterate person who has spent his entire working life growing sugarcane or coffee is going to have much of a chance to get rich here."

History is not on Daniel's side. Canada is filled with the children and grandchildren of illiterate Europeans who came here with nothing more than hope and whose only marketable skills were subsistence farming, woodworking, or the ability to haul heavy loads for long hours. In past years, these labourers were desirable, necessary to build cities and houses for a rapidly developing Canadian middle class. Now, in a changed economy, they no longer qualify as independent immigrants, and it is the independent—the immigrant who can work, pay taxes, buy consumer goods—that Canadian immigration covets.

The problem is that the independent immigrants are a small and shrinking percentage of Canada's overall immigration package. Independent immigrants are, as of July 1993, about 15 per cent, or one in eight, of total immigration into Canada and that, claim some immigration critics, is a problem for now and the future.

In July 1993, the C. D. Howe Institute—a right-wing think tank —released a background paper written by journalist Daniel Stoffman. The title was "Toward a More Realistic Immigration Policy for Canada," and the ink was hardly dry before immigration and refugee groups denounced it as racist.

Race is mentioned only once in Stoffman's report, and in that case he's using the German and French situations as a warning, a vision of a Canada that nobody wants and that a good many Canadians have fought against. But Stoffman sees rapid-fire change caused by the arrival of large numbers of minority immigrants as part of the problem of racism in Canada. He warns that we should not try to combat racism by ignoring "the harm done by too-rapid a pace of immigration."

Forget Meech Lake, the distinct society, and Quebec separation. Immigration, to Stoffman, is the real issue for Canadians in the next century, and much of what he has to say lends credence to the arguments put forward instinctively by people like Liz and Phil and Della and Jack. National unemployment is at unacceptably high levels, and we have increased our immigration to bring in more unskilled and unemployable people. Stoffman's statistics show that, in order to bring in more highly qualified immigrants—those with education, money, and skills—we have to up the numbers of sponsored or nominated immigrants, those brought in by relatives already here. And even with the record numbers, the family members are still threatening to swamp the immigration system, and these immigrants have lower skills and education levels than the independent group.

Furthermore, immigration spending is on the increase. It now costs $1.5 billion a year to process and provide housing and support for refugee claimants; in Toronto alone, language classes cost $100 million. Expert studies, such as that done by Don DeVoretz, an economics professor at Simon Fraser University, confirm what a lot of people have been muttering. While B.C. has benefited economically from the influx of immigrants, most notably the Hong Kong Chinese, into the Vancouver area, Ontario has been a net loser, picking up more problems and costs.

To add to the problems, these new immigrants are not spread out across Canada but are concentrating in three areas—Toronto, Montreal, and Vancouver. None of these cities needs further migrants. Their resources are already stretched, and continued population growth means more pressure on housing, roads, schools, public assistance.

How on earth did we get in such a fix? Simply put, Canada opened the doors.

In the United States it has long been fashionable to talk about "a nation of immigrants." Removal from one country to another is part of the national identity. It is the central fact of American mythology. It is impossible to imagine an America without the Pilgrims, without the wagon trains to the frontier, without the restless movement of people to places. Even at its most destructive—in the dreadful history of slavery and its aftermath—there is an epic quality to the

American experience. Truth or fiction is irrelevant when one looks at books like Richard Wright's *Native Son* or Toni Morrison's *Harlem* or even Alex Haley's migration tale, *Roots*.

According to Freda Hawkins, professor emeritus of the University of Toronto and author of *Canada and Immigration: Public Policy and Public Concern*, Canada also claims to be a nation of immigrants and, more so than America, it is. But here, the immigrant experience isn't part of the national mythology and it's not widely accepted as "an essential element in national development." Hawkins says immigration as an area of public policy has conventional support but "little enthusiasm." The relationship of the two founding races of Canada is the central fact of Canadian life, whereas survival in the wilderness and the North are the foundations of Canadian myth and culture.

In the decades after Confederation, the two largest ethnic groups in Canada continued to be the French and the "British"—Welsh, English, Irish, and Scots. As Hawkins puts it, "the existence of two founding races, each with its own language, culture, and long historical tradition, has preempted the place of immigration in the national mythology." As late as 1968, Pierre Trudeau had to remind voters that there were plenty of Canadians whose first language was neither English nor French.

Before the Second World War, the pattern of immigration remained settled and white. Holders of British passports were entitled to all the benefits of Canadian citizenship. Northern Europeans, especially those who could farm, were encouraged. On the other hand Orientals, considered suspect, were actively discouraged. There was a punitive head tax on each immigrant (to pay for his use of community services, since he could not be expected to contribute in the usual way through taxes) and family immigration was forbidden. Men came to work; the women and children stayed behind in China. The few thousand "Africans," mostly the descendants of free immigrants or freed slaves, were longtime residents of Canada. Despite requests from prospective migrants, there was little immigration from the British West Indies or Africa. The same held true for India and southern Asia. Jews, as recorded in Irving Abella and

Harold Troper's book *None Were Too Many*, were refused entry out of hand. Regardless of how you view it, the immigration system was racist and anti-Semitic. Unlike Australia, which enshrined its whites-only policy in law, Canada's racial policies—with the exception of the rules on Orientals— were unwritten and unspoken. Groups considered undesirable were simply not allowed in.

This characteristic of keeping silent about racial prejudices and conflicts continues in Canada. It's "not nice" to want visible minorities to move to someone else's neighbourhood or some other country. Officially, Canada welcomes all immigrants to its shores. Unofficially, some immigrants are more welcome than others.

The Second World War changed the face of Canada. In the immediate postwar years, Canada took in more than three million immigrants, almost all of them from Europe. Attempts were made even then to keep out some groups. Abella records the favoured treatment given to people from Baltic nations over Jews who had survived the concentration camps. The Chinese, despite having been allies of Canada, were still *non grata*, as were their wives and children. But the door was wedged open because people were needed to work in the factories and farms and construction bonanza of the postwar boom.

It is clear from examining tables of immigration that, although Ottawa claimed to be looking at the overall picture, public opinion and international events really drove Canadian immigration. In 1950, for instance, Canada finally opened its doors to former enemy aliens, the last of the displaced persons from Europe, and groups of hitherto unwelcome Europeans, such as the Italians. European immigration doubled and trebled between 1951 and 1953 during the establishment of the Overseas Service of the new Department of Citizenship and Immigration. Tables show that most of the new Canadians were farmers, in the manufacturing and mechanical trades, or service and recreational workers, a category that included domestic servants.

The establishment of the ministry indicated the importance Ottawa was now placing on immigration. Hitherto, it had been simply an arm of whatever ministry had an extra desk or deputy. As the ministry established itself, the numbers of immigrants to Canada fluctuated with crisis in Europe and economic downturns at home. Immigration reached its highest point (282,000) in 1957, when the Hungarian revolution and the Suez Crisis brought in record numbers of Hungarians and British citizens. The number dropped sharply the next year and fell to a mere 71,000 in 1961 as the economy went into recession. The 1960s marked another expansionary period: immigration peaked at 222,000 in 1968, and then dropped in the early 1970s.

That's when I entered Canada, and it's worth recalling Toronto as it was when I arrived. The immigration hue and cry—and there *was* a hue and cry—was about Americans. There were still draft resisters coming over the border to escape the Vietnam War. Baldwin Street, now the centre of Chinatown, was a tiny American enclave of handicraft shops and secondhand stores. There were American bars and American cafés and concerns that Americans were taking away Canadian jobs.

I lived on Belmont Street, just a stone's throw from the then very untrendy streets of Yorkville where hippies held court and June Callwood ran her Digger House. Just around the corner from my house was Azan's, where elegantly dressed Black women went for their elaborate coiffures. You could walk for miles in Toronto, travel for days on the subway, go in a hundred stores and never see a person of colour. If I hadn't lived by Azan's, I'd have assumed there were no people of African heritage here. I was surprised at the numbers of East Indians who turned up at the opening of the first downtown Indian restaurant, on Yonge Street. There must have been fifty or more.

In those bygone days just twenty years ago, "ethnic" meant Chinese, Jewish, or East European. Chinatown had just been moved west to make room for the spanking new city hall, and the adventurous eater headed down to Sai Woo on Saturday for dim sum. There were jolly little goulash palaces on Bloor West, Granowska's famous cakes and ice creams near High Park, and Ukrainian pierogi and cabbage rolls down at the end of Roncesvalles. Like most immigrants, I can remember my first meal in Toronto. It was a hamburger and fries at Murray's, and the most exotic thing on the menu was strawberry ice cream.

I was lucky. Gino, my Italian hairdresser, recalls Toronto in the early 1960s. "There were no restaurants, no pizza parlours. Just hamburger places with vinegar on the chips. You could smell the vinegar on the street. When I arrived, I remember walking and smelling all that vinegar. You couldn't get oregano, basil, spices for food. Just salt and pepper and vinegar. When the first pizza place opened up, my friends and I rode the subway to the very end. It was at Eglinton then—the back of the world. I remember smelling the store and it smelled so good."

I don't remember pizza, but I do recall celebrating family events at the Noshery on Eglinton, where you could get the largest, gooiest sundae in town, complete with little paper parasols for decoration. If we were feeling reckless, we passed over the chicken and shrimp in a basket or the burgers and tried one of the Jewish snacks—a knish or latkc or blintz. The Noshery was safe, the kind of place where you could order your pastrami or corned beef on white bread with mayo and the waitress wouldn't bat an eyelash.

When I look at the stats for 1972, the year I formally emigrated to Canada, I see that the manufacturing and mechanical trades were already declining and there was a marked rise in the professional ranks. That was me. I came in as an independent; an immigration officer totted up my points on the scale. My seven years of postgraduate education, my limited literacy in French, my command of English, and, most of all, my guaranteed job made me a desirable commodity in those days. Along with my diplomas, Immigration checked my bank accounts, my credit history, my employment history, and my physical health, and cleared me of having any criminal past. Only when I'd passed it all was I declared a landed immigrant. I was selected by Canada. I was part of the chosen few.

When I came here in 1971, Toronto was a city of two and a half million, still predominantly white. It was also quiet, polite, and virtually crime free. The city is ruder now, louder and more aggressive. It grew at a phenomenal rate throughout the 1980s, as the suburbs sprawled across the little villages and farmlands to the north, east, and west. There are nearly five million people in the Greater Metropolitan Toronto Region. Crime seems to have increased. They sell drugs openly on the streets and I've had my purse snatched on the subway. I put all this down to the deleterious effects of urban sprawl.

Some of my friends blame it on "them," the migrants of the past decade. Sondra Carrick, an attractive, well-educated Black woman, is a victim of that change. Despite her education, her charm, and her ten generations of Canadian forebears, she is "them," part of the problem. "It makes me sick to hear what people say. Blaming everything from the dirt on the streets to crime on African Canadians. My family has been here longer than most of theirs and I'm the one they call the problem."

When I came to Canada we Americans were the problem, taking over the universities and gaining a stranglehold on Canadian culture. I came here as a bride, fresh from the deserts of New Mexico, part of the American wave washing across Lake Ontario. Americans in those halcyon days saw Canada as a cleaner greener land. This was the country of choice, with medicare for all, no standing army, and, best of all, no fixed and xenophobic "national identity."

While Canadians agonized over their perceived lack of cultural identity, Americans saw *their* country as a modern Babylon. Faced with a society rent with dissension over the Vietnam War, rife with racial tensions (the fires from the 1968 riots were still warm), and the feeling that there were murderers everywhere after the assassinations of the Kennedy brothers and Martin Luther King, those of us who swam to Canadian shores can be excused for believing that we had landed in the land over the rainbow.

Gathered together in little groups over burgers and beer at Grossman's Tavern on Spadina, we used to speak with wonder about the marvels of Canadian reserve, Canadian lack of nationalist paranoia, the Canadian mosaic. Most of us were veterans of civil rights marches and antiwar demonstrations, and we sipped our Canadian beer with deep satisfaction and referred to Toronto as the great rest home in the sky, a paradise island far from Amerika, with its deaths and disasters. Canada had a Department of Multiculturalism and laws against racism. Canadians were nice caring people, and when they said "burn, baby, burn," they meant the logs in the fireplace.

As I write this, I'm impressed with how unquestioning I was back in those days. Trained from infancy to be a racist, and having spent almost fifteen years attempting to change the most egregious racist attitudes, I simply closed my eyes to events in my new country.

It is January 1972. I have been offered a job with an obscure Anglican organization that hands out Christmas hampers and old clothing to Toronto's poor. The director of the organization and my church rector want to change this, to make the church more socially responsible. Because of my civil rights work and my history of community organization in New Mexico, I have been offered the job, but I am not yet a landed immigrant. If I want to work I have to apply for a work permit. This requires a letter offering me the job and including a statement that there are no qualified Canadians available. After the letter and a cursory search by Employment Canada (the letter and job requirements are couched in such a way that only I can fill them), I have an appointment with Immigration, who will issue or deny the work permit.

The appointment is in a faceless federal building downtown. The waiting room, really just a large hall with some baffles in the centre, is full of South Asians. My husband and I are the only Caucasians waiting. No one talks. After a short time, we are ushered behind the baffles to the officer in charge of my file. I do not know her name and she never bothers to tell me, but she is the usual well-dressed bureaucrat, middle-aged and pleasant, just what I expect a Canadian immigration officer to be.

Ms. X scans my letter and supporting documents, sniffs about the lack of qualified Canadian applicants. Not for a moment is she taken in by the skilfully worded "requirements." She pulls out a form and fills in my name, address, and particulars. At the top of the form is the place for her signature and the all-important nine-digit number that will admit me to the wonderful world of work in Canada. Ms. X puts a digit in a box and then glares at me and my husband and delivers a brief rant about lawyers who jiggle the jobs against Canadian applicants. I'm not distressed. The officer is right.

Then, her voice rising and, I'm certain, easily heard by the waiting applicants beyond the baffle, Ms. X begins a series of completely gratuitous racist comments. "These people coming in from Asia and taking jobs," and she fills in another digit. "No place for me in my own country," and she puts in another. "What about my culture, what about my family? No one cares about what happens to my culture."

We are miserable, my husband and I, but we sit, listening to her and nodding, counting those digits like pearls. My husband, at that time a college lecturer, is planning a large cultural gathering of Native Canadians. He attempts to mollify her by telling her about it. It's the final red flag.

"Those people aren't part of my culture. They don't have anything to do with my culture. They're part of the problem of what's happening in this country. The people who built it, made it, are being ignored."

Ms. X went on and on, and, after each little rant, she filled in another box. At last, and it really did seem like hours, I had my work permit and was free to leave. As I walked past the waiting nonwhites I could only wonder what was in store for them. Still, I never questioned what had happened.

I rationalized it by saying that I would have lost my permit, but in truth I didn't want to rock my newly launched boat. Canadians were better people. That was a statement I needed to believe at that time. I convinced myself that Ms. X was an aberration, a glitch in the superior Canadian system, in the same way that, all my life, I'd been rationalizing the fact that some of the nicest people I knew were also racists at heart. "All countries have people like that. It doesn't really mean anything"— or so I told myself in 1972. It didn't take much for me to convince myself. Perhaps the most vivid thing I remember about that appointment, some twenty years ago, was that I did nothing, objected to nothing, raised no obstacle to the Immigration lady's racist remarks. There was cowardice involved.

But not all my reaction can be written down to cowardice. My reticence was also prompted by her being an official of a country I very much wanted to live in because I found it trustworthy and safe and reliably liveable. Though I didn't realize it at the time, I was already turning away from America. I was readier then than at any recent point in my life to excuse racial peccadilloes and trust the essential goodness of the System.

Looking back, I realize that more than a baffle and good luck separated me from the anxious people in the Immigration waiting room. If I had been less fortunate in job prospects or education, I might have come into Canada by a more difficult route. If I had been turned down by Immigration as an independent immigrant, I could have tried again as a sponsored immigrant. I could do that only if I had a close relative in Canada willing to sponsor me and assure Immigration that I would not become a burden on the state by claiming welfare or unemployment benefits. Sponsorship, long the only route into Canada for the unskilled and uneducated, has always posed problems and been a source of contention for those responsible for immigration planning.

Since 1967, regulations have governed sponsored immigrants. Before 1966, few statistics were kept on who came in, though we can look at broad pictures. Between 1946 and 1966, 2.5 million immigrants arrived in Canada, and of that group, 900,000 were sponsored. Most of these sponsored immigrants were from Italy, Portugal, and Greece, the three countries that also supplied nearly 30 per cent of the immigrants listed as "unskilled labour" in the statistics. Furthermore, there was a concern among immigration officials that, rather than close relations—wives, children, siblings — large numbers of distant cousins and in-laws were being sponsored, immigrants who added to the pool of unskilled labour and were destined to be a problem during periods of high unemployment.

The idea of sponsorship was born of economics, not a noble desire to permit families to reunite. In the postwar years, resources for immigrants were few, and a penny-pinching government figured that families could smooth the problems of adjustment to North American society. In short, if you needed a job but couldn't speak English, a relative could speak for you. If housing was short, live with a sponsor until you could manage on your own.

It all seemed to make perfect sense, but even before 1967, when the sponsorship regulations were tightened, immigration officials saw problems. One 1967 government document quoted by Freda Hawkins cites some of the problems:

> 1. A major bias in favour of national groups already established in Canada and particularly those with strong kinship ties.
>
> 2. An element of explosive growth. During much of the postwar period it was possible to sponsor a wide range of relatives. And there was little to prevent these relatives from sponsoring other relatives in a rapid process of chain migration.
>
> 3. A proportion of sponsors never carry out their full sponsorship responsibilities. Sponsorship served in a great many cases simply as an easier means of gaining entry to Canada.
>
> 4. Sponsorship, while it may provide immediate help and shelter for the immigrant (thus relieving government of this responsibility), is probably not in itself a major factor in satisfactory and long-term adjustment, and reliance upon it for this purpose is illusory.
>
> 5.The sponsorship system breeds pressure. It has been immensely time-consuming for officials and politicians in Canada. It is difficult to control geographic patterns developing within it which are difficult to change. For example, the very large sponsored movement from southern Italy preempted such a large part of the total Italian movement that virtually no promotion of development took place in northern Italy until fairly recently.
>
> 6. The sponsorship system has also contributed powerfully to the growth of large and, to a considerable extent, self-contained ethnic communities in Montreal and Toronto and, to a more limited degree, in certain other cities.

In 1967, the rules governing sponsorship were changed. Children had to be under eighteen; adopted children, particularly adult adoptees, were no longer eligible. (Even young adopted children came under Immigration scrutiny.) Wives and parents were permissible, but siblings and in-laws were often rejected. The migrants most affected by these changes were the relatives of the most recent arrivals to Canada—and those arrivals were from the Caribbean, the Indian subcontinent, Central America, and Africa.

B. P. Singh of Scarborough came to Canada in 1972, the same year I received my landed immigrant status. He is a cheerful gentleman who likes his tidy ranch-style home, his carefully planted and much-loved flower garden, and the cosy warmth of his large and very supportive family. "Yes, I came here and I brought my family," he says. "I don't regret it. Why should they not share what I have? Yes, we Sikhs have strong kinship ties and we tend to live near each other so we can visit. Is this some sort of crime?

"It was very different," he says of those days in 1972. "I had gone to university in Minnesota and so I knew something of the climate, but the United States is very different for people of East Indian extraction. In the six years I was at Minnesota, I don't ever recall a racial slur even though I heard many racial comments about Africans and Orientals. This was during the Vietnam War years and people spoke of gooks, although it wasn't done on campus. Minnesota had many student radicals and people were very aware of racial slurs. There were many articles in the student newspapers about the civil rights in the south. Martin Luther King, Stokely Carmichael. I remember student meetings where these issues were argued most aggressively."

Canada, Mr. Singh discovered, was quite different. "I was here a week and I went into a store to buy some film. The clerk just ignored me. She kept waiting on other people. Finally, I confronted her and told her I had been waiting. She got my film and took my money. As I was leaving the store, she said in a loud voice to someone that Pakis were so rude. I convinced myself that she was an isolated case, but it happened again and still again. People wonder why some of us prefer to stay within our own families, our own friends. This is why.

"I was here less than a year and I cut my hair and shaved my beard," Mr. Singh says. "I've heard about Sikhs being called ragheads, but that's not the reason I did it. A friend told me that I'd never get a promotion on my job so long as I wore a turban, and he was right. I was passed over time and again and nobody would say why. It wasn't my race, because there were other South Asians and they were getting on. Then I realized that I looked different. I wore the same suits and ties but my turban was unacceptable. Things have changed now, but then, that was what you did."

Singh, clipped, cleanshaven, and westernized, prospered. "After two years, I was financially very well off. I had an apartment in Mississauga and I felt the time was right to marry. I told my parents and they arranged everything in India. I went back, married my wife, and then returned to Canada and filled out all the necessary documents to sponsor her. It was an ugly time. The immigration people were not helpful. But, after seven months, she came. The next year, when she was pregnant with our first child, I sponsored her parents to come here to help with the baby."

All in all, over the years, Mr. Singh sponsored ten relatives: his parents, his in-laws, his brothers, and his brothers-in-law. The younger brothers and in-laws in turn sponsored their own wives and in-laws. "When we get together now, we are about sixty people," he says. "All Canadian citizens, by the way, including my father, who is over seventy."

Most of Mr. Singh's sponsored relatives have jobs. "I provided a room to live in and food and money for transportation, but they went to work and paid me back. Every one of them." Even his aged father works part time in a store owned by a relative. "We are not parasites. We are home owners. We pay taxes. We support ourselves. My parents are not eligible for the Old Age Pension and so my father works so they will not be completely dependent upon me and my brothers. I am sick of people saying immigrants take and don't give anything to the economy."

As expected, Mr. Singh is an enthusiastic supporter of sponsorship. "Some people think all immigrants are on welfare. I hear this said all the time. Of course, no one says it to me because they know, but I've heard comments about 'So-and-so's brother came here and went on welfare and brought his children and got all their teeth fixed on welfare and his parents had heart surgery and then they went back to India or wherever.' I don't know any one who ever got welfare. If you are sponsored, you are not eligible for welfare. I even had to sign an undertaking that if my parents were to fall ill, I would pay for their medical expenses. I don't think the people who oppose sponsored immigrants know very much about the program."

There is much in what Singh says. I didn't know much about immigration in 1987 when I was assigned to do a story for a Canadian business magazine on immigrants from Hong Kong. I've spent countless hours since then reading and interviewing and investigating, and I can't say I know very much more. In addition, I find that many of the people who administer the Canadian Immigration Act don't know the ins and outs of it either. The honest ones (and that's by far the majority) admit that they are caught in changing times, when pressure back home and pressures from the Third World are meeting like two bull goats in midstream. One of the major worries for most immigration planners is the effects of political pressure groups on the process. Says one, who refused to be identified, "We wouldn't be in this mess"—with far more sponsored migrants than independents —"if it weren't for politics, and it doesn't matter what the party is. They all want those ethnic votes."

Larry, a smart young financier, says, "I'm not a racist but I'm worried about the numbers and the quality of immigrants to this country and the fact that they're all locating in three areas. This is the result of the Trudeau Liberals and their use of immigration to purchase votes for themselves. It was disgusting then and it's dangerous now."

Larry is just past thirty, born and raised in Regina, eking out an existence in Toronto on unemployment after losing his job in the recent recession. Larry is also of mixed race. "My mother is a Métis, so I know firsthand about aboriginal peoples' problems." It is Larry's contention that Canada should shut the doors on immigrants and funnel the money saved —"billions and billions for immigrants on welfare, immigrants who don't speak English, immigrants' health care"—into rehabilitation programs for aboriginal people. "You could change the whole Ministry of Indian Affairs system, get rid of welfare, get people off sniffing gas and solvents, alcoholism. Native people could teach whites a lot about spirituality and living a more balanced life. It's not a one-way street I'm proposing."

It is in vain to argue with Larry—or any other convinced foe of immigration—that immigrants contribute more to Canada than they cost. "Go to any city," he says. "Just open the telephone book and look at the government services for immigrants. And that's just the ones listed with the government. There are also dozens of groups, all getting government funding from Multiculturalism or the provincial Citizenship branch, who are also serving the immigrant community."

B. P. Singh agrees with Larry on a lot of issues. He thinks Canada's treatment of aboriginal peoples is "nothing short of a scandal." But he doesn't see more government handouts as the answer. "Government money hasn't been the answer thus far. I think pitting one group against another—more money for us and less for them—won't help people have pride in themselves."

Surprisingly, Singh agrees with Larry that there's too much government cash being spent on immigrant services. "I pay taxes too," he says. "Quite high ones, in fact, and I don't believe in having all these services financed by the taxpayer. I think the government should examine the books of every organization, look carefully at what they are doing. In the South Asian community, some of these groups are not doing anything. They are just places for the young people to hang around, pick up undesirable friends, bad habits. I am not against the Black people. Many are fine persons, but I go by their community centre and I see grown men hanging about in the middle of the day. They should be working. If they can't find jobs, they can clean up the community centre or mow grass or tidy up the parks. It sets a bad example to everyone to have them just lounging about, playing cards or dominoes."

Singh is also concerned about jobs. "I think that in a recession people tend to blame the newcomers even if it's false. That's understandable. I think it is very difficult to lose your job, but I think

Canadians are spoiled. If I lose my very good job and I have to find another, I may not get one with as good a salary or benefits. I may have to reduce my standard of living or my wife might have to go to work. These are things that are happening everywhere. But Canadians think that they should be able to get the same job again and they don't want to work at just anything and so they stay on UIC. Meanwhile, immigrants come and take anything they can get. I hear union leaders talking all the time about not giving up the high salaries and benefits they have, and that's all well and good, but if the wages mean the companies aren't competitive and the business goes bankrupt, what good are the benefits then?"

Singh has a point here, one that many Canadians would prefer not to acknowledge: we are spoiled. We are used to our luxurious (by world standards) living, our expensive government services, our social safety net and subsidized trains and airlines and prices. Rather than acknowledge that we may be living a bit too high on the hog, we react by blaming someone else for our own selfishness. We are being asked to share what we have and we're happy to do it, so long as it doesn't cost us anything.

Finally, Singh believes that the immigration process has, indeed, been politicized. "As far as I'm concerned, it always was," he says. "When I first arrived, a member of the Liberal Party came and told me I could be a member, even though I wasn't a citizen. I was signed up, and when the riding meeting was held, I voted on the candidate. Naturally, I was interested in candidates who favoured open immigration.

"I know a lot has been said about instant Liberals and particularly about riding meetings where two or three thousand South Asians come to vote on a candidate. This is unusual, I suppose, but we are very political people. Politics in India is important, and it's important to us here. What I don't like is having a so-called Canadian, which means a man or woman of English or European extraction, as the candidate for thousands of South Asians. I think we should run our own candidates, who represent our interests, and that doesn't mean the narrow scope you might think. We are educated, intelligent people. We have a broad outlook. We have our own views on international events, including what happens in India, but we are also active on the local scene. If I might say so, I think we have a more international outlook than most Canadians. We hear from people all over the world, have ties in Africa, in Asia, in the Middle East, in Europe, even in South America.

"I think that Canadians see these instant Liberals and they are as appalled as I am. They see this as a very cynical attitude. They say that the government is buying votes with grants for cultural centres or festivals or whatever, and I agree. I think that the process is politicized. It is cynical. That doesn't mean I support it as it is. What if a South Asian candidate wants to change that system? It's at this time that I feel a real sense of rage, real helplessness, at people who assume that because of my background, the fact that I'm a Sikh, I don't have anything to offer this country. It is my country, too. Why do they assume that I am not concerned with this cynicism, this abuse?

"Of course, when people first arrive, they are worried all the time about paying rent, getting established, but after years, this rushing about stops and we look around and see things that need to be done. That is why they now are wanting to go into politics."

I called Mr. Singh after the news broke about Jag Bhaduria, the MP for the Toronto suburb of Markham-Whitchurch-Stouffville. Bhaduria was forced to resign from the Liberal Party caucus in January 1994 amid allegations that he lied about having a law degree. Days before, a poison-pen letter written by Bhaduria—a former schoolteacher—in 1989 to his former employers at the Toronto Board of Education was made public. In that letter he wrote that he wished Marc Lepine, the young man who killed twelve young women in Montreal, had killed members of the education staff. The letter had led to Bhaduria being fired from his teaching job.

Bhaduria claimed that at the time he had been under severe stress because he was engaged in a human rights dispute with the board; he publicly apologized for the letter, as well as admitting that he was wrong. Prime Minister Chrétien stood by Bhaduria, saying that the fledgling MP deserved a chance. That chance evaporated when it was revealed that Bhaduria "lied" about having a law degree. On his résumé, he stated that he had an L.L.B. (Int.) from the University of London. The implication is that he holds a degree in International Law from a prestigious university. The truth is that "Int.," according to Bhaduria, stands for intermediate, indicating that he completed two years of study but didn't receive a degree.

After his resignation from the Liberal caucus, Bhaduria announced that he would stay on in Parliament as an independent. Members of all three parties in his riding organized against him, demanding that he resign his seat, but Bhaduria stood his ground, insisting that he had done nothing criminal. The whole episode has left a bad taste in the mouths of people who supported Bhaduria as well as given ammunition to those who assert that ethnic politicians will always be unreliable, nepotistic, and self-serving. Members of the Indo-Canadian community, originally unsympathetic to Bhaduria, found themselves divided over his plight. Some, like Ajit Jain, associate editor of *India Abroad*, called the attacks racist. Others weren't so sure that race was the issue.

Mr. Singh was not eager to discuss the Bhaduria case with me. "I don't know the man. He is not my MP. I don't know all the circumstances of his resignation."

Finally, after some days of deliberation and several discussions with me, Mr. Singh agreed to speak provided I printed his words exactly as he stated them, without any "editorializing" on my part.

"First of all, Jag Bhaduria didn't do anything illegal or immoral. Claiming to have a degree when you've only studied the subject is wrong, and I'm not defending that, but he didn't say he was a doctor and then attempt brain surgery. He didn't injure anyone. He didn't open up an office and start to practise law. There is such a thing in India as an intermediate stage when one is getting a professional degree, and at that stage the person is often allowed to work in a law office or whatever. So there is some background here for Mr. Bhaduria.

"Now, I can think of several reasons why Mr. Bhaduria would do this. First, he wanted to impress the people in his riding. He does have several quite legitimate degrees, so it seems, but many MPs are lawyers and he thought that mentioning his law studies would be of benefit to him. So he said that he had an intermediate degree. He didn't lie. He just didn't correct any misapprehension that might occur."

I point out to Mr. Singh that that might be construed as lying by omission.

"That is ridiculous. A lie is a lie. If he had said that he was a lawyer, he would be a liar. He said that he had studied towards a law degree and that is the truth. So he isn't lying."

I mention that it does seem like we're in the midst of a game of semantics.

"That is not correct. You are a reporter and you want me to help you. You put your best foot forward. You show me your book, your articles. You want to impress me with your veracity and scholarship. Mr. Bhaduria wanted to impress the voters and so he put down everything he thought would influence them. If you tell me you have a degree in journalism and later I find out you don't, then I would be angry because you lied to me. But if you say you've only studied journalism I have no cause for complaint. Besides, it's your work that I'm concerned with, not your studies."

I point out that I did provide Mr. Singh with concrete examples of my work, that he could judge me on my published merits.

"What did Mr. Bhaduria do but that? He has many hours of community service. He has taught physics. He must have had some qualities, other than this one mention of law studies, that impressed the voters. And it wasn't his race, I can tell you. More than Indians voted for him if he was elected to Parliament."

What Mr. Singh is saying does, after a while, begin to make sense. Although I'm still troubled by Bhaduria's rave against the board of education, I can believe that stress causes people to do odd and dangerous things.

Mr. Singh: "If Mr. Bhaduria were a businessman, would this degree be a concern? Certainly not. People would be looking to see if he was delivering the goods. We like to believe that there is a higher standard for politicians, but look back over the past years. There have been all sorts of resignations of Cabinet ministers for all kinds of things—sex scandals, taking bribes, abusing power. Compared to those, what has Mr. Bhaduria done so wrong?

"I have to conclude, and I don't wish to be intolerant, that Mr. Bhaduria's race is an issue. If he had been white, I don't think this degree would have been such an issue. But he is brown. Also, I have to say that in my own researches, I find that Mr. Bhaduria and his wife have publicly accused certain Canadians of acting in a racist manner against them. This is behind the letter that Mr. Bhaduria sent to the board of education, that he was passed over for promotion because of his race. Mrs. Bhaduria, also, has publicly protested this. Now, who released these letters to the press? Someone anonymous. So someone is out to get Mr. Bhaduria in hot water. I don't think that would happen if Mr. Bhaduria was white and his name was Smith, do you?"

I have to confess that I'm concerned about the moral and ethical content of parliament but I honestly don't see that Bhaduria's real or feigned degree makes much difference to his performance. Would the degree have been an issue if Bhaduria wasn't Indo-Canadian? Possibly. But in the past two years there have been attacks on other politicians of colour, including a charge of evading rent controls against Ontario MPP Zanana Akande. The charge was first found to be false; then it was proved that Akande was in fact *undercharging* her tenants. There was also the highly publicized resignation of Carlton Masters, Ontario's agent-general to the United States, after charges of sexual harassment. In April 1994, Akande announced her intention to leave politics and return to teaching. Masters, who resigned from a highly successful career in banking to become agent-general, is said to be embittered by the way the government handled the charges against him as well as by the results of an in-house investigation. (His case was still before the courts when this book went to press.)

Will the treatment of Bhaduria, Akande, and Masters—all of whom have considerable support from within and without their respective ethnic communities—mean that Blacks or East Indians will think twice about public office? Mr. Singh thinks not: "I believe it will stiffen resolve. If, as some suspect, there is racism involved in these attacks on these people, then I think it will encourage more Indians to get out and vote, to work for candidates. It is time for us to stop being children and become adults, to take our place in public life in this country. If we make mistakes, we can live with them and learn from them."

What is a perfectly natural evolution of his community to Mr. Singh —the move into political representation—is the end of the road for Della and Jack in B.C. "These people are fighting out ages-old ethnic wars in British Columbia," says Della. "Bombing planes, killing hundreds of people—their own people. I'm supposed to vote for that?"

Jack is less concerned about incidents of international terrorism than in continued growth of "an isolated and inward-looking community group. I do not see Asians—and I include the Hong Kong Chinese in this—as particularly civic-minded persons. They are out to get what they can for their people and the rest of us are expected to just go along.

"I don't believe it's race that's the problem. I think it's background. I come from a European tradition with a certain code of ethics, a certain moral background. You can call it Judaeo-Christian or WASP or whatever, but it's what I've built my life on and it's what my ancestors built this country on. Now these people come in and it's all just hocus-pocus to them, just like Confucianism or Hinduism is to me. But the laws of this country aren't about Confucianism or Hinduism, they're about British common law and British and French attitudes. The government just gives in and gives in and brings in thousands more each year, and those thousands all want their wives and parents and grandparents and whatever, and as soon as they get here the party who brought them in can count on their votes. So long as Ottawa keeps the floodgates open, they'll get those votes, and it doesn't make a damn that out here in British Columbia we're losing our Canadian identity. Hell, they're already calling Vancouver Hongkouver. Next, it'll be Hongcutta. There won't be any people like us left."

There is the crux. So long as the new arrivals were Europeans— folks like Liz's family, like Phil's grandparents, people like us—race wasn't an issue. True, there were tensions, ethnic slurs, unkind and unwelcome jokes at the expense of the newcomers. And there were fears. When I arrived in 1971, there were bitter outcries against

American professors "taking over" Canadian universities. There were complaints about British and American influence in Canadian literature, Canadian theatre, Canadian film and television. Canadian culture was a threatened entity, a fragile flower in desperate need of protection.

But nationality, not race, was the issue. And there was an easy end to it all. The Americans and the Brits became Canadians, blended in with the mainstream. The new immigrants, the ones who are an issue with Canadians, are black or brown or yellow or a mixture of all these and red besides.

The entire immigration issue can be described as a minefield. There's no argument that this is *the* issue of the next several decades, and it's one that isn't going to go away. But what is the problem?

According to Preston Manning and the Reformers, the problem is that Canada is letting in too many people. The solution is to reduce the numbers to 100,000 and link those numbers to jobs and training. In other words, family reunification and refugees go to the back of the queue.

Sergio Marchi, Minister of Immigration, has yielded somewhat to the Reformers' message, a clear signal that the Liberals have heard and understood the feelings of people like Della and Jack. In November 1994, Marchi announced a cut in immigration levels from 250,000 to 190,000. This is a clear retreat from a Liberal campaign promise not to cut immigration levels. Furthermore, in a break with past Liberal practice, the cuts are to come from the family reunification group. From now on, the fast track will only apply to spouses and dependent children under the age of 19. It will become more difficult for Canadians to sponsor parents and more distant relatives and sponsors will have to post cash bonds as guarantees that their relatives will not end up on welfare. The idea, according to Don DeVoretz of Simon Fraser University, is "to make the family reunification plan be paid for by the immigrants. It will also immediately shrink the family class category. It'll become self-regulating."

The new rules also mean more attention will be paid to independent immigrants—those with language and job skills and good educations—and Marchi actually raised refugee levels slightly. The cuts weren't enough to suit Preston Manning and the Reformers, but they were more than enough to get activists out demonstrating in defence of refugees and family-class immigrants. But the handwriting really is on the wall and Marchi knows it. The era of wide-open immigration into Canada is over.

One of the new voices in immigration is Daniel Stoffman, author of a highly critical 1993 study of immigration policy written for the C. D. Howe Institute. Mr. Stoffman believes that we are letting in too many of the wrong kinds of immigrants. He argues that the effect of immigrants on the Canadian economy is "revenue neutral" (read negligible) and that "if immigration does not affect the incomes of the members of the host community, then it follows that economic self-interest should not be used as a basis for immigration policy." In short, immigration isn't the route to rejuvenating Canadian society and protecting our standard of living. Furthermore, Stoffman argues, current immigration levels are too high, accelerating the pace of change in our cities, contributing to racial tensions and overburdening the social services. Stoffman's solution? Reduce numbers and focus on independents and business immigrants, letting in fewer family-class immigrants.

Prof. DeVoretz, disagrees again. Yes, he says, immigrants cost more at the beginning, requiring more services from education and social services, but these initial costs are far outweighed by the lifetime tax contributions, to say nothing of the consumer benefits, of immigrants. "There's no evidence to say that immigrants are a net draw on the treasury," he says. "All evidence points the other way."

What's remarkable about the four varying positions outlined above is that all of them rely on the same figures contained in an analysis published in 1991 by the Economic Council of Canada. *New Faces in the Crowd: Economic and Social Impacts of Immigration* does show that immigration has a negligible economic benefit. In fact, the figure the council came up with was, for every one million new immigrants, the economy grows by just $71 for each Canadian.

But, working with figures from the 1986 census, the last figures available to them, the council showed that federal and provincial governments spent $432 million on services to immigrants, or just $17 for each Canadian. The researchers also found that the proportion of welfare recipients among recent immigrants was smaller than among people born in Canada, and that immigration does not take jobs away from Canadians because, historically, jobs have been created at approximately the same rate as the level of immigration. The study goes on to say that, although *recent* immigrants have higher unemployment rates than their Canadian-born counterparts, after a few years the unemployment rate was the same as that for other Canadians.

Who gets in and on what criteria? What part does compassion play in the process? Families versus skilled workers. In this climate, it's clear that no hard-and-fast rules can be devised, and it's also clear that, in order to make room for one person, another has to be delayed or denied. If the experts can all read the same figures and come to very different conclusions about the benefits of immigrants to Canada, then what are ordinary people—both those eager to welcome cherished relatives and those who pay the bills to Canadianize those relatives—supposed to do?

In my neighbourhood of Lansdowne and Bloor in Toronto, you can see every hue of the Canadian rainbow. Some of them don't like others and some don't speak. They are not a happy, harmonious mosaic like the multiculturalism czars would have us believe, but we all have something in common. We own our homes and we enjoy our little piece of the Canadian Dream. We want police protection from loiterers, drug merchants, flesh peddlers, and anyone else who doesn't "fit in" to our orderly little neighbourhood.

The most recent immigrants are South American, and it's common to see descendants of the Maya shopping, chatting amiably in Spanish, selling milk and pop in the corner store. You can also see them being rousted by the police for being potential drug dealers. Anyone who looks so obviously South American and Mestizo must be peddling crack, the theory goes.

When a real drug peddler was spotted recently, the neighbourhood fairly shrieked with rage, and I honestly worried that the next step would be some kind of vigilantism. Only promises from the police (and hourly patrols by marked police cars) kept the rage at bay. "The bastards should be shot on sight," was a commonly expressed wish. When Raymond Lawrence, a Black man suspected of being a drug dealer, was shot dead by police just four blocks away, no one, including the Black families on the street, shed a tear.

At a recent public meeting to discuss the problems in the neighbourhood, I met Tamils, Pakistanis, Portuguese, Italians, Blacks, and South Asians. It seemed that every colour of the globe and every language in Babel was present that night. There were kids translating for grandmas and a lot of very worried people who wanted something done. In that room, full of immigrants, the Canadian mosaic was alive. The topic of the evening was crime prevention. The answer for a good many people was to control immigration. There were only three dissenting voices when the group agreed that keeping certain people out would reduce crime. The groups to be banned were Vietnamese refugees and South Americans. "Our" immigrants were good, thrifty, and industrious and should be allowed in.

8

MULTICULTURALISM RUNS AMOK

"JUST WHAT THE HELL IS MULTICULTURALISM, ANYWAY?" asks
Frank Lyons of Kelowna, B.C. Mr. Lyons can be excused for sound-
ing a bit confused about Canada's national policy on relations
between Canadians of varied ethnic backgrounds. Anyone should be
forgiven for getting confused by a lofty-sounding government policy that has turned out to be a major industry, an agent of political
control, a method of cultural dissemination and for manipulating
ethnic groups.

In Kelowna, B.C., for example, Mr. Lyons says Japanese interests
are buying up ski resorts and golf links and turning them into private playgrounds for Japanese tourists—no Canadians allowed,
either as employees or participants.

Mr. Lyons would feel right at home with the North York, Ontario,
shopkeeper who found himself turfed out of his store in an upscale
mall because the new owners—Chinese—wanted stores that would
reflect the new character of the neighbourhood—also Chinese.

Or perhaps he could share views with Michael Valpy, the *Globe and Mail*'s senior columnist, who was surprised to discover that at his son's school, a multicultural Festival of Light, held to replace more traditional Christmas celebrations, wouldn't allow the singing of Christmas carols.

All of these people are happy to support what they see as the benefits of official multicultural policy: benefits that offer lots of diversity in cultural life, from flashy extravaganzas like Toronto's Caribana festival to Dragon Boat races in Regina. But those are urban events. What multiculturalism often means in most of Canada is the local Chinese-Canadian restaurant serving egg rolls alongside the grilled cheese, or a pierogi fundraiser at the local Legion hall.

The catchphrases of multiculturalism abound. There's unity in diversity, or the Tory cry of "community of communities," and even the constitutional angle in "distinct society."

From one place to the next, from one person to the next, multiculturalism has a different meaning depending upon who you are, where you live, where you came from, and how long you've lived in Canada. Its successes—the specialized counselling services for immigrants, the support for community events, the funding of arts and crafts that would otherwise be ignored or forgotten, the support for small cultural enclaves—are often invisible and ignored. Its problems and failures, on the other hand, are writ large, feature stories in the media, sad addenda to the conflicts around immigration policy, money, race, and power.

To see failure firsthand, we need go no farther than Mississauga, Ontario, to a sorry spot on Dixon Road. There are towers as far as the eye can follow. Today, it's raining, a steady, dreary grey drizzle. In the unfurnished lobby of a highrise, two women in hijab— Muslim head veils—stand quietly watching a pair of toddlers chase each other back and forth. The women turn away when I approach. I am not welcome here. This is the place where the bright legal vision of the Multiculturalism Act meets the acid test of reality. Here, multiculturalism has failed.

These buildings are condominiums, part of the great Toronto building boom of the 1980s, the days when the money was going to go on forever, the real-estate prices would go higher and higher, the buyers would fight to be the first in line to buy. That was then.

Now, some of the apartments are vacant, abandoned by people who couldn't carry the payments and who just left the keys and walked away. Others are owned by landlords who bought them as investments, short-term rollovers that would double in price within a couple of years. When the prices crashed, the speculators were left with the apartments. So they rent them out and hope the condo market will improve to the point where they can sell for what they paid. The trend is not hopeful.

Finally, there is a group of owner-residents, mostly older people, so-called empty nesters who have sold the house with the yard and moved into the condo for a peaceful, maintenance-free old age. Mixed in here and there are some first-time buyers, young couples who thought this was the route to the suburban dream of the split-level with the patio, the fruit trees in the yard, and the flower borders along the walk. These people are mostly white, but there are some South Asians and a smattering of Orientals as well.

"I'm sick of being called racist by the Toronto press," says an owner who has lived in York Condominium Corporation for several years. "My husband and I have all we own invested in this place. We saved for five years to get a down payment. We put thousands of dollars in extras in our unit, top-of-the-line everything. And now it's worthless. Just worthless. All because of them."

"Them" are refugees recently arrived in Toronto from Somalia, where thousands of people have died in a vicious civil war that has been raging more than ten years. It is dangerous just to walk down a street in the capital of Mogadishu. Political power changes almost by the day. People are starving by the thousands. If danger to life and limb is the criteria for a "legitimate" refugee, Somalis qualify.

There are three thousand Somalis in York CC, almost all of them tenants. They are all Black and virtually all are Muslim.

"What we left is unbelievable to you here," says Abdullah Udore. "My father was shot in the street on his way to get water. We could not get food, leave our homes. Even in our homes we weren't safe.

Children were killed sitting at the window. There is no law there, no protection for anyone."

Mr. Udore has been in Canada just over a year. His English is not very good and he finds communication with Canadians frustrating because he cannot make himself clear. He wants to tell me that in Somalia he was an educated man, a person with a profession, but he cannot find the appropriate words. He is clearly intelligent and, in his native language, expressive.

Mr. Udore, his wife, and infant son live with another family in a spacious three-bedroom apartment. The adults each have a bedroom and the three children share the third. While his wife prepares coffee and tea, Mr. Udore shows me around. The furniture is somewhat battered secondhand and there isn't much of it, but there is a lovely Somali carving by the door and everything is clean. "My wife washes every day," says Mr. Udore. "The people here say we are dirty. Look around. Floors, walls, even the children's toys. She washes every day."

Mrs. Udore is, indeed, washing. The tub in the bathroom is full of sheets soaking. She doesn't speak any English and "she is very shy," says Mr. Udore. "But she washes by hand because she says the electric machines don't clean enough. After she washes, she puts everything in the machine."

The Udores are very happy to be in this nice place. They found it through the Somali grapevine. Someone moved out and the Udores moved in. The sharing family, who have been here for two years, are the legitimate leaseholders, but they cannot afford the rent unless they share.

Refugees are not allowed to work (this restriction, in force when I met with the Somalis, was lifted in early 1994), so almost all the recent arrivals are receiving welfare. Money is tight, and the Udores admit that it would be nice if they could get another small family into the apartment. There are few cars, not much entertainment. The Udore extended family has a small colour television that they watch without interest. The older children like *Sesame Street*. The Udores watch it to improve their English. Most of their social life consists of conversations with other Somalis about events in Somalia and about how to get along and get ahead in their new country.

Every day, Mr. Udore attends an ESL class at a nearby community centre. He points vaguely in the direction of the centre but cannot tell me much about it because he doesn't have enough vocabulary. I gather that he wishes the pace of the lessons was faster. "I want to get a job," he says. "I need to work."

Mr. Udore knows that the older white residents of the building don't like him and his wife, don't want them in their building, believe that they are lazy, ignorant, and dirty and that their presence drives property values down. "I have no idea where these things come from," he says. "You look. Are we so bad?"

I go through the litany of complaints about Somalis that the Udore's neighbours have listed. They cover the whole range of "us" versus "them" complaints. The Somalis won't learn English. They are hostile and glare at residents. They are unfriendly and stick together. They entertain all night, talk loudly in the halls, congregate in the halls, the lobby, the parking lot. They sleep ten to fifteen in a room, just tossing down mattresses. They spit everywhere—in the elevators, on the floors, out on the walks. They urinate and defecate in the bushes by the buildings, they urinate in the elevators, the halls, the garbage chutes. They have never heard of garbage. The children are brats, out of control, swearing, defiant. The Somalis don't respect Canadian laws, don't abide by Canadian rules, aren't good tenants, good neighbours. These complaints are, almost to the word, identical to comments made by Germans against Turkish immigrants in their country. Some of the same comments were made about East Germans after German reunification.

What is not on this list, but what does influence the thinking of the owner-occupier residents, is that the rapid influx of Somalis, who now total more than 35 per cent of the residents of the condominiums, has been a social and financial disaster. The owners, faced with what they consider a tidal wave of refugees "foisted on us by the damned government," as one owner put it, are losing their shirts and their tempers. "My unit is worth 30, even 50 per cent less than I paid for it. So much for our financial planning. I work full time and so does my husband, and we come home to this."

"This" is a group of Somali teenagers hanging around the lobby. I'm sure there must be a park or a mall nearby. In these developments, there's always a mall or a park somewhere, but I can't spot it. The kids are propped against the walls, chatting and snacking. They aren't loud, but they are ubiquitous and, when they notice us looking at them, shoot us a collective icy glare. "How would you like to get that every time you left home?" asks the owner-occupier.

I point out that it is raining, that the kids may not have any place to go. Teenagers congregate. It's what they do best. "I know," says one owner in a resigned tone. "I know they're crowded into those places. I know there are huge extended families in apartments and I know they don't have any place to just be, but I don't want them in the public spaces of my building. It looks bad. And no matter what you think, they're not nice. They're nasty."

What I think is that both Mr. Udore and the condo owner are telling the truth as they see it. Mr. Udore and his family are doing the best they can with the skimpy resources at their disposal. They are lonely and far from home, don't speak the language, have very little money, and are forbidden to earn more. The resident owners, however, are entitled to quiet enjoyment of their homes.

What is at fault is a government that allows three thousand people from a completely alien culture to settle into six Mississauga apartment blocks, with no support services, and expects everybody to get along. "We don't control where they live after they receive official refugee status," says a spokesperson from Immigration Canada, who refuses to give me a name. "We've heard enough about the Somalis. This is a free country. People can live where they like."

They couldn't always and, in some cases, they still can't. European immigrants of forty and fifty years ago were allowed entry only if they went to specified locations, which in those days meant small farming communities. Today, immigrant entrepreneurs are directed by immigration officers to areas where their particular business has the greatest chance of success in creating Canadian jobs. An entrepreneur, no matter how well heeled, hasn't much chance of emigrating on the promise to start up an upscale Chinese restaurant in Toronto. He may be encouraged to consider Halifax or Winnipeg or

Regina or any of many smaller communities where the local hamburg palace could use some competition.

But these are economic issues, not issues of human rights, and, in truth, the government would be in serious breach of its own human rights code if it attempted to control where immigrants live. Besides, when it all works, as it does in the Chinatowns of Vancouver, the Ukrainian neighbourhoods of Winnipeg, Toronto's "Little Bombay" or "Little Italy," immigrant clustering is a real boon to everything from tourism to dining out. In Canada, ethnic charm is big business.

But the Somalis lack the charm and the money essential to become trendy. They haven't established any little restaurants serving Somali native dishes. They're still too shell-shocked from war to hold dance-fests or community singalongs. In point of fact, the Somalis have been an immigration nightmare for more than six months. They first made the headlines when the owner-residents of the Mississauga complex hired guards and dogs to keep them from congregating in the public areas of the buildings. The Somalis, who abhor dogs on religious grounds, were infuriated, claimed that the guards were deliberately sicking the animals on Somali women. They also said that the guards were harassing them, rousting them as they walked by, ticketing their cars for no reason, insulting their women and children. They complained that the dogs were named Mohammad and Allah. The guards, hired from a local security agency, deny all this.

On the Dixon Road battle line, at a public meeting of owners, a South African Black declared that if she could learn to adjust to life in Canada "so could the Somalis." A man from India said they were "bred" to mob violence. A Pakistani Muslim said they were insulting and aggressive towards her. The meeting ended with a grey-haired woman, a veritable picture of the beloved grandma, standing up and saying, "If the Somalis don't like our rules they should go back where they come from. We don't need them." She was roundly cheered.

Mr. Udore admits that there have been some regrettable incidents on the Somali side. Children have been rude, "but you must understand that that is the exception. And you must understand that some of these children have seen things that no child should see, some have been tortured, terrified. They see guards with dogs and they think of torture. They are frightened and they react." Other Somalis report that their children have been attacked at the local school, that they have been beaten and verbally abused by white youths and by Jamaican gangs.

Reports of excrement, urine, and dirt are all untrue, says Udore. What is true is the overcrowding. "We have large families and we like to live together. We draw our strength from our families." There are also cultural considerations. Somalia is a tribal nation. "Our clan is our history, our place, it is everything to us," explains Udore. "A member of my clan, even if he is not related to me by blood, is a brother. If he comes to me, I treat him well. He can share my home, my food. If he dies and his wife is left alone, I must look after her, see that she is cared for. When a member of my clan comes here, we have a celebration. We invite other clan members. We don't question these things. It's the way life is."

The cultural divide between Mr. Udore's tribal consciousness and the average North American idea of life and entertainment is vast but, if the forces of multiculturalism were working, it should be bridgeable. There should be a way to explain Mr. Udore's lifestyle to other residents and to develop a working consensus that everyone can live with. That's what should happen in a perfect world.

Yet multiculturalism is not about cobbling out a consensus between dissenting groups. It is about politics and votes and jobs and power. Once the Somalis are established in Canada, past their refugee period, multiculturalism will give them grants to start up community newspapers, to hold community festivals. There will be grants for salaries to members of the community to serve other Somali newcomers. None of this will do much for the hatred and rancour on Dixon Road, but it will pull the Somalis, along with other ethnic groups, into the multicultural industry. It will also ensure that, when votes are needed, the Somali voters will remember who sent those grants and financed those newspapers and bought advertisements in them, and support the party who provided them.

The next time I speak with Mr. Udore, some weeks after our first meeting, he is in what can only be described as a state of controlled rage. He has had a relative telephone me because he is afraid that he will not be understood. He wants me to write an article for the Toronto *Star* and the *Globe and Mail* and to call the television stations. He and the entire Somali community have been the victims of the "most serious lies."

When we meet, the atmosphere is considerably changed. No more coffee and sweets, no more open atmosphere. Mr. Udore has three men with him. No one gives me a name. One man sits beside me and tells me he is going to interpret. He is also reading my notes as I write. I explain that I have no access to the media, but I promise to put what the men say in my book.

The genesis of their rage is two separate but related news accounts. The first is a report, widely disseminated, that the children and one of the several wives of Somali warlord Gen. Mohammed Aidid are living in London, Ontario, as refugees on welfare. The gentlemen in the room regard this—correctly, I might add—as a dreadful invasion of privacy. Mrs. Aidid has been hounded by reporters day and night. Aidid, who, at this time, is widely regarded in the West as the fiend incarnate of Somalia, "is not an evil man," says Mr. Udore. "There are many complicating issues that are hard to explain." Whatever the issues, however, he feels that the safety of Aidid's wife and children shouldn't be jeopardized by the Canadian and American media.

Then there is a report from Immigration Canada, an internal report assembled by the immigration intelligence branch and written by an employee of the department's Eastern Ontario office, that says, among other derogatory statements, that Somalis are running welfare scams, "pillaging" the Ontario welfare system to send millions of dollars back to Somalia to fund the civil war. "How can such lies be printed?" asks one of Udore's companions. "Why were they read out in the Ontario Legislature?"

These are excellent questions for which I have no answers. A copy of the report was obtained by Lyn McLeod, leader of the Liberal opposition. Ms. McLeod, believing it to be an accurate account, read out sections in the Legislature, a venue protected from

Canada's libel laws. You also cannot libel a group. Since no individual Somali was named, no libel occurred. That is why special hate legislation is so important.

Immigration Canada and the newly appointed minister for immigration, Sergio Marchi, acted quickly to deny the allegations and to point out that the report was in error on many grounds, that it was not part of immigration policy, and that it had no influence on the acceptance or rejection of refugee applications. Mr. Udore and his companions don't believe a word of this.

"These are lies, just lies. They have been in every newspaper, on television. People believe them. They believe that all Somalis are stealing from Canadians, that we are buying guns, that we don't belong here. If life was hard before, now it is even harder. If the members of the refugee boards think we are criminals, 'pillaging' the welfare funds, then it will be that much more difficult to get refugee status. They have made criminals of every Somali in Canada."

This is a tiny bit over the top, but not much. The report, whose content is enough to enrage any taxpayer, is couched in language that can at best be called racist and at worst downright inflammatory.

Everyone, from the minister to the Eastern Ontario divisional bureaucrats, have since admitted that both the content and the tone of the report were wrong, but the Somalis believe it is part of an attempt to discredit them, to show them as less desirable immigrants, unworthy refugees. It is "a smear campaign," as one calls it. They are deeply offended that Liberal Leader McLeod, who was responsible for making the report public, has never apologized. "She has said that she was misled," says Udore, "but she never said she was sorry."

The result of this sorry affair is that things at York CC have degenerated further. Residents who formerly saw the Somalis simply as unwanted tenants are enraged at the idea of living with what they perceive as a gang of warmongering welfare cheats. "How do they expect us to fit in when they single us out as criminals?" asks Mr. Udore. "Would they write the same things about white Bosnians?"

That is a truly loaded question. There have been dozens of reports of atrocities and counteratrocities on all sides in the former Yugoslavia, but, to give Udore his due, there have been no reports insinuating that Bosnian refugees in Canada are engaging in welfare fraud or that funds sent to relatives in Bosnia are going to support the civil war. Bosnian children are seen as victims of violence, not brats. Bosnian Muslims are seen as victims of religious oppression, not "nasty" outsiders. But then, there are no condo complexes with three thousand Bosnian refugees crammed into them—possibly because Bosnian immigrants and refugees can rely on well-established relatives and community services to assist them in integrating into Canadian life. The Somalis have none of these.

What is clear at York CC is that trust, both in the individual and in the government, has broken down on both sides. The owners have the right to the peaceful enjoyment of their homes. The Somalis, who came here in good faith, have the right to have their persons and their religion respected. The cultural clash, however, is a different issue. The owners see themselves as victims of a faceless and heartless government policy that has cast thousands of people with completely alien habits into their community. The Somalis see themselves as victimized twice—once by the war that forced them out of their homes, and now by the Canadians who don't want them and don't like them. "Just what is multiculturalism about in this circumstance?" asks Mr. Udore.

A resident owner replies: "This is multiculturalism run rampant."

Multiculturalism is the first thing any new immigrant learns about Canada. It is what makes Canada different from the assimilate-or-leave attitude of America. Here, so the policy goes, many racial and ethnic groups can live together in harmony, maintaining their cultures and heritages. There are heritage languages in the schools, Caribbean festivals in the east, Ukrainian fêtes in the west, and Dragon Boat races in Vancouver harbour. From sea to shining sea, Canada celebrates its diversity.

Well, sort of.

The fact is that multiculturalism policy is recent, its roots are shallow, and its fruits not fully ripe. It began, as so much in

Canada does, with a compromise between the two founding races over the use of French and English. The 1963 Royal Commission on Bilingualism and Biculturalism was appointed to recommend "what steps should be taken to develop the Canadian confederation on the basis of equal partnership between the two founding races, taking into account the contribution made by other ethnic groups."

This was the first recognition by a royal commission of the dramatic change in Canadian society created by post–Second World War immigration. From a tidy little Franco-British colony, Canada had evolved into a multiracial, multilingual, multiethnic mélange. When language was an issue, ethnic groups whose first languages were neither French nor English wanted to be recognized and they didn't want their contributions to the building of Canada ignored.

The royal commission agreed. It recommended much higher priority, attention, and support for ethnic groups, provided it was done in the context of Canada's two charter groups and two official languages. This policy, called "Multiculturalism within a Bilingual Framework," was announced by Prime Minister Pierre Trudeau in 1971.

There was also a less noble motive for enshrining multiculturalism in government policy. The Liberals had traditionally drawn much of their electoral support from their base in Quebec, but Quebec was volatile. The Parti Québécois was building strength, and there was change afoot. Who knew how long the Liberals could count on Quebec. Multiculturalism ensured the support of the ethnic communities of Canada for the Liberals. They were the backup force if Quebec voters turned against the party.

This may seem a shade cynical, but politics is a cynical business. The fact is that multiculturalism suited the Canadian times. There was a vague feeling of goodwill towards Canadians of non-British and non-French origin and a belief that their concerns should have the recognition recommended by the royal commission.

But the Liberals never intended multiculturalism to be anything more than a modest program, a contribution to the community, and a way to keep the government's relations with the ethnic communities manageable. Anything more, the Liberals knew, would be unalterably opposed by Quebec, which was at that time opposed to multiculturalism of any kind. There could be no increased influence or status for multicultural groups within Canadian politics, and the budget and aims of the program were to be kept small.

As envisioned by the Trudeau Liberals, multiculturalism was to be mainly a function of grants to cultural groups, some establishment of Canadian ethnic studies, the writing of some ethnic histories, and the inclusion of ethnic materials in the national museums, the National Archives, and the National Film Board. There was also the Canadian Consultative Council on Multiculturalism, with 101 members from forty-seven ethnocultural backgrounds.

There is a tendency to regard multiculturalism as motherhood, a warm and fuzzy feeling we get when we have dinner at a good Thai restaurant or attend an ethnic conference and see dozens of cultures on display, and, had the Liberals' original vision held, that's about what it would be. But the ethnic community wanted more and they got it.

Multiculturalism is the state policy of Canada for dealing with other races and ethnic groups within this country. It is an official act of Parliament known as the Act for the Preservation and Enhancement of Multiculturalism in Canada, passed in 1988.

According to that act, the multiculturalism policy of Canada is designed to:

> *(a) recognize and promote the understanding that multiculturalism reflects the cultural and racial diversity of Canadian society and acknowledges the freedom of all members of Canadian society to preserve, enhance, and share their cultural heritage;*
>
> *(b) recognize and promote the understanding that multiculturalism is a fundamental characteristic of the Canadian heritage and identity and that it provides an invaluable resource in the shaping of Canada's future;*
>
> *(c) promote the full and equitable participation of individuals and communities of all origins in the continuing*

evolution and shaping of all aspects of Canadian society and assist them in the elimination of any barrier to such participation;

(d) recognize the existence of communities whose members share a common origin and their historic contribution to Canadian society, and enhance their development;

(e) ensure that all individuals receive equal treatment and equal protection under the law, while respecting and valuing their diversity;

(f) encourage and assist the social, cultural, economic, and political institutions of Canada to be both respectful and inclusive of Canada's multicultural character;

(g) promote the understanding and creativity that arise from the interaction between individuals and communities of different origins;

(h) foster the recognition and appreciation of the diverse cultures of Canadian society and promote the reflection and the evolving expressions of those cultures;

(i) preserve and enhance the use of languages other than English and French, while strengthening the status and use of the official languages of Canada; and

(j) advance multiculturalism throughout Canada in harmony with the national commitment to the official languages of Canada.

In addition, this act establishes the Canadian Human Rights Commission and makes French and English the legal languages of the country. There are eleven implementation programs as well as advisory committees and recommendations for work with provincial human rights commissions. Everything, in short, would seem to be covered.

There has been a lot of motherhood talk and multicultural money under the bridge since 1971.

From the first, multicultural policy and multicultural implementation were at odds. In truth, the Liberals had never really thought through what multiculturalism was to be. They wanted a patronage conduit to insure votes and a recognition of ethnic diversity, but what the Liberals wanted to keep modestly small, the ethnic communities wanted large. Early on, there were unrealistic expectations of grants, ill-defined roles for both community groups and government, as well as the shifting of multiculturalism from one ministry to another, keeping it fragile. The Consultative Council on Multiculturalism, largely a token body, was too unwieldy to accomplish any action and was replaced in 1983 by the Canadian Multicultural Council.

Throughout its history, multiculturalism has achieved some successes. It does affirm the role of ethnic communities in Canada and it does provide a way of handling the relationship between government and those communities. It has funded some worthwhile cultural projects and provided status and security for the newest and smallest members of Canada's cultural mosaic.

The most important contribution, however, is in the area of language. Multiculturalism has given us the words to describe, in a completely neutral and non-pejorative way, the ethnic diversity that surrounds us. It has had a beneficial and a civilizing effect on our world, and we should think very carefully about it before we abandon or change the policy.

But multiculturalism, in that idealistic and inventive vein, was born at a time when there was money for grants and services and facilitators and bureaucracies. The immigrants whose leaders made their submissions to the 1963 royal commission were by and large Europeans. They may not have been British or French, but they were white, Christian, and nurtured on Western democratic principles. They were not Black Africans with clan ties to deposed warlords. And they were not what multiculturalism has become.

There are as many critics of multiculturalism as there are supporters. There are those, like the members of the Association to Preserve English in Canada, who insist that multiculturalism is no more than a guise to destroy the mother tongue. Preston Manning and the Reform Party see multiculturalism as the great equalizer, the way to make Quebec just another province and French just one language among many. The French, of course, see it as the opposite, a way to control other languages in Quebec, keeping French paramount.

There are those, usually recent arrivals, who see it as too little and those, usually "old" Canadians, who think that it is an expensive frill that we can no longer afford. It has been seen as a platform for ethnic minorities to seize political power and as a cynical attempt to divide and conquer Canadian minority groups. Not surprisingly, some of multiculturalism's most vocal critics are members of the multicultural intelligentsia.

Is multiculturalism the forum to combat racism in Canada? Marlene Nourbese Philip says it's not. In the essay "Why Multiculturalism Can't End Racism," in her collection *Frontiers*, Philip states the conflict inherent in the concept of multiculturalism: "The configuration of power appears to be designed to equalize power among the individual satellite cultures, and between the collectivity of those cultures and the two central cultures, the French and English. The mechanism of multiculturalism is, therefore, based on a presumption of equality, a presumption which is not necessarily borne out in reality."

Ah, reality. The real world of Somali refugees intruding into the rosy vision.

Philip goes on: "Because it pretends to be what it is not—a mechanism to equalize all cultures within Canada—it ought not to surprise us that multiculturalism would be silent about issues of race and colour."

The flaw in the mechanism, for Philip and other members of visible minorities, is Canadian systemic racism, the fruits of European racism that travelled with Europeans wherever they settled: "He took with him this particular gospel—that the Native and indigenous peoples he encountered, who were also not white, were to be brutalized, enslaved, maimed, or killed and, where, necessary, used to enrich him personally and/or his particular European country.

"Wherever you find the European outside Europe, there you will find this particular pattern and method of settlement. The settlement of Canada was no exception to this rule."

Philip calls racism the "glue that holds the edifice of white supremacy together." It permeates our society, creating prejudices between multicultural groups "because racism is not restricted only to relations between white and Black people."

The net result of all this is that "Black people of African heritage will be found at the bottom of the multicultural pool. And below them will probably be found Natives....

"When you are black-skinned, it often matters little if the person refusing to rent to you is Polish, Anglo- or Italian-Canadian. The result is the same. And multiculturalism, as we presently know it, has no answers to these or other problems such as the confrontations between the police forces in urban areas like Toronto and Montreal and the African Canadian communities that live there....

"In short, multiculturalism, as we know it, has no answers for the problems of racism...unless it is combined with a clearly articulated policy of antiracism, directed at rooting out the effects of racist and white supremacist thinking....But despite it's many critics, multiculturalism will not disappear. Too many people benefit from it, and it is far too fancy a piece of window-dressing for a government to get rid of."

Philip's stinging indictment should make people sit up and listen. When she talks about the people who benefit, she's talking about, literally, tens of thousands of jobs that range from the cheery bureaucrats in federal and provincial offices to the reporters at the local ethnic newspaper. There are the consultants and the planners and the translators and the myriad other small community businesses hiring people who are often newcomers themselves. This is an industry that has direct economic benefits that people can see at the local level, and so Philip's comments about window-dressing have more truth than anyone, particularly those engaged in the multiculturalism industry itself, will admit.

Philip's more equitable and antiracist, multiracial New Jerusalem is not at hand, not in this decade of deficits, cutbacks, and shrinking government resources. In the 1993 election, Jean Chrétien and the Liberals ran their usual appeals to the ethnic voters. There were nomination meetings that turned into ethnic free-for-alls as one group's supporters—"instant Liberals"—slugged it out to see which potential candidate could drag in the most bodies to vote. There were the ads in the ethnic newspapers—ads which, in some cases, are the major source of funding for these papers—and visits to important ethnic ridings.

And it all paid off. In the year the Liberals knew the Quebec vote was lost, and when they were beset by Reform in the west, the ethnic vote came through. The window-dressing was enough.

Another critique of multiculturalism is that it keeps the ethnic community divided, prevents the creation of a Canadian identity by allowing new Canadians or hyphenated Canadians to become simply "Canadians." The writer Neil Bissoondath, who was born in Trinidad and is of East Indian origin, is an outspoken critic of multiculturalism, for he believes it fosters the kind of tribalism that separates groups and races.

Bissoondath, who lives in Montreal, differs from many ethnic writers in another way. While Nourbese Philip, and the East Indian author Bharati Mukherjee, see Canada as an extremely racist society, Bissoondath does not. Speaking to Aruna Srivastava in the book *Other Solitudes*, a collection of short fiction by and interviews with authors of many heritages, Bissoondath states: "I think every country is racist, unless it is a country that has only one race living in it. But Canada is less racist than most countries I can think of."

Bharati Mukherjee has often criticized Canada for being more racist than the United States, a position Bissoondath doesn't share. Bharati, he says, "she prefers the United States because there everything is up front. An American doesn't like you because of the colour of your skin, you will know it, whereas in Canada people will smile and be polite and not let you know it. And therefore Canada is a more racist country. I would much rather have a racist behave in the Canadian way: smile and be polite....Canadians, even when they are racist, realize that it's not a nice thing to be."

As for multiculturalism, Bissoondath sees it as a barrier to becoming a Canadian. He's not for the absorption model of the U.S., but he doesn't think hiving off the ethnic communities each into their own "ghetto" is productive either. "People who arrive and find themselves living in their little ethnic community, never engaging with society. That's what I think has to be avoided because a person ends up in a way caged by their cultural baggage. I know too many people from the Caribbean who insist on living here as if they were still back there, and then resenting being told that there are certain ways of doing things here."

Our ways, our laws, our rules. These are the words one hears from opponents of multiculturalism. Ethnic groups will not become Canadianized if they continue to live in their cultural enclaves. Bissoondath: "I don't think we should expect the greater society to adjust to our ways; I think that's calling for a kind of anarchy because there are simply so many groups. There has to be an across-the-board standard of what it is to be Canadian. And that's where immigrants have to make a certain adjustment, just as society has to make an adjustment too. But sometimes I think we ask the society to go too far."

Bissoondath is "wary" of the assertion of ethnic identity, an identity that, he points out, can be misconstrued. The hyphenated Canadian is not for him. "To be called a Trinidadian Canadian to me conjures a picture of someone who, in March or April, whenever they have the carnival in Toronto, dresses up in a costume to jump and dance in the streets, while drinking illegally That has nothing to do with me."

As expected, Bissoondath's stand isn't popular among defenders of Canadian multicultural policy. They are particularly incensed that he, as a major Canadian author, a winner of the Governor General's Award for fiction, a prime recipient of the perceived cultural benefits derived from the increased ethnic visibility, should have criticisms of the program and the policy. These are the polite critics. Others, less refined, simply claim that Bissoondath himself is indulging in a bit of racist gibe, a position taken to satisfy the white powers who read and publish his books.

Bissoondath doesn't see it that way and he's not supportive of cries of racism in the police force or the education system either.

"I'm fearful of people overreacting: screaming racism simply because the two people involved happen to be of different races or different colours. Whenever there's a problem in Toronto between the police and a Black man, it's always claimed to be racism. I'm afraid of people overusing the word. I got tired of the screams of racism. I'm very wary of that because there are truly racial incidents—but if you cry wolf often enough, people will not pay attention any more, and racism is such a powerful charge, it's got to be reserved for when it clearly is needed."

The confusion between what is multicultural, what is racist, and what is simple cultural survival has reached its apex in the simmering cultural stew of Quebec. In Quebec, culture is French. Multiculturalism, once seen as a possible Trojan Horse to erode the foundations of French, is now seen by some Quebec intellectuals as a trivial side issue. Novelist, essayist, and journalist Jacques Godbout, in an interview in *Other Solitudes*, refers to it in terms of consumption.

Godbout's vision of Quebec is what he calls pluri-ethnic; there will be many cultures and races in a Quebec unified by one language. "Pluri-ethnicity considered as a diversity of expressions seems to me a concept which is inappropriate and in fact politicized. It is part of a pluricultural vision of the world which sees each writer as a kind of deputy of his or her cultural group....I think that multiculturalism is something like those ethnic fast-food areas you find in shopping centres of the third generation across Canada. Life, thought, literature would become a bit like these super-cafeterias. When you feel the need for a bit of Italianness, you could go out and get the literary equivalent of a pizza. This is a reductive conception of ethnicity, culture, and food."

What stands in the way of this pluri-ethnic vision, the enlargement of the Quebec cultural life, is the instability of the French language. "The unfortunate aspect of the yet unresolved language problem here—and it is unlikely that it will be resolved soon— is that it keeps writers and intellectuals from doing their work. The quality of French in Quebec is in certain milieux quite correct, but in others it's quite mediocre. The language which is spoken and taught in schools should be challenged. But how can I talk about the kind of French which will be taught to immigrants, of the passage from the idiomatic spoken language of the past to a more open kind of code, how can I begin to question these norms when French is not yet a stable and recognized reality? And even more, how can we approach the normal intellectual questioning of self in relation to others, of racism and of multiculturalism?"

Godbout points out that important Quebec cultural institutions that should be asking the questions, engaging in the education process of immigrants, are not doing it because "they are still fixed on the question of survival. Just as the French-Canadian Catholic clergy kept us in a state of suffocation by obliging us to think about sin and the utopian vision of a non-existent world, English-Canadian society is now obliging us, by its laws and its policies, to focus our attention on a single and sterile issue. We are still living the legacy of Pierre Elliott Trudeau."

Trudeau, the Northern magus. The visionary who imposed his will on a squabbling and divided land. Two cultures, two languages, one vision, with room for the rest at the table. Nourbese Philip is right: in the multicultural mosaic, the others were supposed to be the also-rans, the bridesmaids. Trudeau the fierce federalist saw politics as an opening to rectify a collection of cultural mistakes. He made French essential to the public service, created a demand for bilingual education, took the smart young Montrealers into politics and turned them into cabinet ministers and deputies and ambassadors. He repatriated the Constitution and fought like a bobcat against the Mulroney concept of the distinct society as laid out in the Meech Lake accord.

On the rare occasions that he emerges from his Montreal redoubt, Trudeau hurls a thunderbolt, reducing the politicians who have succeeded him to pygmy status. In the west, they still hate him because he rammed French down their throats, and in Quebec they rail against him because he didn't ram it far enough.

"In many minds, Trudeau and multiculturalism and the slap in the face from English Canada are linked," says Guy (not his real name), a Quebec entrepreneur. "He is both revered and hated. I detest what he says about federalism but I respect him more than any other politician in Canada."

I met Guy when I went to Montreal to speak to a group of businesspeople about Hong Kong immigration. At that meeting I said, as I have said before, that I don't understand the language issue in Quebec. As an American, even after twenty years in Canada, I just don't get it. Guy, whose mother is American and who attended American universities, offered to explain it all to me. So, whenever I'm in Montreal, if we have time we meet for lunch or a drink and talk about business or films or plays and, of course, Quebec.

When I began working on this book, Guy was a nose-holding federalist. He believed in the system but felt it didn't work for Quebec, that they were, even after the gains of the Trudeau years, second-class citizens in their own country. Now, four years later, Guy believes that the only route for Quebec is to get out. "It is clear that English Canada doesn't want to reach an accord with us, is not concerned about the issues which are passionately ours. This is no longer tolerable to me."

Guy doesn't want to be identified because he genuinely feels that it could damage his business to be labelled as a separatist. "This is not the first time I've been through this."

I ask about multiculturalism. He quotes Bloc Québécois Leader Lucien Bouchard: "Now it's all on the table. We know where everyone stands. Meech Lake was the last word we'll hear from English Canada. The Bloc stands for Quebec's interests first, last, and always. We are ready to negotiate separation from Canada. Multiculturalism is a Canadian idea, not a Québécois concept."

Guy's discussion turns to the constitutional questions that still rage in Quebec. Like many English Canadians, I glaze over at the mere thought. It is part of the divide between the two solitudes. To Guy, the constitutional agreement in the Meech Lake accord was a step towards redressing wrongs and establishing a new "working relationship" between the cultures of Canada. "You cannot have rights for the Inuit, for the Natives, for the Blacks, unless you have a foundation that is built on respect for French, and you cannot respect French unless you understand that it is a distinct society, one that is long-established, with its own cultural matrix, it's own goals, its own life.

"We are not Anglo-Canadians, we are French-Canadians. We think, write, read, watch movies, listen to the radio, everything we do, we do in French. Language does influence thinking. Claude Lévi-Strauss calls this process *mentalisme*. In English you call it structuralism. These are not interchangeable words and ideas. They mean different things in the different languages."

If language is culture, then it stands to reason that multiculturalism should be multilingual. More than a hundred languages are spoken in Toronto alone. Are we, in the name of multiculturalism, to preserve and advance them all? For Guy, this isn't an issue. "Culture in Quebec is Québécois and the language is French. It doesn't matter if you are a Haitian novelist or a Senegalese poet, the images can be anything the imagination construes, but the language of expression, the mode of thinking, is French. We are committed to the survival of our language and our culture, and if that means forcing allophones [persons whose first language is neither French nor English] to learn French, so be it. I don't care any more what people outside Quebec think. If the allophones don't want to live in French, don't want their children educated in French, don't want to make their contribution to French, then they can leave."

Despite Guy's strong views, views he insists are shared by a majority of Québécois, many members of minority groups report that there is less prejudice in Quebec than in other parts of Canada. This seeming anomaly, according to Guy, is because survival of language and culture are essential. "I don't care what a man's skin colour is. I care that he shares my commitment to my country, Quebec. If he is a Black Haitian taxicab driver, fine. I know there is prejudice against Blacks in Quebec. We have been a closed culture defending ourselves for two hundred years. There is even prejudice against me because I am not a *pur laine*, but that is not racism. To say I can't speak my language in court, or to force my children to learn English and to see my children and grandchildren losing the culture and language of Cartier or Laurier—that is racism to me."

But isn't forcing allophones to learn French just as destructive? What about their cultures? Their heritage? "This is Quebec, not Hong Kong or Beirut or New York. When an immigrant comes to Toronto, you expect him to learn English. Now, he might continue to speak Chinese or Greek at home in his family, but when he goes to school or to work, he speaks English. Well, the language of Quebec is French. We are doing the same thing here that you are doing in Toronto or Calgary or Vancouver. You can speak whatever you like in your home, keep your cultural heritage, your customs, dress, foods. No one is quarrelling with that. When you are in public, you are living in French."

As always, Guy manages to make all this sound very reasonable, very fair. Separate but equal. Two languages, one country, at least for the time being. So what is Mordecai Richler so exercised about in his polemical essay *O Canada! O Quebec!* Among other targets in this book are Quebec's sign law, which Richler labels "infamous," pointedly nasty comments about the late Maurice DuPlessis ("thuggish"), and what Richler calls Quebec's long history of anti-Semitism, fostered and inspired by the Catholic Church. For good measure, he compares the pre-Second World War anti-Semitic articles in *Le Devoir* with those in racist prewar Nazi newspapers.

"I cannot discuss that man with any degree of objectivity," says Guy. "He hates my country and everything it stands for. He has access to podia in the United States, across Canada, and he uses his influence to degrade and defile. He sees nothing good about Quebec society and digs deep into the past to find whatever is bad. Were we anti-Semitic? Yes, we were. In those days, so were the Americans and the rest of Canada. This was wrong and I know that saying everyone else was the same is no defence, but Quebec is not an anti-Semitic culture now. In fact, the influence of religion is much reduced here. We are more free of prejudice and religiosity than we have ever been, and that's good."

But the Jews remain a stone in Quebec's craw. Whenever multiculturalism comes up, sooner or later Jews get mentioned. Traditionally, Jews have been seen as a threat in Quebec. Mostly

English-speaking, they were nevertheless cut out of the rarified Protestant world of the Montreal business elite. When they moved into the professions, they were seen as a threat to the French. According to Guy, this has all changed. "I have a Jewish lawyer. He speaks perfect French, better than my own, I sometimes think. Jews are at ease here, if they understand the language. Richler just hates Quebec."

The same cannot be said of Esther Delisle, author of *The Traitor and the Jew: Anti-Semitism and the Delirium of Extremist Right-Wing Nationalism in French Canada from 1929 to 1939*. This book has caused a genuine uproar in Quebec because Delisle equates virulent anti-Semitism with nationalism during that period. Richler included some of her research in his book, including the damning research into the anti-Semitic and racial theories of Abbé Lionel Groulx and the racially charged language of *Le Devoir,* now the newspaper of choice for the Quebec intelligentsia. Many of the intelligentsia see Delisle's work as an implicit criticism of the sovereignty movement, reinforcing the image of Québécois as xenophobic provincials intent on creating a racially and linguistically pure state.

"Esther Delisle is not like Mordecai Richler. She is a serious scholar," says Guy. "I think this whole thing is simply overblown. I repeat, in those days there were anti-Semites in Quebec. Some of them were very nice, highly respected people. But Ms. Delisle takes pains to point out that the ordinary people, the man in the street, were not anti-Semitic.

"In fact, I think she does the nationalists a service. She points out that all that twaddle about Quebeckers all being of the same racial stock is hogwash. There are some *pur laines*, but the majority of Quebeckers have an American or a Native or an English ancestor somewhere. We're just as ethnically mixed as people in Toronto or wherever, and it's time to lay the *pur laine* myth to rest. We are multicultural, multiracial, multireligious, all those multis. Just like the rest of Canada, except that it's in French."

I want to believe my Québécois friends who tell me that sovereignty is just another name for peaceful coexistence, that it won't materially affect my life, that I won't have to have visas and new currency and internal passports to travel from Kingston to St. John's. I want to believe them for another, more fundamental reason: I like my few Québécois friends. I do not want to see them go away from me, from all of us.

That said, I'm also troubled by the idea of Quebec nationalism. The truth is, I'm troubled by any form of passionate nationalism. Put it down to my jingoistic American upbringing or my love of the absence of jingoism in Canada, but I always look askance at nationalistic movements. Just to the edge of the cheers for Czechoslovakia's Velvet Revolution are the screams of terror from the ethnically incorrect residents of Bosnia and Serbia. Boris Yeltsin's pro-Russian demagoguery has led to Vladimir Zhirinovsky's neo-fascist imperialist dream of a Russian state incorporating the old Russian borders that include the Baltic states of Lithuania, Latvia, and Estonia.

Somewhere, at the cutting edge of nationalism, there always seems to be a calling together of the tribe, an assembly of those who belong, and then we hear the music, beat the drums, and raise the flags of nationhood as we prepare to exclude, deport, deny, and destroy those people who are not part of our culture, our tribe.

To me, nationalism always has racist overtones, and linguistic purity might just be the first step towards ethnic cleansing. The defence against this kind of thinking is true multiculturalism, a community in which many races, creeds, and religions coexist in mutual respect and dignity. It is the vision outlined in the Multiculturalism Act, not the hodgepodge of ethnic fairs and racial committees that now pass for multiculturalism. What we now have, as Nourbese Philip says, is "a mechanism whereby immigrants indulge their nostalgic love for their mother countries." Multiculturalism isn't antiracist. It can, in fact, perpetuate racism by keeping old hatreds and old prejudices intact.

Journalist Zuhair Kashmeri saw this firsthand in Canada during the Gulf war and recorded it in his book *The Gulf Within*. Kashmeri recounts the saga of Canadian citizens of Arab descent who were investigated by CSIS—Canada's secret security agency—as suspected terrorists, children who were beaten and verbally abused at school, a community vilified in the most abusive and vulgar language.

Kashmeri writes of the fallout of Canada's participation in the Gulf war, and its mark on our Arab-Canadian community: "As they watched the massacre of more than a hundred thousand Iraqis in the Middle East and the persecution of Arabs and Muslims in Canada, they began to raise some interesting questions. Foremost among them: Was multiculturalism simply a selling job?...Or did multiculturalism bring with it the need for Canada to consider the damaging effects within the country of getting militarily involved in foreign conflicts? As the Gulf war shows, there is a tremendous potential for long-term damage to Canada's social fabric and for fanning the flames of racism, hatred, and intolerance."

The Gulf war exposed Canadian suspicion of the Arabs in our midst. Perhaps wars always do that, but we are not a warlike people. We're the peacekeepers of the world, prepared to take action for the right in the name of the United Nations. If we joined George Bush's crusade against Saddam Hussein, it was because we believed the Kuwaitis in need of rescue. We are, after all, the good guys, the ones in the blue berets.

I've never been overfond of armies; I'm a product of the Vietnam War era. My heart doesn't pound to the tunes of a military march. Still, I know armies are necessary for those times when wars must be fought. My father and uncles went willingly off to Africa and Normandy and Okinawa to rid the world of Hitler and the Japanese warlords.

The army is the one place that I truly believe should be multicultural in the truest, most general sense of the word. It should genuinely protect the interests of the entire country. The War Measures Act and the standoff at Oka were not the Canadian Forces' finest hour. As well, Kashmiri and the Arabs offer some compelling evidence that the interests of Canada—and the Arab world—might have best been served by sending medical and humanitarian aid rather than joining with the Americans and British to bomb and blast.

Or so I thought before the Canadian Airborne Regiment went off, with pipes humming, to make war-ravaged Somalia safe for food shipments to reach starving children. In a country rent by tribal animosities and anarchy, Canada was going to save the day. As I watched the troops leave from CFB-Petawawa, I assumed that they were nice lads, good fellows out to do a good deed.

So, like a lot of other Canadians, I was stunned when four boys from the Airborne were charged with crimes against a Somali civilian. Shidane Abukar Arone was arrested in the hamlet of Belet Huen on March 16, 1993, for attempting to sneak into the Canadian military compound there. Three hours after his arrest, his body was found in his cell. He had been beaten to death.

A military investigation ended with charges against seven men, including two officers. Master Cpl. Clayton Matchee and Pte. Kyle Brown were charged with torture and murder in the second degree, which means the crime was not premeditated. Sgt. Mark Boland and Pte. David Brocklebank were charged with torture and negligent performance of duties. Matchee attempted suicide while under arrest and sustained major brain damage.

Less serious charges were laid against Sgt. Perry Gresty, two counts of negligent performance; Maj. Anthony Seward, unlawfully causing bodily harm and negligent performance; and Lt. Col. Carol Mathieu, negligent performance of duty. Two other men were charged with related offences against Somalis.

Meanwhile, the Department of National Defence conducted an investigation into the Airborne Regiment. What the investigation revealed was a disturbing picture of a rebellious unit given to flouting authority and plagued with disciplinary problems. There were a few enlisted men who openly supported such racist organizations as the Ku Klux Klan. The 2nd Commando Unit of the regiment was considered the most problem-laden. There were incidents in Canada of insubordination to officers, firearms infractions, problems with alcohol, the flying of Confederate flags as the unit's symbol even after officers banned it. Attempts to ferret out wrongdoers in the unit were met with the classic military code of silence, according to investigators. It was this troubled group who had the most day-to-day contact with Somali civilians.

The investigation led to other charges, against higher-ranking officers in the Airborne, but it was the first trial—that of Pte. Kyle Brown—that brought the real horrors of war home to Canada. Day after day, as Brown sat silent and stoic, prosecutors brought in witnesses who told of hearing screams that were ignored. There were grisly photographs of Brown and another soldier displaying Arone's beaten body like that of a captured animal. Witnesses told of how Arone was bound and blindfolded, how he called out "Canada, Canada" before he died.

It surprised no one when Brown was sentenced to prison for life. Hearing the evidence, it's difficult not to agree with Haitian Prime Minister Marc Bazin, who publicly referred to Canadian soldiers as "a pack of Nazis."

But, in all the hue and cry about the Airborne, about Brown and, later, Clayton Matchee's evildoing, one question kept coming up. Why? Why would two young men, charged with keeping the peace in a war-ravaged country, senselessly and savagely kill a teenaged boy?

That question wasn't really answered in the testimony from the Airborne but some clues did surface. The Airborne is, by and large, a white male institution. There are only a handful of visible minority members. Both Matchee, born in Meadow Lake, Saskatchewan, and Brown, from Edmonton, are of aboriginal heritage. Matchee was subjected to endless racial taunts. His nickname was Geronimo. He heard comments about Indian welfare bums from non-commissioned officers. At one point, Matchee considered leaving the military, but his parents urged him to hang on, to prove he had the right stuff. In the old, cold code of the military, shit always flows downhill. In Belet Huen, Shidane Arone happened to get caught at the bottom of the racist hill.

Hard on the heels of the revelations about Belet Huen came the case of Cpl. Matt McKay, who served in Somalia, formerly (so he claims) a member of the Aryan Nations. Wolfgang Droege couldn't claim McKay as one of his Heritage Front members, but he did say that there were "a number" of Canadian Forces members in the Front. "We have many of the same ideals," he said. He denied a rumour that McKay, or any other Forces member, was in charge of guerrilla training for Heritage Front members.

A 1990 photo of McKay shows a good-looking young man with a Vikingesque moustache and build standing at attention under a swastika banner. He is dressed in an Adolf Hitler T-shirt and is giving a smart Nazi salute.

At some point along the line, McKay made a choice to dress up that way, to have his picture taken. At some point, he learned how to act out the visual language of racism, its iconography, even as he had earlier learned to speak its verbal language. This we know, because racism is, above all, a way of speaking of the world that leads to deeds that appear to the non-racist to have nothing to do with the world, to come from some other realm of existence, poisoned and bleak. Where are we to begin eliminating that world-picture if not in the larger field of intellectual formation—the schools, the universities, the museums, entertainment?

There is a real message to be learned from Corporal McKay and his buddies at Petawawa. It is that we have to get past the motherhood statements about "community of communities" and see the eradication of racial prejudice as a common goal. We have to do it because it's necessary if we're to continue to live together in this country, and we have to do it at a time when there is no money for programs, when every dollar for essentials is being tested, and at a time when tribalism—from the west and from Quebec—threatens the very fabric of the country that immigration and multiculturalism have built.

Half a world away, the people who weren't safe in Somalia are trying to adjust to life in Mississauga, a place they presumed was safer and more hospitable.

As I left that depressed and depressing place for the last time, I passed a pair of Somali teenagers standing in the parking lot. They were next to my car and, since I'm not the world's best driver, I asked them to move. They told me to fuck off and stayed where they were. I explained why I wanted them to move. They ignored me. Eventually, our little standoff was resolved when the security guard came along and ordered them to move. They left, but as they went, one turned and made a little gun with his fingers, aimed it at me, and fired. I suppose it was a joke, but I think he meant it. When tribes are attacked, they fight back.

CONCLUSION:
THE STONE IN THE HEART

I FINISHED WRITING THE FIRST DRAFT of this book on a hot, clear Sunday morning in September 1993. Behind me at last were the racist nightmares, the faces of victims and brutal victimizers, the painful ambiguities of my own feelings about the subject I had chosen. I wanted to escape, and did. With my husband and daughter, I drove out of Toronto to a place that had over the years become a refuge from all the troubles and cares of city living, the beautiful farm of a dear friend. The occasion was an annual cornroast, that quintessentially Canadian experience—the iron cooking pot full of freshly shucked ears, the potatoes baking in the pit, tables laden with fresh breads, fruity pies and crumbles. It was a day to cherish, to celebrate being fortunate enough to live in this large, rich country.

The Collins family cornroast is, like most, a time to gather, reflect, and say goodbye to summer. The guests cover three generations, the entire political spectrum, and an assortment of professions, talents, and careers. There's always a lot of good conversation, and this year, with an election hovering, the state of the nation is the main topic. Among the gathered—poets, writers, teachers, social workers, homemakers, businesspeople—every race and creed is represented.

Here, on a sunny September day, one can fantasize that Canada really is a country that works, that the racial conflicts of America, the endemic racial hatreds of Britain, the former Yugoslavia, and Germany don't exist. We are the people of the twenty-first century, the one where these old shibboleths are passé. But in the midst of tractor rides and pick-up softball games, kids roving in the raspberry canes or climbing the apple trees in search of the perfect late-summer Macs, bigotry dropped in for dessert.

Jason, scion of a Canadian Black family with hundreds of years in this country behind him, is thirtyish, educated, elegant, intelligent, a loans officer for one of Canada's largest banks. Jason is telling me about an experience he had at work recently, an experience that he assures me is part and parcel of his everyday life.

"I had a customer who was overdue on his loan payments and he'd come in to explain and to renegotiate the loan, set up a new schedule. He came in and told me that he'd borrowed the money to put a basement apartment into his house. He'd rented the apartment out to a young Black woman. She'd brought in a bunch of her friends. They were all smoking dope, not paying the rent, so he was behind.

"Now, I have situations like this a lot and I like to push a little, get the racism out in the open. So I had him repeat:

" 'You borrowed the money to build the apartment.'

" 'Yes.'

" 'And you rented it to a young woman.'

" 'Yes.'

" 'And she was Black. And she brought in her friends.'

" 'Sure, man. You know what these niggers are like.' "

Nigger. The word runs across the back of my mind like fingernails on slate. I haven't heard that word used in public for more than thirty years. It is part of a past life, not part of the land of cornroasts and bobsledding. I do not know what to say to Jason, so I ask the obvious. "What did you do?" I don't hear the answer because no matter what he says, the n-word hangs in the air between us. For Jason, it's another anecdote in a lifetime of discrimination, which has taken the peculiar form of pushing him towards becoming a "white" person—that is, one who has emptied himself of the traits traditionally associated in racist imagination with being Black. For me, this imposed perversion of the soul is perhaps the ugliest manifestation of a hatred as old as Cain.

I had been three years on this book by the time of that cornroast and I thought that by this time, I was impervious. I'd spoken with dozens of Jasons encompassing every conceivable combination of religion and race. I'd documented hundreds of reports of jobs lost for lack of "Canadian experience," of apartments suddenly rented "just minutes before you arrived." There were South Asians who'd had excrement smeared on their doors, the mixed-race couple who were denied service in upscale restaurants, the clever Chinese accountant who didn't get the promotion because he didn't know that one of the requirements was being Caucasian.

I'd attended celebrations of Hitler's birthday with pretty young women in Toronto who told me, quite genuinely, that the Nazi Holocaust never happened and that the white race was at the top of the evolutionary ladder. I'd met women in Vancouver who believed that having turbanned Sikhs in the RCMP was a plot to destroy Canada and genteel pensioners from Halifax who swore that Hong Kong business immigrants were the vanguard of an Asian crime wave that would bring tong wars to the Annapolis Valley. I'd met people who lived their lives in the darkest corners of the human imagination, and I thought I'd seen it all.

In all my talks over the past thirty-six months, I hadn't heard anyone other than the Heritage Front members talk about niggers or kikes or Pakis or Chinks. They might have thought the words, but they didn't say them to my face. So Jason's story took me aback. There, amidst all the autumn plenty, surrounded by people I know and love, respected and cared for, Jason reminded me that he is the Other. Forever. And that this fact is due to only one thing: I was born white, he was born Black. And, in a world where racial discrimination is a constant fact of life, this accident of birth is the most important reality of all.

In the beginning, I said this book was a journey. I began my personal odyssey believing that racism existed in Canada. I didn't like to believe it, but I did. I knew a lot about anti-Orientalism because of my book *China Tide*. I knew about Black racism because I've lived with it all my life. I knew about Native racism because of Oka and Elijah Harper and the James Bay Cree and the other Native groups fighting back. I'd also seen racism firsthand, in the Skid Row shelters of Toronto and on the icy streetcorners of Winnipeg and Vancouver. So I can't say I was unprepared for what I found.

And still, this book has been a thirty-six-month trip to Calvary. I have, quite literally, hated many of the people I've met with, loathed them with a visceral hatred that sits in my stomach like a stone. And I've been frightened, afraid I'd end up as the target of some Heritage Front security man's truncheon or dead on a sidewalk like Leo LaChance.

When I spoke of these fears to friends, they thought I was losing my mind. "You're dramatizing," said one. "You can't be serious," said another. I knew what they meant. After all, this is Canada, the peaceable kingdom. We're safe here. People don't die just because of the race they belong to. What they meant was that we—the white middle-class majority—don't die because of race. They didn't know that's what they meant. They really believe that the police are here to serve and protect, that the army is the defender of the downtrodden, and schoolteachers are nice ladies and gentlemen who read Louisa May Alcott's *Little Women* and tell children about truth, justice, and the Canadian way.

But once you've crossed over the divide and moved into the invisible empire, even only into its margins, you can't ever go home again without locking the door. I want to find positive things to say, to ease my own fears. We have the Charter of Rights as a first public line of defence against all forms of discrimination, but court challenges take years and cost money. Who will finance the antiracist challenges under the Charter? Native people are doing so, for each other. But what about the other Others?

I comfort myself with anecdotes about education. I've always believed in the power of education to change thinking. You can learn yourself out of any dilemma. The truth shall set you free. Knowledge is power. I became a teacher more than thirty years ago because I believed all of that, and I've continued to teach because I still believe it. For me, journalism is an extension of teaching, a way of reaching people by other means. Boards of education in Canada's major cities have tried to rise to the challenge. They've established Festivals of Light to replace the traditional Christmas parties in the schools. They've created inclusive language and incorporated long-forgotten histories into the curriculum. Today's children can learn about the Black soldiers who fought in the Great War along with Greatgrandad and the Vandoos. They can read about the contribution of the Chinese to the building of the west—not just the ones who died to build the transcontinental railroad but the ones who ran the farms and built the roads and worked the mines. There are Estonian festivals and West Indian steel bands, right along with Mozart and Handel.

And, with all this, in 1993, we still have a society in which a thirteen-year-old East Indian boy, walking in Grenville Park in Oakville, a wealthy suburban community west of Toronto, can be set upon by two white youths, subjected to racial taunts, and have a lit firecracker jammed in his mouth. The boy suffered severe burns to his face. The culprits weren't caught. Where were they when the teachers were finishing lesson forty of the antiracism curriculum?

Another positive step: the provincial human rights commissions. Despite their difficulties, they have been successful at breaking down discrimination in the workplace. But jobs are disappearing at an alarming rate. Affirmative action may be the only route to real equality in the workplace, but this strategy plays into the hands of the kids and their parents who see themselves cut out because of racial quotas. Reverse racism and backlash aren't theoretical. They are real.

Something else is real: the chasm between all those grand public gestures and the private resentments and uncertainties harboured in the hearts of Canadians. Before me are the results of a national survey on ethnic relations in Canada conducted by the Canadian Council of Christians and Jews. In it, nearly three-quarters of Canadians reject utterly the notion of this country as a multicultural mosaic: 72 per cent of Canadians rejected a policy that has been in place for more than twenty years, saying that new immigrants should "adapt to the value system and the way of life of the majority in Canadian society." Forty-one per cent thought that Canadian immigration policy "allows too many people of different cultures and races to come to Canada." Fifty per cent agreed with the statement "I am sick and tired of some groups complaining about racism being directed at them," and 41 per cent agreed that they were "tired of ethnic minorities being given special treatment."

Karen Mock, chairperson of the Canadian Multicultural Advisory Committee, tried to put the best possible face on the survey, claiming that the "value system and way of life" in Canada includes respect for diversity, freedom of religion, equal opportunity for everyone, and integration into society. At least, that's the committee's definition of Canadian values.

But Ned Goodman, president of the Council of Christians and Jews, disagreed, saying Canadian are frustrated with the mosaic and "want to try the melting pot."

Michael Sullivan, senior vice-president of Decima Research, which conducted the survey for the council, was even more explicit. "My sense is respondents were probably saying that they [minority groups] should become more like Canadians," he said. And those respondents know what a Canadian is: a "white Catholic or Protestant model."

White Catholic or Protestant. The facts about Canadians show a different picture. In the 1986 census, there were 1.6 million members of visible minorities out of Canada's population of 26 million. By 1991, the number was more than 2 million. Members of the population whose heritage is neither British nor French made up 38 per cent. The number is expected to rise to 50 per cent in a decade. Vancouver is already a Eurasian city. More Italians live in Toronto than live in Rome. There are more Estonians here than in Talinn.

But what difference has this profound ground-shift in reality made to our perceptions, and to what we do as a result of these perceptions? We whites stand today just where we were when we arrived in this country: in full possession of the Eurocentric cultural and racial baggage that M. Nourbese Philip calls "white supremacy," a concept she believes isn't limited to a handful of hardcore neo-Nazis in an isolated corner of the Canadian prairie but is an irrationality thriving in homes and schools all over this land.

Speaking of Canadian understanding of issues in the Gulf war, a United Church minister quoted in *The Gulf Within* by Zuhain Kashmeri, seemed to underscore Philip's point. "There is race involved in judging who is an enemy and who is a friend," he wrote. "Canadians will never think of America as an enemy, and neither can they think of the British or the French as enemies, and nowadays, even Germany. But it is so easy for Canadians to think of Arabs as the enemy. And if you start to classify the subconscious psyche of Canadians—who can and who cannot be the enemy—it so turns out that most of the countries with which Canada cannot engage in war are white...and so it cannot be wrong to advocate their policy."

But does this make Canada a profoundly racist country? Not if one's definition of profoundly racist is Bosnia or Serbia or South Africa. Not if one grew up in the Southern United States under segregation. Not if one has seen the human wreckage in the racial ghettoes of Detroit or the burned-out remains of south-central Los Angeles. If we define racism as the numbers of dead, Canada is still salvageable. And surely as important as any of the criteria above is the fact that Canadians do not see themselves as racist—that is, we have not become emotionally comfortable with the discrimination among us. In the same survey where two-thirds of Canadians said immigrants must adapt and 40 per cent want the immigration doors closed, 68 per cent said that one of the best things about this country is that it accepts people of all races and ethnic backgrounds.

This result is reassuring, even a ground for hope. But, in the present, we must keep asking ourselves the hard questions. How well do our systems work to protect "people of all races and ethnic backgrounds" from those who would harm them? Are all our citizens treated equally before the law? Is the history of all races taught in our schools? Are the literatures, cultures, philosophies of Africa, Asia, our Native people taught in our schools? Who teaches our children? What messages are passed along to them?

It is here, in the great well of systems, that racism is thriving in Canada. We may not be calling people nigger or Chink or kike or raghead on the street, but we make it clear that the values we want enshrined in our institutions are the values of the founding races— white, Catholic, Protestant, European culture, Western philosophy. We might add an African author or two to a reading list or take the kids to a Spike Lee film. We can drop in on the Chinese Cultural Centre in Vancouver and walk through a Ming garden and then stop off at the mall to buy a Thai silk scarf for Grandma. But if a Sikh war veteran shows up at some Legion Halls, he won't be welcome if he wears his turban. We can buy, eat, and consume the multicultural mosaic without ever believing in it at all.

The consequences of this attitude for Canadians are not good ones. We do not, as we are so often told these days, live on an island. We are part of a global economy, a global communications network. We are part of the dominant power group on this planet and subject to all the dangers that power presents. Europe is a closed shop with the European Community. Economic power is heading east to the emerging industrial nations of Southeast Asia.

We are now part of a huge multinational trading bloc called the North American Free Trade Agreement. If that agreement is eventually extended to South America, as many economists believe and many businesses hope, it will incorporate huge populations of visible minorities.

At the same time, our international prestige, once so high, has dropped. Our peacekeepers may be appreciated in Sarajevo, but the smell of Belet Huen hasn't dissipated. Hard times at home mean less money for foreign aid, and so our humanitarian presence is lowered. As well, members of ethnic communities in Canada see "their" countries being ignored, hear the cries of "charity begins at home" and "cut off foreign aid." Retreating into our own little borders is an appealing fantasy, particularly in these times of high taxes and reduced services. Cutting off the Other is always an option. This is the ground that Preston Manning and the Bloc Québécois occupy, and it is truly a siren's song leading us to destruction.

Race and questions of race, and the conflicts precipitated by the vast movements of people in flight from war or in search of better economic prospects, are almost certain to be the dominant social issues facing the world in the twenty-first century. Wealth and power are increasingly concentrated in western Europe and in the emerging economic powers in the Far East. The massive migrations to these centres of enterprise and high living standards will almost certainly continue as the emerging states and statelets of eastern Europe and Africa continue their decline into tribal warfare, officially sanctioned genocide, and social misery. Where only a few years ago we hailed the end of the cold war and spoke eagerly about spending the "peace dividend" on improving life for the world's poor, we now, with fear in our hearts, watch wars and hear rumours of wars. The shift from ethnic solidarity to ethnic cleansing has involved only a change of a word.

What this means in Canada is a transformation of the face of the country. As Jacques Godbout puts it (his comments are about Quebec but apply to all of Canada), until now "there has never been the mass arrival of immigrants racially different from the people here. The European immigration caused cultural difficulties which were resolved within a generation or a generation and a half. But now you have immigration from Asia, Africa, the Caribbean, and Latin America who are visibly different, have different religions, different attitudes towards women, etc., and who are arriving in great numbers. And more than half of these immigrants have come as refugees. I think this is a very complex situation which will certainly preoccupy us for the next twenty-five, thirty years. It is a phenomenon which concerns the human race and the planet. We are so unprepared for this that everything is possible. We may invent a way of integrating these people which will solve all our problems or we may fail miserably."

Canadians are doomed to fail if the existence of racism coiled in our hearts is not acknowledged, frankly and fully. We cannot otherwise hope to curb its power over us or reduce its violent place in our world. I would like to think that my children might live in a country that is free of racism, but I no longer believe that eradication is possible. We can limit the public damage, we can legislate public decency and put teeth into the laws. If we can, to some extent, regulate the relationships among people, we cannot be so optimistic about making radical changes to the hearts and inner thoughts of men and women.

"It used to make me so angry," says my friend Howard States of the subtle and not-so-subtle racism that has marked his passage through his land. "I was angry all the time and it wasn't good for me. I had to give that up and, after a struggle, I did. But it never goes away. Racism is always there, and the hurt is like a stone in my heart."

If I long ago gave up on my quest to make the world perfect, I'll settle for a certain place—say, Canada—in which all people, including Howard States, feel safe when they take an evening walk, and in which his children and mine will neither be rewarded nor rejected for having been born a certain colour. I'll settle for a place in which future generations will know a little less of the hurt and a little more of the hope that lie inextricably tangled in the heart of the human condition.

CHAPTER NOTES

Racism is not a new issue in Canada. Over the years, there have been hundreds of examinations of various aspects of racial conflict and racial integration so a comprehensive listing is not possible in this work. My own book is a journalist's overview—not intended as the last word on any of the issues—and, as such, relies more on firsthand observation, interviews, and news stories than on scholarly research. Fortunately, superb research has been done—and is continuing—on racism in Canada and elsewhere in the world. The following authors are ones who influenced my work. Some appear only as background. Others are mentioned in the texts. This list is less than 10 per cent of the studies, books and monographs available on the subject.

Abella, Irving, and Harold Troper. *None is Too Many:
Canada and the Jews of Europe 1938-1948*. Toronto:
Lester and Orpen Dennys, 1982.
Bolaria, B. Singh, and Peter S. Li. *Racial Oppression in
Canada*. Toronto: Garamond, 1988.
Cannon, Margaret. *China Tide: The Revealing Story of the*

Hong Kong Exodus to Canada. Toronto: HarperCollins, 1989.

Davies, Alan, ed. *Antisemitism in Canada: History and Interpretation*. Waterloo: Wilfrid Laurier University Press, 1992.

DeLisle, Esther. *The Traitor and the Jew: Anti-Semitism and the Delirium of Extremist Right-wing Nationalism in French Canada from 1929 to 1939*. Montreal: Robert Davies Publishing, 1993.

Fanon, Frantz. *Black Skin, White Masks*. New York: Grove Press, 1967.

Harris, Michael. *Justice Denied: The Law Versus Donald Marshall*. Toronto: Totem, 1987.

Hawkins, Frieda. *Canada and Immigration: Public Policy and Public Concern*. Kingston: McGill-Queen's University Press, 1988.

————. *Critical Years in Immigration: Canada and Australia Compared*. Kingston: McGill-Queen's University Press, 1991.

Hutcheon, Linda, and Marion Richmond, eds. *Other Solitudes: Canadian Multicultural Fictions*. Toronto: Oxford University Press, 1990.

Kallen, Evelyn. *Ethnicity and Human Rights in Canada*. Toronto: Gage, 1982.

Kashmeri, Zuhair. *The Gulf Within*. Toronto: James Lorimer, 1991.

Kilgour, David. *Inside Outer Canada*. Edmonton: Lone Pine, 1990.

Kinsella, Warren. *Web of Hate: Inside Canada's Far Right Network*. Toronto: HarperCollins, 1994.

Langlais, Jacques, and David Rome. *Jews and French Quebecers: Two Hundred Years of Shared History*. Waterloo: Wilfrid Laurier University Press, 1991.

Lemann, Nicholas. *The Promised Land: The Great Black Migration and How It Changed America*. New York: Knopf, 1991.

Levine, Marc V. *The Reconquest of Montreal: Language Policy and Social Change in a Bilingual City.* Philadelphia: Temple University Press, 1990.

Li, Peter S. *Race and Ethnic Relations in Canada.* Toronto: Oxford University Press, 1990.

Malarek, Victor. *Haven's Gate: Canada's Immigration Fiasco.* Toronto: Macmillan, 1987.

McCall, Nathan. *Makes Me Wanna Holler: A Young Black Man in America.* New York: Random House, 1994.

Philip, M. Nourbese. *Frontiers: Essays and Writings on Racism and Culture.* Stratford: Mercury Press, 1992.

————. *Showing Grit: Showboating North of the 44th Parallel.* Toronto: Poui Publications, 1993.

Porter, John. *The Vertical Mosaic.* Toronto: University of Toronto Press, 1965.

Priest, Lisa. *Conspiracy of Silence.* Toronto: McClelland & Stewart, 1989.

Richler, Mordecai. *Oh Canada! Oh Quebec! Requiem for a Divided Country.* Toronto: Penguin Books, 1992.

Robertson, Heather. *Reservations Are for Indians.* Toronto: Lorimer, 1991.

Sartre, Jean-Paul. *Anti-Semite and Jew.* New York: Schocken Books, 1965.

Scheier, Libby, Sarah Sheard and Eleanor Wachtel. *Language in Her Eye: Writing and Gender. Views by Canadian Women Writing in English.* Toronto: Coach House, 1990.

Theweleit, Klaus. *Male Fantasies: Volume 2. Male Bodies: Psychoanalysing the White Terror.* Minneapolis: University of Minnesota Press, 1989.

Trinh, T. Minh-ha. *Woman, Native, Other: Writing Postcoloniality and Femininism.* Bloomington: Indiana University Press, 1989.

Webb, James. *The Occult Establishment.* La Salle, Illinois: Open Court Paperbacks, 1976.

Williams, Patricia J. *The Alchemy of Race and Rights: The*

Diary of a Law Professor. Cambridge: Harvard University Press, 1991.

Wistrich, Robert S. *Antisemitism: The Longest Hatred.* London: Thames, Methuen, 1991.

Woodsworth, J.S. *Strangers Within Our Gates.* Toronto: University of Toronto Press, 1972.

INTRODUCTION: ENCOUNTERS WITH THE OTHER

ViVi Leimonis and Todd Baylis were killed as I prepared this book to go to press. For that reason, most of the material regarding the cases came from newspaper and television accounts in the *Toronto Star* and the *Globe and Mail* newspapers, both of which covered the murders and the subsequent arrests and funerals in detail. Stories on ViVi Leimonis were in April 1994. The surveillance photos and the "Urban Terrorism" headline appeared on April 7, 1994, in the *Toronto Star*. Constable Baylis was killed in June 1994. I did not attend Ms. Leimonis' funeral. I did go to Constable Baylis's funeral. I was looking for a young Black man to interview and I found Clive. Like most of the people interviewed for this book, he asked that his full name not be used.

The sad story of Tin Wah Lui, the forgotten victim of crime, was recounted in "The Crucial Social Lesson of the Just Desserts Tragedy," by Thomas Walkom, *Toronto Star*, April 10, 1994.

The reaction against young Black men, and the furore over the deportation of criminals continued right up until press time. Among dozens of articles in all three major Toronto newspapers were "We're all Targets, Black Students Say," by Rita Daly, *Toronto Star*, April 14, 1994; "Blacks Speak Out: Anyone Listening?" letter to the Editor, *Toronto Star*, April 16, 1994; "Father Tells what It's like for Black Kids in Metro," by Philip Mascoll, *Toronto Star*, April 15, 1994; "Young Blacks Brace for Crime's Aftermath," *Globe and Mail*, April 16, 1994; "Young Blacks Wear a Stranger's Guilt on their Faces," by Rosie DiManno, *Toronto Star*, April 11, 1994; "Good People and Bad People," by John Barber, *Globe and Mail*, April 12, 1994; "Ottawa to Kick out Foreign Criminals," by Allan Thompson, *Toronto Star*, Friday, July 8, 1994; "Getting Tough on

Immigration May Beget Injustice," by A. Alan Borovoy, head of the Canadian Civil Liberties Union, *Toronto Star*, August 3, 1994; "How We See Crime is Changing—and that's the Big Danger," by Catherine Mulroney, *Toronto Star*, April 14, 1994; "Hard Line on Deportation Backed Here Poll Shows," by William Walker, *Toronto Star*, August 16, 1994; "Face Up to Crime, Jamaican PM Says," by Allan Thompson, *Toronto Star*, July 15, 1994; "The Gentle Art of Conciliation on a Lazy Sunday," by Rosie DiManno, *Toronto Star*, August 8, 1994; "Doing Time for Immigrant Crime," editorial, *Globe and Mail*, June 21, 1994; "Deportation Controversy 'a Big Mess'," Staff and Canadian Press, *Globe and Mail*, June 21, 1994; "'Sharing the Guilt Appalling,' Blacks Told," by Rosie DiManno, *Toronto Star*, April 18, 1994; "Don't Blame Me; Work with Me," by Erma Collins, *Toronto Star*, April 19, 1994.

Two additional notes: In late August 1994, the Leimonis and Baylis families launched a civil suit against Immigration Canada. The suit is backed by the Metro Toronto Police Association. On August 13, 1994, the *Globe and Mail* headlined the story of Malachy McAllister, "Judge Orders Release of Terror Suspect." McAllister, a refugee claimant living in Cambridge, Ontario, was convicted of murdering a Belfast police officer in 1981. McAllister has a long record in Northern Ireland for firearms offences and assault. He immigrated to Canada after serving his sentence for killing the police officer. He has been ordered deported but is currently free to fight his deportation, thanks to the Federal Court of Canada.

CHAPTER ONE: THE OLDEST HATRED

Interviews for this chapter were done between 1991 and 1994. Most people interviewed preferred that their names not be used. People do not like to be publicly identified as anti-Semites, unless, of course, they're members of any of the various far right groups. During 1991 and 1992, I attended several Heritage Front rallies and meetings, as well as information evenings like the lecture by revisionist historian David Irving. I did not identify myself as a journalist and, in all cases where I quote, I do not use a name. In other cases of quotes, I have left the name out because, as in the case of the lawyer in the opening section, he was being interviewed for something else. Many casual anti-Semitic references were picked up in passing and I just made notes.

There are thousands of excellent works chronicling the history and rise of anti-Semitism. Of all the ones I read, I preferred Wistrich's *The Oldest Hatred* and *The Occult Establishment* by James Webb.

There were several small stories about the ScotiaMcLeod and Simon Israel affair. The most extensive was "Brokerage Firm Still Taking Flak over Firing," by Stevie Cameron, *Globe and Mail*, September 28, 1992.

The best source on the Heritage Front, and all ultra-right organizations is Warren Kinsella's book *Web of Hate*. I called the Heritage Front many times to listen to the messages on the Hot Line. The personal information on Gary Schipper came from "The Face of Hate," by Lindalee Tracey, *Toronto Life*, March 1994. A mention in a later article in August 1994 indicated that Mr. Schipper had given up Nazi regalia for cross-dressing. When the media needed interviews from Front members after the CSIS story broke, Mr. Schipper was available.

The Winnipeg incident is documented in "Temple Defaced" in the *Globe and Mail*, November 2, 1992; the Montreal incident in "Vandalism," *Globe and Mail*, October 22, 1992. The sorry saga of Zvonimir Lelas appeared in "White Supremacist Given Stiffer Prison Sentence," *Globe and Mail*, September 1, 1990; "Supremacist's Jail Sentence Appealed," by Donn Downey, *Globe and Mail*, August 24, 1990; "Police Hold Man in Desecration of Synagogue," *Globe and Mail*, July 1, 1989.

The importance of, and development of, ZOG is well documented in Wistrich and Webb.

Over the years, there has been extensive coverage of Ernst Zundel's activities, his trials, his role in continuing Canadian anti-Semitism. I have a copy of his interview with Victor Malarek that aired in the spring of 1993 on *fifth estate*. He also appeared in a Swedish documentary on the rise of neo-Nazi activity in Germany. A German government official confirmed Zundel's role in supplying hate literature in Germany. His role has also been confirmed by the B'nai Brith, Klanwatch, the Canadian Society for Yad Vashem, and a host of other groups.

Some of the articles on Zundel used in this chapter are: "Law Struck Down in Zundel Case," by David Vienneau, *Toronto Star*, August 28, 1992. I also relied on various accounts of Zundel's trials, including his own, over the years.

The role of anti-Semitism in the creation and fostering of racial hatred has been extensively discussed. Again, I relied on Wisteria, as well as Webb, and the essay *Anti-Semite and Jew* by Jean-Paul Sartre.

Carney Nerland was unavailable for interviews when I began this piece. Since his release from prison in 1993, according to Warren Kinsella, he's been in the RCMP Witness Protection Program. One of my major sources for the Nerland saga was "Fuhrer of Saskatchewan" by Lisa Kowal (a pseudonym) in *Saturday Night* magazine, April 1993. Ms. Kowal's real name and location were hidden for her protection. There are many accounts of Nerland's trial and all were admirably summed up in *Web of Hate*. There are some minor language discrepancies between his book and the *Globe and Mail* accounts of Nerland's activities. Where discrepancies exist, I have chosen the version which my research deems most accurate.

In January 1993, I was at the Heritage Front rally. Background information on the Heritage Front, Klanwatchers, David Duke and David Irving et al., is readily available. Some of the major articles are: "Mild-mannered, but Not One to Back Down from a Fight," by Catherine Dunphy, *Toronto Star*, January 31, 1993; "White Rights Advocate Learned it all at Grandpa's Knee," by Michael Tenzen, *Toronto Star*, February 21, 1993; "Will Media Game Pay Off for Canada's Racist Right?" by Kirk Makin, *Globe and Mail*, February 6, 1993; "The Klansman who Came Calling to Canada," by Julian Sher, *Globe and Mail*, November 9, 1991. Also, printed sporadically and available by mail from the Front or at Front meetings is "Up Front: the Voice of the Heritage Front."

Background on neo-Nazi activity worldwide has been a major news story. One of the best analyses was "Racism's Back," *The Economist*, November 16, 1992.

The Julius Melnitzer information came from my own article in the *Report on Business* magazine of the *Globe and Mail*.

CHAPTER TWO: EQUAL RIGHTS FOR WHITES

Again, I attended all Heritage Front meetings from 1991-1993. I also listened to, and made notes of the casual conversations of several dozen members of the Front, as well as those of assorted hangers-on. "Lorne" is a pseudonym for the young man who wanted to join the Klan. Also on the subject of why young men join the Klan, "Young, White and Racist," by Raymond Familusi, *Globe and Mail*, April 24, 1991.

The Elisse Hategan story was covered by the Toronto media, including me. The new Ontario policy on hate in the schools was announced by Education Minister Dave Cooke in "Ontario Zeros In on Hate in Schools," by James Rusk, *Globe and Mail*, June 3, 1994.

Droege's case in the Human Rights Commission was extensively covered. The most interesting article is in "Racist Comments about Whites Ignored, Court Told," by Rudy Platiel, *Globe and Mail*, January 26, 1994.

A partial listing of articles on the csis contretemps: "Front Member Manning's Shadow," by Kirk Makin, *Globe and Mail*, August 23, 1994; "Ottawa Probes Claims about csis Informant," by Amber Nasrulla, *Globe and Mail*, August 16, 1994; "Agency Fostered Racism, Activist Says," by Dale Brazao, *Toronto Star*, August 17, 1994; There were also several major stories in the *Toronto Star* during the week of August 20, 1994. The best of these are: "Ex-aide Admits Leaking Spy Note," by David Vienneau, Rosemary Speirs and Shawn McCarthy, August 26, 1994; "Who's Watching Whom?" by Speirs and Vienneau, August 27, 1994. At this time, csis is demanding that the *Star* return certain documents mentioned in those letters and the former journalist-civil servant who leaked them is under investigation by the RCMP.

At the time of writing, there was little more than newspaper reports and conjecture about the relationship between csis and the Front. The parliamentary subcommittees and sirc have just begun their investigations into the affair. Elisse Hategan appeared on Vision TV in Toronto in a long interview about her life with the Front. She was also interviewed on news broadcasts. She is in hiding and says she is in fear for her life.

Articles about the csis-Front controversy abounded. "csis Told to Clear its Name Publicly," by Rosemary Spiers, *Toronto Star*, August 24, 1994; "Who's Watching Whom?" by Rosemary Spiers and David Vienneau, *Toronto Star*, August 27, 1994; "Ex-aide Admits Leaking Spy Note," by David Vienneau, Rosemary Spiers and Shawn McCarthy, *Toronto Star*, August 26, 1994; "Tory Aide Admits csis Leak," by Kirk Makin, *Globe and Mail,* August 26, 1994; "Bristow Inquiry Missing Bristow," by Jeff Sallot, *Globe and Mail,* September 15, 1994; "Reform Shaken By More Allegations of Ties to Racist Group," by Tu Thanh Ha, *Globe and Mail,* September 16, 1994; "Whistle Blower," by Kirk Makin, *Globe and Mail,* October 1, 1994; "Do Canadians Have Reason to Be Worried about CSIS?" by Peter Marwitz, *Globe and Mail,* October 10, 1994; "Lewis Tight-lipped on CSIS Allegations," by Tu Thanh Ha, *Globe and Mail,* October 19, 1994; "I Wanted to Kill, Ex-racist Tells Group," by Cal Millar and Gail Swainson, *Toronto Star,* September 30, 1994; "Seven Released after Raid on Home," Canadian Press, *Globe and Mail,* October 31, 1994.

A good examination of the conflict between the Heritage Front and the ARA is to be found in *This* magazine by Clive Thompson, November 1994. A short form of this article appeared as "In Your Fascist Face," *Toronto Star,* November 6, 1994.

CHAPTER THREE: MOULD THE CHILD AND YOU HAVE HIM FOR LIFE

Professor O'Driscoll's story has been covered by the Toronto newspapers in some detail. The most intriguing article on O'Driscoll in class is "My Prof's Jewish Conspiracy," by David Layton, published in the March 1994 issue of *This* magazine. In the August 1994 issue of *This* magazine, Professor O'Driscoll wrote a stinging response to this article claiming, among other things, that David Layton consistently cut class and had a grudge against him because O'Driscoll had "a terrible row" with Layton's father, the poet Irving Layton, at a Christmas party in 1971. At the end of the letter, O'Driscoll points out that the Adamowski Investigation at U of T found no evidence of anti-Semitism in his work, that he was found guilty of a "pedagogical error" and compares himself—favorably—to Peter Abelard and Thomas Aquinas. As of publication, O'Driscoll was planning a new book on the same topics and was still on the faculty of St. Michael's.

The documentary with the Scarborough teenagers was produced by CBC *Prime Time* and aired February 22, 1993.

The story of Jim Keegstra has spawned dozens of articles across the country, as well as three books. This history is drawn largely from Steve

Mertl's book, *Keegstra: The Trial, the Issues, the Consequences*, as well as nine years of articles from the *Globe and Mail*. Again, the Keegstra affair is covered in *Web of Hate*.

Malcolm Ross's works and story are covered extensively in *Web of Hate*. Mr. Kinsella and I have used many of the same sources and come to most of the same conclusions. At this point, Mr. Ross is free to teach in the Moncton schools. The final chapter of the Malcolm Ross case was reported in "N.B.'s Top Court Allows Teacher Back in Classroom," *Globe and Mail*, December 21, 1993. There were also front page stories in the Moncton and Fredericton papers. In an attempt to explain why a proven anti-Semite could be cleared to teach in the public schools, "The Issue Is Who May Teach," by A. Alan Borovoy, *Toronto Star*, February 2, 1994, is the best source. Some of the most extensive and controversial studies of the issues in the Ross case are from the Canadian Association for Free Expression (CAFE) which defended Ross vigilantly in its quarterly newsletter. CAFE is an adjunct of C-FAR and both organizations originate with Paul Fromm.

The information about Matin Yaqzan appeared in "Professor Sparks Flap by Saying Date Rape is Natural," by CP, *Toronto Star*, November 9, 1993, and in "Jewish Group Wants Teacher Investigated," by Kevin Cox, *Globe and Mail*, November 19, 1993.

I attended Paul Fromm's lectures and spoke with him on those occasions. I also have his C-FAR newsletters—*The Canadian Immigration Hotline*—and pamphlets as mentioned in the story. The three I used are all from the C-FAR Canadian Issues series. They are: "Race, Evolution and AIDS: What Rushton Really Said," edited by Fromm and published in Toronto, 1990; "Over-population and Third World Immigration," by W. Harding LeRiche, M.D., FRCS(C), published in Toronto in 1983; and "The Vietcong Front in Quebec," by Gilbert Gendron, B.A., published in Toronto, 1987.

CHAPTER FOUR: WORDS AND MUSIC

For this chapter, I interviewed more than twenty people during 1992–93.

Many of them, for obvious reasons, remain anonymous. "Harriet," the woman who grew up in Africville and who now lives in Vancouver was interviewed in June 1993. For more information on the "glass ceiling," turn to "Chinese Canadians Fight Racism," by Virginia Galt, *Globe and Mail*, April 26, 1991. I also interviewed four Indo-Asian women in Vancouver who told esssentially the same story as Harriet. On the record are the members of the Coalition for Truth about Africa. Other incidents, like the one on the *Dini Petty* show, the casual slurs, were related to me by individuals too numerous to mention. I am indebted to people like Althea Prince who were bringing my attention to this issue long before I started this book and years before political correctness in language was conceived. One of the more interesting discussions of this entire issue occurred on the *Oprah Winfrey Show* in October 1993.

The *Dini Petty* show incident occurred in March 1992 on live TV. It was covered the next day by the Toronto newspapers and protested by the Canadian Jewish Congress Ontario Region and B'nai B'rith. It did not become a cause célèbre and was soon forgotten.

Michael Coren's article on Archbishop Ambrozic, "Pope's Choice," appeared in *Toronto Life* magazine, June 1993 and provoked much discussion. "Why an Archbishop Made the News," by Jack Kapica appeared in the *Globe and Mail*, May 26, 1993; I spoke with Mr. Coren in August 1994 to confirm his views and he pointed out that the entire interview was taped by the Archbishop. Had the derogatory comments not been uttered, Archbishop Ambrozic had only to produce his own personal copy of the interview and challenge Mr. Coren. That he did not speaks for itself. My calls to the Archbishop requesting clarification or comment were ignored. The only press officer who returned my call refused to give her name and informed me that the issue was closed.

On the knotty subject of French language rights in Quebec, I do not, even after more than twenty years of living in Canada, profess to completely understand the issues. My own views have been influenced by my friends and colleagues in Quebec, as well as by *The Reconquest of Montreal: Language Policy and Social Change in a Bilingual City*, by Marc V. Levine and the works of Jacques Godbout.

* * *

The conflict over "Into the Heart of Africa" was covered in detail by the Toronto media. I attended most of the major news conferences in 1990 and have more than 200 press releases of all sorts from both the Coalition and the ROM, as well as other groups concerned with the issues. Despite the hue and cry, the best and most fair coverage of the issue was "The Heart of Into the Heart of Africa" by Robert Fulford, *Rotunda*, the magazine of the Royal Ontario Museum, Summer 1991. Professor Cannizzo refused to be interviewed at all times and has since left Canada.

Further information on the role of non-whites in Canadian museum circles came from John Bentley Mays, art critic for the *Globe and Mail*. On the subject of white control of the media see "Nation's Newsrooms a Pale Reflection of our Diverse Society," by Irshad Manji, *Toronto Star*, August 9,1994.

The best coverage of the *Show Boat* controversy was "Rocking the Boat," by Cecil Foster, *Toronto Life* magazine, November 1993. The most perceptive was M. Nourbese Philip's series of essays in *Showing Grit: Showboating North of the 44th Parallel*. Garth Drabinsky's views were aired in a speech to the Empire Club of Canada, February 2, 1994, a speech which was excerpted in the *Globe and Mail*, February 11, 1994. Other articles on *Show Boat* include: "Harmony Lost over Musical," by Cecil Foster, *Globe and Mail*, October 19, 1993, which recounts the conflict within the Toronto United Way over the *Show Boat* gala. "School Kids Too Young to Discern *Show Boat* Racism, Teachers Told," by Allan Thompson, *Toronto Star*, October 1, 1993; "Black History Group Rejects *Show Boat* Offer," *Globe and Mail*, February 10, 1994. I am deeply indebted to Ms. Sondra Carrick for assisting me in long interviews to sort out the *Show Boat* issues from the media frenzy. I am also indebted to a young Black actress who gave me the best defense of *Show Boat* as a musical and explained its important role in the history of theatre. Aviva Kemper is a student at York University who volunteered this information to me. For the discussion of the conflicts and differences between the various Black groups in Canada, I spoke for many hours over many years with the late Dr. Wilson Head, founder of the Urban Alliance on Race Relations and a long-time professor of Social Work at York University.

Lost in all the frenzy over *Show Boat* was a protest by the Oriental community against *Miss Saigon*, which many Oriental Canadians considered a perpetuation of the derogatory stereotype of Oriental women as passive sex objects. For coverage of the *Miss Saigon* protest, "East Meets West Meets Stereotype," by Keith Lowe, *Globe and Mail*, May 27, 1993; "*Miss Saigon/Madama Butterfly* Love Story Makes Great Theatre," by William Littler, *Toronto Star*, April 2, 1994; "Demonstrators Protest Against *Miss Saigon* Stereotypes," by Ann Fuller and David Hilderley, *Globe and Mail*, May 27, 1993. I attended the demonstration and spoke personally with members of "Asian Revisions; Beyond *Miss Saigon*," the coalition protesting *Miss Saigon*.

Chapter Five: Jobs and Power

For this chapter, I interviewed several former members of the staff of Nellie's, as well as a number of users of the facility. I spoke with several community spokespersons and, in one case, have not used a name for obvious reasons. I interviewed Cleta Baines, along with several other visible minority women. I have used her quotes because she was the most articulate of them all and because all the women I interviewed told me similar versions of Baines's account. I also relied on my own first-hand knowledge of Nellie's formation and history. By the time I began work on this chapter, most of the major players were no longer speaking to anyone from the media. Carolann Wright said what she had to say in "Challenging the Status Quo on all Fronts," by Lynda Hurst, *Toronto Star*, August 9, 1992; I did not call Ms. Callwood because I was told that she was coping with a major family crisis and didn't need any more discussion of what was surely one of the most awful incidents in her life. Instead, I relied on the extensive interviews she gave in "Battered Woman," by Elaine Dewar, *Toronto Life*, March, 1993 and in "Women, Race, and Power," by Adele Freedman, *Saturday Night*, April 1993. Nourbese Philip has said on more than one occasion that she said all she had to say about the PEN incident in her writing. I took her at her word and used her version of events as recorded in *Frontiers*, her collection of polemical writings. The Writer's Union conflict continued in the Union newsletter for several months over the summer and fall of 1994. The newsletter, which is private, is not available for reprint-ing. The best recounting of the issues was "What Kind of Way is that for Canada's Writers to Talk?" by Bronwyn Drainie, *Globe and Mail*, February 26, 1994. Further conflicts within the Union surfaced in "George Orwell, Call your Office," by Robert Fulford, *Globe and Mail*, March 30, 1994. One of the best discussions of the concept of "white privilege" is "Unpacking a Lifetime of White Privilege," by Michele Landsberg, *Toronto Star*, Feb. 20, 1993.

The saddest, to me, footnote to the Nellie's debacle comes in "Strife Shuts Down Women's Shelter," by Lourie Monsebraaten, *Toronto Star*, July 24, 1994. This story recounts the failure and closure of Shirley Samaroo House, a shelter in the City of York, named for a woman who was raped and then stabbed to death by her abusive husband. Shirley Samaroo House, opened in 1987, was set up to deal especially with the problems of immigrant women and was based on the same feminist-collec-tive model as Nellie's. Conflicts at Shirley Samaroo were very similar to Nellie's, including charges of power-mongering, racism (despite the fact that the staff and board were all members of minorities) and violence. The province claimed that Shirley Samaroo house was destroyed by a combi-nation of political ideology and incompetence. When it closed, Martha Ocampo, a founder and board member said that the reason Shirley Samaroo house was closed and Nellie's survived was because "at Nellie's there were some privileged white women involved."

CHAPTER SIX: THE REAL WORLD

For this chapter, I interviewed more than a dozen members of visible minority communities in Vancouver and Toronto. I made several trips to the neighbourhoods mentioned in the chapter during the spring and sum-mer of 1992. Interviewees included Harry Lee, Randall Wang, Howard States, two Native Canadian streetworkers who preferred that their names not be used, and several individuals in the Toronto communities mentioned in the book. These interviews were all conducted in 1992–93. Tran was interviewed in Vancouver in early 1992. The information on Ben Eng came from my previous book, as well as the news conference when Eng announced his resignation from the Toronto police force and subsequent public appearances when he announced his candidacy for MP in February, 1993. The statistics he revealed were in "Officer May Have Violated Police Act," by Nicola Pulling, *Globe and Mail*, July 26, 1991.

Officer X, the law enforcement officer, agreed to an interview only if his location, rank, race and all other identifying information was concealed. I met him once in person, through another officer whom I interviewed on an unrelated matter. After that, our discussions—more than 12 hours in all—were conducted by telephone. He taped these sessions, including my repeated promises to never reveal any information about his identity. I have complied with his requests in every possible way. I will say only that he is NOT a member of the Metro Toronto Police Force. His views were echoed by numerous police officers who refused to give me interviews on or off the record.

The Dwight Drummond incident was covered by all the Toronto media. The quotes here are from "Toronto Editor's Story One of Racism," by Colin Vaughan, *Globe and Mail*, October 25, 1993. Some people may have thought—or hoped—the Dwight Drummond episode would end with an "inside the force" inquiry, but it didn't. In late January, 1995, Deputy Police Chief Bob Kerr, one of the highest ranking members of the Metro Police Force, ordered a public inquiry into the case. Kerr did this after an internal investigation cleared the two officers of any wrong-doing. Clearly Kerr was dissatisfied with the police version of events. The Metro Police quickly and publicly voiced their dissatisfaction of Kerr, a 29-year force veteran who very nearly became police chief in autumn, 1994. First, officers at 52 Division pulled off a wildcat strike, closing the division for several hours. Then, police spokespersons and union representatives turned on Kerr, holding a rally and voting non-confidence in his leadership. There were threats—later withdrawn—of a city-wide strike by police. The police spokespersons then claimed that all the hubbub was really about police dissatisfaction with working conditions and resentment of the civilian review process. In all the eyewash and pro-police rhetoric, one fact seems to have been ignored. If a police force is here to "serve and protect," then that protection should extend to residents of every race, and when that force ignores its most fundamental mandate, someone—in this case a deputy chief—has to remind police that they have to obey the laws as well as enforce them.

The Vancouver police story is documented in "B.C. Rights Groups Protest 'Terrible Wrong'," by Deborah Wilson, *Globe and Mail*, May 26, 1992. Details were confirmed by Victor Wong of the Chinese Community Centre in Vancouver.

There have been many discussions—some of them highly public and acrimonious—about the keeping of crime statistics by race. See "Colouring Crime Stats by Race," by Lynda Hurst, *Toronto Star*, November 27, 1994; "Shying Away from Reporting on Race is Understandable but Wrong," by William Thorsell, *Globe and Mail*, April 9, 1994; "Rowlands' Speech Heralds an Ugly Election," by David Lewis Stein, *Toronto Star*, April 13, 1994. I also attended this community meeting and heard and saw Ms. Rowlands in action.

Professor Tony Hall's views are expressed in "As Long as the Sun Shines and the Water Flows," *Globe and Mail*, July 7, 1990.

One of the more trenchant commentaries on justice and race is "Raising Questions about Racial Bias in the Courtroom," by Clayton Ruby, *Toronto Star*, May 18, 1994.

The firefighters and equity dispute was covered daily. One of the best analysis of the issues was "Firefighters Using Old Ploy in New Effort to Discriminate," by Michele Landsberg, *Toronto Star*, February 23, 1993.

There have been myriad charges and counter-charges of racism in the Toronto police force. Some of the most serious occurred when it was discovered in February 1994 that the police intelligence unit had been gathering information on Black "activists." These included people like Dudley Laws, head of the Black Action Defence League, but also included community leaders like Dr. Wilson Head. This raised many questions that were still unanswered at press time; some articles on this subject are "Black Activists Probed by Police," *Toronto Star*, February 11, 1994; "Police Target: an Individual or a Community," by Roger McTair, *Toronto Star*, April 18, 1994; "Eng Queries Secret Study on Blacks," by Jack Lakey, *Toronto Star*, February 12, 1994; "Sixteen Steps Toward Improved Policing," a letter to the Editor by Peter Rosenthal, *Globe and Mail*, November 20, 1993; "Racism by Police Unproved, Chief Says," by Philip Mascoll, *Toronto Star*, March 19, 1994; "Officer's Girlfriend Says Police Wanted to Get Laws," *Globe and Mail*, February 17, 1994.

The Donald Marshall case is notorious and has been covered and re-covered. Most of my information came from *Justice Denied: The Law Versus Donald Marshall* by Michael Harris. For information on the Betty Jean Osborne story, I used *Conspiracy of Silence*, by Lisa Priest.

The J. J. Harper case, along with the Aboriginal Justice Inquiry, and assorted side cases, cover more than 500 articles in the Winnipeg Free Press alone. For this chapter, I have used information from "The Shooting of J.J. Harper," by Don Gillmor, *Saturday Night*, December 1988 and "Recoil," May 1992. For background to the situation between the police and the Winnipeg Aboriginal community: *Reservations Are For Indians* by Heather Robertson. "Indians Deplore Treatment by Police," by Canadian Press, *Globe and Mail*, April 21, 1990; "A Tale of Two Schools," by Geoffrey York, *Globe and Mail*, April 21, 1990; "Policing the Prairies," by Timothy Appleby, Miro Cernetig and Geoffrey York, *Globe and Mail*, April 20, 1990; "Investigation Sparked by Racist Calendar," by Geoffrey York, *Globe and Mail*, February 3, 1990; "Native Sex Comment Condemned as Racist by Manitoba Métis," by Geoffrey York, *Globe and Mail*, November 23, 1989; "Police Recruits Made Remarks that Were Racist, Inquiry Told," by Geoffrey York, *Globe and Mail*, November 7, 1989; "Racist Town Shielded Men, Osborne Probe Told," by Geoffrey York, *Globe and Mail*, October 3, 1989; "Constable Related Joke about Shooting Indians, Manitoba Inquiry Told," by Geoffrey York, *Globe and Mail*, August 29, 1989; "Key Piece of Evidence Kept Secret at Harper Inquest, Inquiry Told," by Geoffrey York, *Globe and Mail*, August 22, 1989; "Manitoba Native Justice Inquiry Opens Review of Harper Case," by Canadian Press, *Globe and Mail*, August 21, 1989; "White Residents Didn't Yell Enough after Native's Murder, Inquiry Told," by Timothy Appleby, *Globe and Mail*, August 9, 1989; "Judicial Reform: Manitoba Natives Tell their Story," by Geoffrey York, *Globe and Mail*, October 8, 1988.

Conclusions of the aboriginal justice inquiry: "Judges Urge Separate Native Justice System," by David Robert and Geoffrey York, *Globe and Mail*, August 30, 1991; "Inquiry Sought Out Alienated," by Geoffrey York, *Globe and Mail*, August 30, 1991; "Native Justice Reports Gather Dust while Canada Builds New Jails," by George Oake, *Toronto Star*, February 16, 1993.

The Harvey Pollock case first came to my attention in a column "The Winnipeg Police and the Wrong Arm of its Law," by John Dafoe, *Globe and Mail*, September 21, 1991. The bulk of the information on the Pollock incident comes from the "Report of The Honourable E.N. Hughes Q.C., with Respect to the Process and Procedure in the Investigation, Charge, Arrest, Prosecution, Stay and Subsequent Action of the October 3, 1990, Harvey I. Pollock, Q.C. Case," issued in Winnipeg, September, 1991.

The Audrey Smith case received extensive publicity in Toronto and was front page news in Jamaica for weeks. Sources here are "Strip Search Inquiry Disbanded," by Gay Abbate, *Globe and Mail*, April 28, 1994; "Woman Describes Strip Search Done by Police," by Gay Abbate, *Globe and Mail*, April 27, 1994; "Police Confirm Strip Search, Lawyer Says," by Henry Hess, *Globe and Mail*, October 14, 1993; "Strip Search Report Ready," by Henry Hess, *Globe and Mail*, October 13, 1993; "Chief Refers Strip Case to Tribunal," by Henry Hess, *Globe and Mail*, October 15, 1993; "Triggered Probe Jamaican Leaving," *Globe and Mail*, October 2, 1993; "Strip Search Probe Urged to Speed Up," by Henry Hess, *Globe and Mail*, September 30, 1993; "Strip Search Investigation Criticized," by Henry Hess, *Globe and Mail*, September 29, 1993; "Woman, Chief Meet over Stripping Allegation," by Henry Hess, *Globe and Mail*, September 22, 1993.

I attended several Reform Party rallies in Toronto and its suburbs throughout 1992. I also attended Reform meetings in Vancouver in 1990 and 1991. As well, I spoke at length with members of Reform in Edmonton, Calgary, Ottawa, and Toronto. Bill and Maggy were at the Reform rally in Mississauga. I interviewed them there.

The Huband comment comes from the article "Native Justice Reports Gather Dust while Canada Builds New Jails," by George Oake, *Toronto Star*, February 16, 1993.

CHAPTER SEVEN: HOW MANY IS TOO MANY?

The conflict between immigration supporters who want numbers raised and those who believe that quality, not quantity, is the issue came to a head in November 1994, with a highly public media attack on Michael Schelew, deputy chairman of the Immigration and Refugee Board, the group that oversees those who investigate refugee claims and decide who gets admitted. Individuals on the IRB have accused Schelew, a long-time refugee activist and head of the Toronto chapter of Amnesty International, of pushing his own agenda on the IRB. Friends of Schelew claim this is ludicrous, that the IRB members are independent and that all decisions are final. The best, if biased, work on this subject appeared in "Open Door Travesty," by Daniel Stoffman, *Saturday Night*, November 1994. On November 2, 1994, Mr. Schelew was suspended from his post pending an investigation. That report was in "Refugee Board Suspends Deputy Chairman Indefinitely," by Lila Sarick, *Globe and Mail*, November 3, 1994.

One of the major background books for this chapter is *Inside Outer Canada* by David Kilgour, an examination of Western Canadian alienation. As a resident of what Mr. Kilgour terms "inner Canada," I disagree with much of what he says and I dislike many of his ideas. However, I heard the same ideas expressed dozens of times by Western Canadians of all political and racial hues. To understand the phenomenon of Reform, one has to accept the fact that Western Canada feels left out. Now that same alienation is coming east. That's what the interviews with Liz and Phil and the continuing interest in and rise of the Reform Party is about.

I conducted more than thirty interviews with individuals across Canada before settling on the ones in this chapter. Many of the persons interviewed expressed ideas and opinions far more derogatory and damaging than the ones I used. I chose the interviews that were most representative of the opinions and ideas expressed. The same thing applies to the Della and Jack and to Daniel.

For more information on immigration policy and the history of immigration in Canada, I turned to *Canada and Immigration: Public Policy and Public Concern* by Professor Frieda Hawkins. This is the source for the figures related up to 1988. After that time, the figures come from Immigration Canada or Statistics Canada. Additional information on immigration can be found in *Haven's Gate: Canada's Immigration Fiasco* by Victor Malarek and my previous book *China Tide: The Revealing Story of the Hong Kong Exodus to Canada*. Since that book, I have also done further research on business immigration into Canada and those figures appear here.

David Baines, Business columnist for the Vancouver *Sun* has made it his personal crusade to expose investor immigrant funds that are used to defraud the investors. My own exposé, entitled "The Great Canadian Rip-Off," appeared in the *Report on Business* magazine of the *Globe and Mail*, November 1994.

Articles of use in this chapter are: "Coalition Attacks Immigration Policy," by Estanislao Oziewicz, *Globe and Mail*, June 23, 1992; "Race, Religion, Economics and Immigration," an editorial, *Globe and Mail*, July 6, 1991; "Closing the Door," by Allan Thompson, *Toronto Star*, January 3, 1993; "The Immigration Door Swings Both Ways," an editorial in the *Globe and Mail*; "Immigration: Striking a Balance," by Daniel Stoffman, *Toronto Star*, September 24, 1992; "Refugee Board Member Resigns, Protests Racism," by Donovan Vincent, *Toronto Star*; "Sending the Serious Criminal Element Home," by Estanislao Oziewicz, *Globe and Mail*, February 21, 1991; "Influx of Immigrants Largest Since 1957," by Canadian Press, *Globe and Mail*, December 15, 1992; "Call to Cut Immigration Unbalanced, Critics Say," by Allan Thompson, *Toronto Star*, September 28, 1992; "Richer Nations Told to Brace for 'Tide of People'," by Southam News, *Toronto Star*, July 5, 1993; "Report Slams TV Portrayal of Immigrants," by Allan Thompson, *Toronto Star*, July 5, 1993; "Whisper Campaign Against Immigrants," an editorial in the *Toronto Star*, September 26, 1992; "Immigration, though Undebated, in our Best Interests," by Richard Gwyn, *Toronto Star*, July 4, 1993; "Asylum Seekers Find New Walls around North," by Allan Thompson, *Toronto Star*, July 24, 1993; "Immigration Shifting," by Estanislao Oziewicz, *Globe and Mail*, December 9, 1992; "Ottawa Girds for Big Battle over Future Immigration Policy," by Allan Thompson, *Toronto Star*, December 28, 1993; "Illegals Besiege Europe's Gates," by Neely Tucker, *Toronto Star*, December 28, 1993; "Times Are Hard and They're Not A-changin'," by Mohammed Aslam, *Globe and Mail*, February 1, 1994; "Putting a Price on Immigration," by Robert Mata, *Globe and Mail*, February 11, 1994; "How Many Immigrants Should Canada Admit?" a discussion between Daniel Stoffman and Peter Gzowski on "Morningside," printed in the *Globe and Mail*, February 4, 1994; "Immigration Policy Review Won't Discuss Numbers," by Richard Gwyn, *Toronto Star*, July 17, 1994;

"Economic Realities Demand a Reduction in Immigration Quotas," by Stan Sudol, *Toronto Star*, August 16, 1994; "Who Should Canada Accept as Immigrants?" by James A. Brander, *Globe and Mail*, November 15, 1993; "It's about Colour, Not Numbers," by Peter Calamai, *Toronto Star*, July 20, 1994; "Let's Take Another Look at the Immigration Data," by Michael Valpy, *Globe and Mail*, July 14, 1994; "Immigrants an Asset," an editorial in the *Toronto Star*, July 14, 1994; "Attitudes on Immigrants Harden," by Murray Campbell, *Globe and Mail*, March 10, 1994; "Canadian Dream Sours for Immigrants," by Sandro Contenta, *Toronto Star*, January 22, 1994. "Clampdown on Immigration," by Tim Harper and David Vienneau, *Toronto Star*, October 29, 1994; "Marchi's Big Change Is to Factor in National Interest," by Daniel Stoffman, *Toronto Star*, November 6, 1994; "The Volumes and Kinds of Immigrants," Editorial, *Globe and Mail*, November 3, 1994; "Marchi Denies Betrayal of his Roots," by Edward Greenspan, *Globe and Mail*, November 3, 1994.

My interview with Mr. Singh (this is a pseudonym) took place in September 1993. I met with him against in March 1994 after the Jag Bhaduria story had been headline news. Other articles on the Bhaduria affair are: "Bhaduria: Rush to Judgement," by Andrew Cardozo, *Toronto Star*, February 11, 1994; "Embattled MP Says He's Done Nothing Criminal," by Philip Mascoll and Peter Small, *Toronto Star*, February 11, 1994; "Bhaduria Asked to Resign Because He Lied, PM Says," by Rosemary Speirs, *Toronto Star*, February 1, 1994; "Many East Indians Now Defend Bhaduria," by Philip Mascoll and Peter Small, *Toronto Star*, February 11, 1994. There were also two pages of letters to the editor of the *Toronto Star* on the Bhaduria affair.

CHAPTER EIGHT: MULTICULTURALISM RUNS AMOK

Mr. Lyons spoke to me at a Reform Rally in Vancouver. Michael Valpy told me about the "Festival of Light." I also heard the same story from several other parents of children in the Toronto public schools. The issue of celebrating everything but the Christian holiday became a minor cause célèbre in December 1993, when some Ontario government offices refused to set up the traditional Christmas trees and Nativity scenes, claiming that these displays were politically incorrect. One of the more insightful articles on this subject was "Christmas Can Be a Trying Time for Non-Christians," by Mark Gerson, *Globe and Mail*, December 12, 1993.

For background on multiculturalism policy, as distinct from practice, I relied again on Frieda Hawkins's study of immigration policy. Equally important were *Frontiers* by M. Nourbese Philip, *The Gulf Within* by Zuhair Kashmeri, and *Other Solitudes: Canadian Multicultural Fictions* edited by Linda Hutcheon and Marion Richmond. Quotes from these books are cited in the text. Multiculturalism has very different meanings in America. One of the best examinations of American multiculturalism was a two-voice essay, *Beyond PC, the Canon, and Multiculturalism*, by Louis Menand and Rosa Ehrenreich in *Harper's* magazine, December 1991.

The Somalis on Dixon Road in Toronto were extensively covered by the media, including all the major television stations. My own interview was set up through a Somali friendship organization. I am most grateful to Mr. Udore who spent much time with me, despite the fact that the language problem made communication slow and halting. I am also grateful to the other residents of Mr. Udore's condominium who spoke with me about the problems in the community.

Other articles about the Somalis include: "Troubles of a Neighbourhood in Flux," by Rosie DiManno, *Toronto Star*, August 2, 1993; "Ignorance Fuels Culture Clash at York Condos," by Rosie DiManno, *Toronto Star*, August 9, 1993; "Caught in a Strange Racial Divide," by Ali Sharrif, *Globe and Mail*, September 21, 1993; "As Somalis Learned: No Clout, No Apology," by Cecil Foster, *Toronto Star*, December 29, 1993.

There was much coverage of the fact that Khadiga Gurhan, wife of Somali warlord Mohammed Aidid was living in London, Ontario with children of the warlord. Most of the stories focused on the fact that Ms. Gurhan was receiving welfare and that she travelled to meet her husband outside of Somalia. In some minds, this lent credence to the reports that Somalis were contributing welfare money to the warlord. "Secret Reports Allege Aideed Funded by Drug, Welfare Money" (Moira Farrow, *Toronto Star*, March 4, 1994) was one of the most hurtful articles to the Somalis. "No Widespread Scam to Fund Somali Warlord, Marchi Says," by Canadian Press appeared in the *Toronto Star*, March 5, 1994. After the articles appeared, Gurhan's welfare was cut off. "Aideed's Wife Asks to Be Left in Peace," by Bob Massecar, *Toronto Star*, August 18, 1994; "General Aideed's Wife Urges Reporters to End Scrutiny," by Henry Hess, *Globe and Mail*, August 18, 1994.

Conflicting views of multiculturalism abound. The view out west is, again, articulated by *Inside Outer Canada*, by David Kilgour. Preston Manning's Reform speeches were another source. Articles for this section include: "Ethnic Minorities Realize Assimilation's the Best Route," a letter to the editor by Helmut F. Manzi, *Globe and Mail*, and on the same page: "Multiculturalism Counters Discrimination, Ignorance," by Karen R. Mock; "It's Disastrous to Focus on Differences," by Douglas J. Buchanan; and "A Policy that Encompasses our Values," by Dan Iannuzzi; "Capitalist Agenda Fuels the 'Multiculti' Fad," by Andrew Nikiforuk, *Globe and Mail*, April 22, 1994; "Most Think Immigrants Must Adapt, Survey Says," by Allan Thompson, *Toronto Star*, December 14, 1993; "Is Multiculturalism Becoming Multinationalism?" by Richard Gwyn, *Toronto Star*, February 28, 1993; "Multiculturalism Could Do With Another Look," by John Dafoe, *Globe and Mail*, November 17, 1990.

On Quebec anti-Semitism, I relied on *Jews and French Quebecers: Two Hundred Years of Shared History* by Jacques Langlais and David Rome. On Quebec multiculturalism, I chose to go with Jacques Godbout's idea of "pluri-ethnicity" because it makes sense. That cannot always be said about Quebec Language policy and Quebec's immigration and multiculturalism policies. My interview with Guy took place in late 1992, shortly after the elections. *Oh Canada! Oh Quebec!* is by Mordecai Richler. He wrote of his newly established reputation as a racist in "My Life as a Racist," in the *Globe and Mail*, February 16, 1993. Esther DeLisle's book *The Traitor and the Jew* was much discussed in Quebec for its controversial stand on the relationship of nationalism and anti-Semitism. Ms. DeLisle was interviewed by Marcus Gee in "Daring to Use the A-word," *Globe and Mail*, November 25, 1993.

The actions of the Canadian peacekeepers in Somalia and the death of Shidane Arone have been extensively covered for months by all the major

media. The best analysis of the entire event, including the trials and con-
victions, was "Canada...Canada," by Peter Cheney in collaboration with
Darcy Henton and Peter Watson, *Toronto Star*, July 10, 1994. Peter
Cheney also examined the history of the Airborne Regiment in "The Gung-
ho Regiment that Met Disaster in Somalia," *Toronto Star*, January 15,
1994; "Unit Sent to Somalia Rebellious, Report Says," by Geoffrey York,
Globe and Mail, September 1, 1993; "Airborne Unit Beset by Rebels,
Probe Finds," by Tim Harper, *Toronto Star*, September 1, 1993; "Somalia
Inquiry Raises New Questions," by Tim Harper, *Toronto Star*, Spetember
1, 1993.

CONCLUSION: THE STONE IN THE HEART

On the day I completed the final rewrite of this book, the Toronto Police
announced that hate crimes—most specifically those targeting Jews and
Blacks—had risen dramatically. At the same time, figures for all other
crimes were down 5 per cent.

The story of the boy who had the firecracker jammed in his mouth
appeared in the *Toronto Star*, May 26, 1993.
  Nourbese Philip's quotes are from *Frontiers*.
  The United Church Minister's words are from *The Gulf
  Within* by Zuhair Kashmeri.
  The figures and quotes are from "Most Think Immigrants
  Must Adapt, Survey Says," by Allan Thompson, *Toronto
  Star*, December 14, 1993.

Acknowledgements

Any attempt to personally thank or name all the individuals and organizations who assisted me with this book would take many pages. When I found the material too daunting, the subject too over-whelming, I considered shelving the project. At those times, I was urged on by my husband John Mays, my editor Sarah Davies, and my agents Lee Davis Creal and Jan Whitford.

I also owe a great debt to the late Dr. Wilson Head, founder of the Urban Alliance on Race Relations and former Chairman of the York University Department of Social Work. When I was first approached by Random House with this project, I discussed it many times with Dr. Head. He encouraged me to take on the book and to dig into my own background as part of the story. I was able to share with him an early version of the manuscript and I deeply regret that he was unable to see the finished book. Many of the ideas in the text are inspired by his suggestions. I hope I have done them—and him—justice.

Over the three years I spent researching the book, I conducted more than two hundred interviews with individuals across Canada. The vast majority of those interviews do not appear here, not because they weren't important, but because I could not include everyone. What I attempted to do was to select a representative set of individuals speaking on the issue along with all their disparate points of view. I am deeply grateful to all the people who took the time to talk with me, share their thoughts and feelings and give me insight into how racism works in Canadian society. In many cases it took considerable courage to talk with me, to put forward ideas and thoughts that are unpopular, or occasionallly, downright dangerous. In all cases where anonymity was requested, it has been preserved. Sadly, the climate of the times has made it necessary to give pseudonyms to several people, who at the time of the interview, did not so request. Two and three years ago, it wasn't always necessary to protect sources. My own investigations have convinced me otherwise, now.

Finally to all my friends, family and colleagues who listened to my problems, helped me to sort out my ideas, and kept me going: thanks to you all. I couldn't have done it without you.

Margaret Cannon
February, 1995

Index